A CASE STUDY APPROACH TO CLASSROOM MANAGEMENT

RICHARD T. SCARPACI

St. John's University

Boston   New York   San Francisco
Mexico City   Montreal   Toronto   London   Madrid   Munich   Paris
Hong Kong   Singapore   Tokyo   Cape Town   Sydney

Senior Series Editor: *Arnis E. Burvikovs*
Series Editorial Assistant: *Erin Reilly*
Marketing Manager: *Tara Kelly*
Production Editor: *Annette Joseph*
Editorial Production Service: *Publishers' Design and Production Services, Inc.*
Composition Buyer: *Linda Cox*
Manufacturing Buyer: *Megan Cochran*
Electronic Composition: *Publishers' Design and Production Services, Inc.*
Cover Administrator: *Kristina Mose-Libon*

For related titles and support materials, visit our online catalog at www.ablongman.com.

Between the time website information is gathered and then published, it is not unusual for some sites to have closed. Also, the transcription of URLs can result in typographical errors. The publisher would appreciate notification where these errors occur so that they may be corrected in subsequent editions.

Library of Congress Cataloging-in-Publication Data
Scarpaci, Richard T.
  A case study approach to classroom management / Richard T. Scarpaci.
    p. cm.
  Includes bibliographical references and index.
  ISBN 0-205-39225-3 (alk. paper)
    1. Classroom management—Case studies.   I. Title.

LB3013.S29 2007
371.102'4—dc22   2005054974

Printed in the United States of America

10 9 8 7 6 5 4 3 2 1   10 09 08 07 06

CONTENTS

CHAPTER TWO

Management Styles: What Teachers Bring to School   25

CHAPTER THREE

Identifying Successful Teachers   37

CHAPTER SIX
Group-Guidance Models   87

CHAPTER SEVEN

Individual-Guidance Management Models   107

PART III   CASE STUDIES FOR ANALYSIS   129

CHAPTER EIGHT
Case Studies from the Fields   131

Dealing with behavioral problems in the classroom is a major cause of teacher dissatisfaction. Nearly one-half of all new teachers in U.S. inner-city schools leave during their first five years of service, and many cite behavioral problems and classroom-management issues as influential in their decision (Ingersoll, 2004). This book addresses the issue of classroom management in both a theoretical and practical fashion. Written to be accessible to students as well as the novice practitioner, it seeks to provide readers with a proper perspective on classroom management. The objective is to make available a supporting framework to assist teachers in surviving their initiation and becoming effective classroom managers. Based on the author's forty years of experience and research, the text offers a set of approaches, strategies, and concepts relating to effective problem-resolution. It introduces readers to the IOSIE case study analysis method (Identifying problems, determining Objectives, proposing Solutions, Implementation and Evaluation; explained in Chapter 1), which enables teachers to construct their own case study approach to classroom management.

The book is the end result of a lengthy holistic process; it began as a first aid kit and evolved into a practitioner's management toolbox. Solutions may differ from situation to situation but the underlying concepts and beliefs remain the same. IOSIE is presented as a rubric for interpreting case studies, or real-life scenarios. To become effective managers, teachers need to understand the behavior-management strategies available and how to implement them. This process is similar to that of a painter, who must choose the right brush, color palette, and stroke before painting the desired picture.

An educator's management style depends to a significant degree on teaching personality, the driving force behind practice. The teachers we become, and the management styles we utilize, reflect our individual personalities, just as the work of particular artists can be recognized based on their individual styles. Just as different artists will use the same materials in various ways, individual teachers will apply the same strategies in their own ways. But all teachers need a variety of strategies—a toolbox—to draw from and adapt to the various situations they face.

Readers are introduced to the three basic ways to approach problem-resolution: through a consequences, group-guidance, and individual-guidance approach. Generic management strategies requiring varying levels of teacher intervention are explained, as are specific management strategies, presented on a spectrum of most to least teacher control.

The strategies comprise a road map for use with the case study approach to behavior analysis. Their purpose is to create learning environments in which misbehavior is deterred and education enhanced. Addressing behavioral problems before they result in violence is one of the objectives of the case study approach.

Readers are encouraged to understand the psychological precepts that support the various management strategies. The research base for this book is broad, suggesting an eclectic approach to classroom management.

That so many new teachers are leaving the profession so early in their careers is disheartening. This negative momentum must be reversed if we hope to secure our children's future. We know that the expertise of teachers is of primary importance to student achievement. It is crucial, therefore, to address the issue of student behavior, to aid teachers in effective classroom management and enable them to pursue their vocation. The underlying philosophy of this text is that learning to teach is a career-long developmental process that occurs best in collaborative environments, aided by dedicated mentors. It is hoped that this book will provide teachers with some measure of support and guidance in that process.

The text is designed to provide readers with a working understanding of the behavioral analysis method and its use in resolving student misbehavior, taking into account two primary goals and their accompanying objects. *Goal number 1* is to assist and support readers in understanding and implementing an effective classroom-management program. The objectives here are to

- enable readers to turn sound classroom management theories into practice;
- assist readers in becoming effective classroom managers through an understanding of the IOSIE case study approach to behavioral analysis;
- aid teachers in developing and preparing a practical plan that can be implemented in classrooms;
- encourage effective teacher behaviors with regard to classroom management.

Goal number 2 is to provide readers with an understanding of classroom management from basic theory to practice, utilizing a case study approach. The objectives here are to

- impart to readers an understanding of the basic concepts upon which a case study approach to classroom management is based;
- support readers in utilizing the IOSIE method and generic and specific management strategies to resolve behavioral problems in the classroom.

The basic concepts upon which the case study approach is based are categorized according to three specific areas: (1) effective teacher behaviors, (2) discipline, and (3) behavior management. They form the theoretical construct of the IOSIE method.

BASIC CONCEPTS OF BEHAVIOR MANAGEMENT

Effective Teacher Behaviors

- Effective classroom teachers have a teaching personality that enables them to bring to their classrooms beliefs, skills, and practices that discourage misbehavior and enhance learning.

- Effective teachers understand the need to master content, the importance of management and pedagogical methods, and the need for high student expectations. Finally, they have a teaching personality that successfully engages their students.
- Effective teachers apply positive, rather than negative, discipline. Effective teachers manage a classroom; ineffective teachers punish students.
- Effective teachers meet students' psychological needs.

Discipline/Essential Understandings

- Discipline can be positive or negative.
- The goal of positive discipline is self-discipline (internal control).
- The number one problem in classrooms is not the lack of discipline but the lack of procedures.
- Students choose their behavior and teachers their management style.

Behavior Management/Specific Strategies

- There are three approaches to resolving behavioral issues: a consequences approach, a group-guidance approach, and an individual-guidance approach.
- To determine causality we must understand the different categories, types, and causes of misbehavior.
- Individuals are an accumulation of choices and experiences. The IOSIE method allows for an analysis of student behavioral problems based on past experiences and trial and error.
- A management toolbox consists of six generic strategies: (1) authoritarian, (2) behavior modification (e.g., intimidation), (3) instructional/eclectic, (4) group guidance/group process, (5) socio-emotional, (6) tolerant/permissive, and specific classic management models such as assertive discipline, judicial discipline, and choice theory.

The classroom is essentially a gestalt, in need of several interdependent components in order to be successful: (1) effective instructional practices and an engaging curriculum; (2) high expectations on the part of teacher and students; and (3) effective classroom management approaches, strategies, and practices that can deal with anger, frustration, resistance, conflict, stress, and depression. If any of these components is neglected, the process becomes compromised, and compromise results in dysfunction.

ORGANIZATION OF THE TEXT

The book is organized into three parts: Part I: Introduction to a Case Study Approach to Classroom Management; Part II: Management Approaches and Models; and Part III: Case Studies for Analysis. The text is balanced between theory and

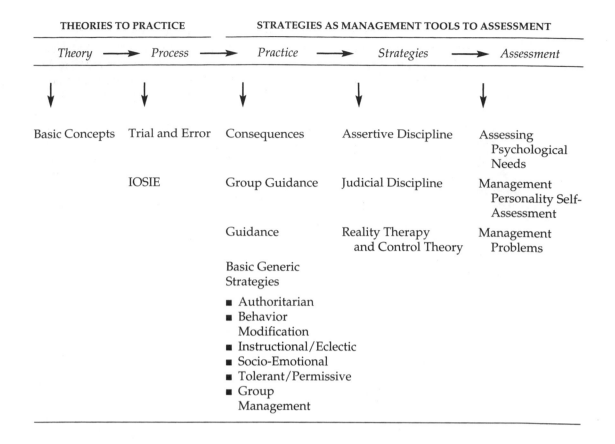

THEORIES TO PRACTICE		STRATEGIES AS MANAGEMENT TOOLS TO ASSESSMENT		
Theory ⟶	Process ⟶	Practice ⟶	Strategies ⟶	Assessment
Basic Concepts	Trial and Error	Consequences	Assertive Discipline	Assessing Psychological Needs
	IOSIE	Group Guidance	Judicial Discipline	Management Personality Self-Assessment
		Guidance	Reality Therapy and Control Theory	Management Problems
		Basic Generic Strategies		
		■ Authoritarian ■ Behavior Modification ■ Instructional/Eclectic ■ Socio-Emotional ■ Tolerant/Permissive ■ Group Management		

practice. The teaching personality, which is viewed as what teachers bring to the classroom, is discussed throughout the book. Teaching personality is understood to be a combination of character, values, and philosophy culminating in one's emotional commitment to teaching. This commitment accounts for the enthusiasm that engages students, discourages misbehavior, and encourages learning by facilitating instruction. It is not the management strategy that is seen as making the difference. It is the teacher who understands and selects the management strategy who makes the difference.

The text presents, in a logical sequence, the general topics of classroom management, and is intended for use by the undergraduate and graduate student as well as the practicing teacher. All materials have been tested in graduate management and methods courses, as well as staff development programs. Each part begins with an introduction that provides an overview of the specific chapters and sets out expectations for the reader. Each of the chapters in Parts I and II concludes with sections titled Key Terms to Focus On, Discussion Questions, Mini Cases from the Field, and References. In Part III, each case study concludes with sections titled Discussion Topics and Questions to Ponder, and What Would You Do If . . .?

Part I introduces the IOSIE method and general approaches to management, with a focus on teaching personality and teachers' individual management styles. Part II provides an in-depth view of management models and strategies, discussing particular classroom contexts and the strengths and weaknesses of models used by teachers to deter violence in the classroom. Classic approaches are reviewed along with specific procedures that can bring these approaches to life within the classroom. Part III gives readers an opportunity to apply their learning of management styles and approaches to particular case studies. No behavior-management program can be effective unless its theories can be brought to bear on actual experience. The goal is to develop, from theories and practices, a useful diagnostic, corrective, and prescriptive tool.

Appendix A looks at the most severe forms of behavioral problems that teachers face, discussing the types of violence in today's schools, including youth violence, bullying, gangs, suicide prevention, child abuse, and sexual harassment. Appendix B presents a Classroom Management Quiz, which is an opportunity for the reader to reflect on and evaluate his or her own management style after reading the different classroom management methods presented in Chapters 4 through 7.

Case Studies for Analysis

The case studies in this text are written from a teacher's perspective. Chapters 1 through 7 contain mini case studies that present real-life scenarios that the reader must analyze and apply the specific classroom management style just described. The generic and specific management strategies discussed in Parts I and II then aid the reader to resolve the identified problems presented in the case studies in Chapter 8. Each case opens with a guide, Keys to Analyzing This Case. Readers are asked to use the IOSIE method, which is presented in Part I, as a framework when beginning to analyze the difficulties confronted in each episode. Other keys to understanding the case follow. Concluding questions provide direction for student thought and reflection.

It is hoped that the information presented in this text will assist and support readers in becoming effective classroom managers. It is important to understand that there are no simple answers to the complex problems facing schools and teachers today. Many methods claim to offer salvation with a quick-fix solution. Instead, teachers must understand and utilize a variety of approaches, adapting them to individual students and circumstances. There is no one answer to behavioral problems. This book encourages teachers to be flexible, providing a toolbox of classroom management strategies that facilitate the ultimate goal of instructional learning.

SUPPLEMENTARY RESOURCE MATERIAL

A Case Study Approach to Classroom Management comes with an Instructor's Guide and Resource Manual to assist the instructor in the organization and presentation of classroom management classes and workshops. The Guide provides an abundance of strategies and materials that can be used in facilitating instruction. The various items in this Guide are designed to be altered and modified to meet individual instructional needs.

The Instructor's Guide is divided into two parts. Part I offers a model syllabus for which this book might be used. Instructors can use this model and adapt it for their own course. Due to individual time considerations, number of students, and individual preferences, there is no single way to organize the course. The instructor should decide what will work for their class based on the content and the activities they expect to use. Part II includes chapter-specific instructional resources. For each chapter, the following sections are provided:

Learning Objectives describe the behavior, understandings, and specific strategies that should result from the study of the chapter. The purpose of these objectives is to assist in planning lessons for instruction in the chapter.

Teaching and Instructional Strategies provide the teacher with practical and specific ideas for presenting each chapter in class. Each chapter could provide for two to six hours of instruction. Each teacher can choose the ideas and strategies that best suit his or her students.

Suggested Instructional Materials are aimed at suggesting a variety of supplementary materials that can and should be used to enliven and enhance instruction related to text material.

Assessments highlight both objective test items (multiple choice and true and false) as well as subjective assessments (essays, case study analysis questions, and performance-based assessments).

ACKNOWLEDGMENTS

I would like to acknowledge the support staff at Allyn and Bacon who worked with me in shaping the content and structure of this book. I realize that this text is only as good as the editors behind it. I am grateful for all their help and support. My editor, Arnis Burvikovs; editorial assistant, Kelly Hopkins; marketing manager, Tara Kelly; production editor, Annette Joseph; composition buyer, Linda Cox; and manufacturing buyer, Megan Cochran, all contributed to this project coming together as a whole. I extend my sincere appreciation for all the suggestions and encouragement in the development of this book that were given to me by Denise Botelho. The reviewers of this text provided useful comments and thought-provoking professional suggestions: James C. Brown, Southern University at Shreveport; Robert Hohn, University of Kansas; Sheila K. Jones, Miami University of Ohio; Marie Kraska, Auburn University; Lawrence Lyman, Emporia State University; Brian McCadden, Rhode Island College; Judie Rhoads, Western Oregon University; Bruce Smith, Henderson State University; Sharon L. Smith, West Virginia

Wesleyan College; Harry Weisenberger, Minnesota State University–Moorehead; and Ron Zigler, Pennsylvania State University–Abington.

A special thanks to Allan Ornstein a colleague and dear friend whose sage advice I followed throughout writing this manuscript.

I also want to thank my beautiful wife Lucille, without whose help and understanding this text might never have been completed.

REFERENCE

Ingersoll, R. (2004). Why do high-poverty schools have difficulty staffing their classrooms with qualified teachers? Center for American Progress Retrieved December 16, 2005 at www.american progress.org/site/pp.asp?c=biJRJ8OVF&b= 19382.

PART I

INTRODUCTION TO A CASE STUDY APPROACH TO CLASSROOM MANAGEMENT

How does one develop a strategy for classroom management that fosters self-discipline in students and enhances learning? This question is of prime concern to teachers. Behavioral problems in schools have always existed, and teachers have traditionally anguished over the lack of discipline, cooperation, and respect in their classrooms (A Public Agenda Report, 2004). They have worried along with parents that the education of the majority suffers because of a misbehaving few. The good news is that student needs can be addressed through understanding and effective teaching. Teachers have strategies at their disposal to identify and treat the causes of misbehavior. There *are* solutions to classroom-management problems.

Part I of this text introduces readers to the IOSIE case study analysis approach to classroom management. It provides an overview of classroom management and the case study approach, and discusses teaching personality and management style, as well as the particular attributes associated with effective teaching. Management strategies and management models are also introduced. Essential understandings related to successful classroom management are explored. The teacher is seen as of primary importance in creating an environment that leads to student achievement. A correlation is drawn between effective teaching and management style. Effective teachers are viewed as having a teaching personality and management style that facilitate student achievement.

Specific strategies that can be implemented to manage behavioral problems within the classroom are also explored. These strategies provide a basic menu from which a management style can be developed. Efforts toward discipline are expected to lead to student self-discipline. A systematic and creative approach to classroom management encourages students to take responsibility for their behavior. Through the development of self-control, students can be the persons and students they want to be.

Discussed are effective teacher behaviors necessary for today's classrooms. An effective teacher is one who successfully manages the classroom and meets the needs—psychological, cultural, and academic—of students; an ineffective teacher uses negative disciplinary behaviors in an attempt to enforce control. The number one problem in classrooms is not the lack of discipline, as commonly thought, but the lack of procedures, because most behavior problems result from the teacher's failure to establish and maintain effective classroom procedures.

At the conclusion of Part I readers will understand that the goal of discipline (self-discipline) is met primarily through the teacher's teaching personality and management style. The major advantage teachers have is that they can adapt their behavior to meet the needs of any situation. Student misbehavior is frequently instinctive; effective teacher response is based on method and practice.

REFERENCE

A Public Agenda Report. 2004. *Teaching interrupted.*
New York: Public Agenda (May). www.public
agenda.org/research/research_reports.cfm

CHAPTER ONE

CLASSROOM MANAGEMENT AND DISCIPLINE

FOCUS POINTS

1. The goal of discipline is self-discipline (internal control).
   - The only person one can control is oneself.
   - External controls may produce unwanted results.
2. Discipline can be both positive (leading to self-discipline) and negative (imposed from without).
3. An effective teacher manages (positive discipline); an ineffective teacher punishes (negative discipline) a classroom.
4. The number one problem in classrooms is not the lack of discipline but the lack of procedures.
5. To effectively manage a classroom teachers must understand the types, categories, and causes of misbehavior.
6. Individuals are an accumulation of their choices and experiences. The IOSIE method allows for an analysis of student behavioral problems based on past experiences and trial and error.

DEVELOPING A DISCIPLINARY STRATEGY: ESSENTIAL UNDERSTANDINGS

Goal of Discipline

"Discipline" has various meanings. It can be defined as the enforcement of obedience or order. "Enforcement" implies external correction or punishment for bad behavior. When discipline is positively defined, the goal is self-discipline. Discipline is defined here as building responsibility and self-control. Discipline takes on a negative connotation when it is achieved by means of punishment or a system of penalties and rewards. An effective procedural system is not based on penalties or rewards and is readily acceptable to students. Procedures support the instilling of self-discipline, and consequences support procedures. Consequences are not punishments, but mutually agreed upon actions applied fairly. Students accept consequences they have chosen; they respond negatively to arbitrarily enforced rules.

Getting a ticket for going through a red light is not a punishment, it is a consequence of an individual's violation of a traffic law. Likewise, losing points on a grade for not doing homework is a consequence and not a punishment. When children comprehend the consequences for their actions they must consider personal responsibility. Punishment can be perceived as arbitrary and capricious and should be avoided; it rarely leads to the ultimate goal: self-discipline.

Role of Punishment

The terms *discipline* and *punishment* are often used interchangeably to refer to any negative sanction administered by an authority. Although in this text punishment is defined primarily negatively, not all educators look at punishment in a negative way. Goodman (2003) advocates the modest use of punishment as a vehicle for moral education. Here punishment is understood as a subcategory of discipline. It goes beyond behavioral reform and is intended to induce remorse or moral culpability. Discipline, defined positively, attempts to influence behavior. Punishment attempts to influence conscience. The breach of a conventional rule (lateness) may warrant some type of disciplinary corrective to deter behavior; the breach of a moral code (stealing, cheating, lying, vandalism, injury to others) merits punishment to engage the conscience. It would appear that Goodman, when using the term *disciplinary corrective,* is implying the use of corporal punishment, which in this text is never viewed as appropriate. The mission of punishment according to Goodman is to change character, not just induce behavioral conformity. In this view, punishment is seen as a valuable tool for fostering children's moral growth. Goodman does believe, however, that punishment must be reserved for deliberate offenses against the welfare of others.

Managing Children's Behavior

Two general approaches can be used to manage children's behavior: coercion and persuasion. Coercion involves using threats or physical force to compel behavior. Persuasion involves getting the child to believe that the desired behavior is in their best interests, or appealing to their core values, ideals, and beliefs.

Diane Gossen (1993), in a rather humorous vein, categorized these approaches into five specific "types": the punisher, the guilter, the buddy, the monitor, and the manager. The accompanying strategies have all, to varying degrees, been used by teachers to deal with improper classroom behavior.

1. **Punisher** is one who enforces control by using such negative behaviors as criticizing, threatening, hurting, sarcasm, or isolating. The punisher's behavior usually results in rebellion on the part of the child.
2. **Guilter** is one who controls by making children feel guilty about their behavior. The guilter uses sighing, moralizing, silencing, and expressions of disappointment as negative means of enforcement. The child is meant to in-

FIGURE 1.1   Positive Discipline versus Negative Discipline

POSITIVE DISCIPLINE	NEGATIVE DISCIPLINE
Based on procedures	Based on punishment
Focus is on how things are done	Focus is on individual student behavior
Utilizes consequences as reinforcement	Based on penalties and rewards
Builds self-control and self-esteem	Reinforces failure
Consistent, expected	Arbitrary, unexpected
Perceived as reasonable and fair	Can be perceived as unfair, overly severe
Strengthens relationships	Weakens relationships
Based on self-evaluation	Based on external evaluation
Strengthens the individual	Isolates, discomforts the individual
Agreed upon, self-imposed	Externally imposed
Proactive	Reactive

ternalize guilt and feel bad about himself. The result to the child is poor self-concept and low self-esteem.

3. **Buddy** is one who gains the child's compliance by using positive controlling behaviors such as complimenting, encouraging, and overextending. The result to the child is overdependence on the teacher to elicit appropriate behavior.

4. **Monitor** uses positive controlling behaviors such as rewards to offset negative controlling behaviors such as punishments to achieve student compliance. Children understand that the teacher will impose consequences, positive and negative, for their behavior. The result to the child is reliance on the teacher to determine behavior; children behave well only when being "monitored," rather than of their own volition.

5. **Manager** creates an environment in which children are expected to control themselves (develop and practice self-control). The object is to have children understand that they are responsible for their actions. The teacher guides and assists the child in developing self-control and self-discipline.

Teachers who excel at classroom management use various noncoercive techniques to help students reflect on and accept responsibility for their actions. They avoid criticizing and emotional manipulation ("guilting"), while moving children toward self-assessment in an environment in which classroom beliefs and expectations have been clearly established and mutually agreed upon.

Categories, Types, and Causes of Misbehavior

Misbehavior is a general term for any action that deviates from an accepted norm—in this case, appropriate classroom behavior. Conduct outside the parameters of accepted behavior is considered misbehavior. Misbehavior in the classroom can be described in terms of category, core type, and cause.

Categories. The two main categories of misbehavior are (1) acting-out behaviors and (2) withdrawal behaviors. Acting out is defined as giving overt expression to internal conflicts and emotions that one does not have sufficient understanding of or insight into. Withdrawal involves a denial of or flight from responsibility. *Acting-out behaviors* are related to some form of physical violence directed at others, while *withdrawing behaviors* are directed at oneself. The behaviors imply a diminished acceptance of responsibility for one's actions.

Violence can occur in either category: in acting-out behaviors it tends to be physical aggression, while in withdrawing behaviors the focus is the self. Examples such as suicide and sexual promiscuity are both physical behaviors aimed at hurting oneself and others.

Types. The five core types of classroom misbehavior are (1) moral; (2) personal; (3) legal; (4) safety; and (5) educational. Misbehavior of the moral type involves some sort of ethical lapse, such as lying or cheating. Personal misbehavior results in physical or emotional hurt to another. Legal misbehavior involves breaking established rules or laws. Safety types of misbehavior include actions that put oneself or others at risk of physical injury. Educational misbehavior is behavior that negatively affects one's learning or one's classmates' learning.

Clearly, these types are not mutually exclusive. Legal can overlap with moral (cheating on an exam). Safety misconduct (e.g., shoving while on a staircase) may have a personal and moral overlap (intent to harm). "Educational" is an umbrella

---

FIGURE 1.2 **Categories of Behavior**

Acting-Out Behaviors

- Fighting or physical violence
- Verbal assaults, threats
- Damaging property (vandalism)
- Sexual promiscuity/threatening suicide
- Stealing
- Swearing or use of inappropriate language

Withdrawal Behaviors

- Inattention
- Unsociability/uncommunicativeness
- Truancy
- Abuse of drugs, alcohol
- Disregard for personal appearance, hygiene
- Sexual promiscuity/threatening suicide

---

term that can include refusal to do homework as well as disrupting classroom lessons (by acting out).

Causes.   There are three major causes of misbehavior: (1) frustration, (2) conflict, and (3) rules. Again, these are not mutually exclusive. Frustration results when a student has little or no control over resolving a problem or issue. For example, if a student is unable to understand content, through failure of the teacher to clearly present the content, the student may become frustrated and begin to misbehave, either by acting out or withdrawing. Children may be frustrated because of classroom rules that they believe to be unfair, or if they are the subject of hurtful teasing. Another cause of misbehavior is conflict, which is simply part of the human experience. Two children may act out because there is a conflict over who gets to play with a particular toy. Related to these causes is displacement, which is a psychological process in which an emotion or impulse is redirected from its original object to something or someone else. For example, a child might withdraw from a bearded teacher because the child identifies the beard with an uncle who mistreated her.

Diagnosing Misbehavior

A prime objective in resolving student misbehavior is in properly identifying it by category, type, and cause. For example, a child demonstrating acting-out behaviors (threatening violence) might be understood to be frustrated (because he is the subject of name calling). The teacher diagnoses the type of misbehavior as personal (personal threat to another child). Once the cause is related to the category and type, the misconduct can be understood and solutions proposed.

Misbehavior and Psychological Needs

Glasser (1986, 1998) sees the causes of misbehavior as related to the teacher's inability to meet the psychological needs of students. All human beings have genetically programmed needs and drives. People need love and acceptance, and classrooms should be created to be warm, caring environments in which children have the freedom to express themselves and the opportunity to make positive contributions to the learning environment. Human beings are social creatures, and a sense of community should be present in the classroom, with time for personal interaction, fun, and laughter. When students' psychological needs are met in this way, learning is enhanced and misbehavior discouraged.

Performance Discrepancy and Inadequate Performance*

Many teachers describe as misbehavior what is really **performance discrepancy** or **inadequate performance**. This confusion often stems from teachers' failure to

*© 1997, CEP Press, 1100 Johnson Ferry Road, Suite 150, Atlanta, GA 30342. *www.ceppress.com* 800-558-4237. Adapted from *Analyzing Performance Problems* by Robert F. Mager and Peter Pipe. All rights reserved. No portion of these materials may be reproduced in any manner without the express written consent from The Center for Effective Performance Inc.

establish well-defined classroom expectations and procedures. In the absence of well-defined procedures for classroom behavior, a student who is caught chewing gum might be seen as misbehaving, when in fact the behavior is simply inconsistent with the teacher's expectations (a performance discrepancy). Another teacher might not have a problem with children chewing gum in class. Teachers must establish collaboratively with their students what is expected in terms of proper classroom behavior.

There are many reasons children do not perform as teachers expect them to; they may not understand what is expected of them, or they may lack the ability to carry out the required task. They may be confused about instructions or procedures. In some cases they are rewarded when they do a task wrong, because the teacher does not want to negatively impact self-esteem, or they may receive little or no teacher input whether they are right or wrong. Teachers should not equate inadequate performance with misbehavior. Often, giving feedback about the quality of the performance and modeling expectations brings expected behavior in line with actual behavior.

Reasons for Poor Performance

- Expectations are unclear or nonexistent
- Student lacks ability, skills, or knowledge
- Student lacks feedback and modeling
- Student has been rewarded when wrong in the past

IDENTIFYING AND RESOLVING MANAGEMENT PROBLEMS THROUGH CASE ANALYSIS

Theoretical Models of Human Behavior

Case analysis focuses on both immediate and long-term intervention. It requires critical reflection in which a situation is viewed from various perspectives and through a number of theoretical lenses. Danforth and Boyle (2000) have developed a research-based rationale for four models of human behavior that can be used with case analysis.

1. **Behavioral**
2. **Psychodynamic**
3. **Environmental**
4. **Constructivist**

These models differ in the way that they define causes and in the types of intervention they prescribe. It is helpful to understand them from the perspective of a general social systems theory, in which individuals are seen as social beings who are influenced and defined by their relationships with others.

Behavioral Model

Behaviorists hold that external variables dictate behavior; that behaviors are conditioned by external stimuli. For behavior to be modified, interventions must employ external stimuli such as reinforcement and rewards. A behavior-management plan based on this model would include the following steps:

1. Determine the specific behavior to be changed.
2. Introduce an appropriate reinforcer.
3. Monitor behavior as necessary.

For example, to address a child's inappropriate calling out in class, the child would be given positive reinforcement for following the correct procedure, raising his or her hand when he or she wanted to speak. The teacher would monitor the child's behavior to ensure that a positive change occurs.

Psychodynamic Model

This model views behavior as reflective of an individual's emotional state. The role of the teacher is to help the student build social skills and develop self-esteem, personal insight, and self-control. Intervention would be based on counseling techniques such as active listening and emotional support. A behavior-management plan based on this model would include the following steps:

1. Soothe the child and encourage him to explore his feelings.
2. Restructure the incident and locate the central issues that led to the misbehavior.
3. Guide the student in accepting responsibility for his actions.
4. Involve the student in developing a solution or resolution.

With respect to a child who habitually calls out in class, the teacher would speak privately with the child and address possible emotional considerations, such as impatience or frustration. The teacher, while being understanding of the child's need to express himself, would reason with the child, explain how calling out disrupts the class and is unfair to the other students. The child would be urged to take responsibility for the disruptive behavior and encouraged to help come up with a solution.

Environmental Model

This model focuses on working with (or helping to develop) the positive aspects of a child's immediate environments (home, school, and neighborhood). The model is based on the understanding that a person's environment influences behavior.

Intervention would acknowledge that the environment provides structural support and regularity, and the environment would be adapted to meet the behavioral needs of the child. A behavior-management plan based on this model would include the following steps:

1. Analyze the environment (time, space) in which the behavior occurs.
2. Determine the quality of human interaction that the environment supports.
3. Adapt the environment to better meet the needs of the child.

This approach addresses both the physical and social environments in which the behavior occurs. In the example of the child who disruptively calls out in class, the child might be reseated next to a student who follows appropriate classroom procedures.

Constructivist Model

This model was developed from the work of Jean Piaget and others. It is based on the assumption that individuals construct their own knowledge base, shaping their thinking to fit experiential constraints and existing beliefs. When viewed from the perspective of classroom management, the students' conceptions, based on their experiences, influence their behavior. Knowledge is not "fixed" in individuals but can develop or be modified based on additional experiences. Common ground for individual ideas is achieved through social interaction. A behavior-management plan based on this approach would include the following steps:

1. The child is reminded that her behavior is out of line with class rules, which she helped establish and signed on to.
2. The child is encouraged to voice any problem she has obeying the rules.
3. The child is guided toward taking responsibility for her actions and resolving the problem.

In this model, the child participates in constructing a response to her misbehavior. For example, the child who calls out in class is reminded that she participated in the development of classroom procedures and agreed to them along with her classmates. She is encouraged to explain why she has difficulty following the established procedure and how she will go about bringing her behavior in line with that procedure.

THE IOSIE METHOD

The **IOSIE method** is a five-step process for analyzing student behavioral problems. The term *IOSIE* is a mnemonic using the first letter of each step in the process.

1. *Identify* the problem.
2. Determine the *objectives* that you want to achieve.
3. Propose a *solution.*
4. *Implement* the solution.
5. *Evaluate* results.

Identifying the Problem

The analysis of problem behavior is essential to effective classroom management. Behavior problems may change daily but solution formats remain the same. The first step in the IOSIE process is always to identify the problem. One can't address what one does not recognize or understand. Identifying the problem is not as easy as it might seem, however. Interventions often require that teachers size up a situation fairly quickly. They must strive to look at a situation objectively, being wary of jumping to conclusions based on their own biases and preconceived notions. For instance, in a situation in which a large male student is arguing with a petite female, the teacher might infer, based on notions of size and gender, that the male is the instigator or aggressor. This may turn out not to be the case. Teachers must be careful not to assign blame before the facts are known.

Identifying the problem also involves gauging its seriousness. Behaviors that include violence or threats of violence obviously require immediate response. The seriousness of other types of misbehavior is typically a measure of the extent to which the behavior impinges on the learning process. It is up to the teacher to decide what constitutes a problem and how serious the problem is (Glasser, 1990, 1998; Mager and Pipe, 1997). The identification of some types of misbehavior is straightforward. Returning to the five core types discussed earlier, some misbehaviors of the moral type, such as cheating on an exam, or of the personal type, such as slandering a fellow student, or of the legal type, such as theft, or of the safety type, such as pushing students on a stairway—these are all rather easy to identify and judge in terms of seriousness. However, sometimes it will not be immediately clear to the teacher who is at fault, and there may be many elements of the incident to sort through. And some teachers will find fault with behaviors that others would let slide. This is especially true with respect to the educational types of misbehavior, or behavior that is seen to negatively affect the learning environment. One teacher might feel that inappropriate dress qualifies as misbehavior of this type, while another might feel that censoring dress is inappropriate.

Determining Objectives

In the IOSIE method of behavioral analysis, objectives are viewed as desired outcomes that remedy the immediate problem and provide for long-term improvement in student learning and self-discipline. Objectives are centered on resolution of the problem, improvement in student learning, and, ultimately, movement toward self-discipline. Objectives should be *specific, measurable, attainable, results*

FIGURE 1.3   **SMART Guidelines for Designing Objectives**

S	Specific	Desired outcome can be clearly described, based on particular actions required for performance to meet or exceed expectations
M	*Measurable*	Desired outcome can be easily observed and monitored
A	*Attainable*	Response meets student's skill level and maturity
R	*Results oriented*	Focus is on benefit to student
T	*Time frame*	Time allotted to achieve outcome is clearly identified

oriented, and capable of being met within an established *time frame* (SMART). (See Figure 1.3.)

Proposing Solutions

It is expected that, in most cases, the IOSIE method will be followed sequentially. However, the formula is not rigid and allows for teacher creativity. Typically there is more than one specific solution to any classroom-management problem; the idea is to best address the immediate problem while furthering a student's movement toward self-discipline. Solution strategies are described in depth later in this book. It is important to note that effective classroom management is both preventative and interventional; good management strategies are comprehensive in design. The goal of classroom management is to prevent or discourage behavioral problems; effective management strategies are utilized to promptly deal with misbehavior when it occurs.

Implementation

After the problem has been identified and the objectives and solution decided upon, the most difficult step, implementation, occurs. Four basic questions must be addressed before implementation:

1. Who will implement the solution?
2. Is it possible to gain the cooperation and support of everyone involved?
3. How long before a positive result can be achieved?
4. What happens if the solution does not work?

In most classroom situations, the teacher is the one who implements the solution, and often cooperation and support for the implementation involves the student or students and the teacher. However, sometimes it is necessary to solicit the cooperation and support of parents, staff, and other professionals outside the classroom. The time needed for success depends on the seriousness of the problem, the objectives set, and the expected level of resistance. The last question is an acknowledgment that teachers must be adaptive; there are always several ways to approach a problem, and some ways may be more successful than others. The questions asked with respect to implementation provide a natural bridge to the final step, evaluation.

Evaluation

Evaluation or assessment of results is the step most often left out of the IOSIE process, or it is done incorrectly. The most logical way to evaluate is to return to objectives. If objectives were well thought out—specific, measurable, attainable, results oriented, and achievable within a specific time frame—assessment should be straightforward. Has the desired outcome been realized? Did you achieve what you set out to achieve? If success was short-lived and the bad behavior returned, or manifested itself in a different way, the problem was incorrectly identified, or the solution was not adequate to the problem diagnosed. Let's say your effort involved a child who often got into fights at lunchtime. Your objective was for this behavior to stop. If your solution resulted in the child no longer fighting at lunchtime, but now getting into fights after school, the problem was incorrectly identified and the objective was too narrow. Therefore the solution was ineffective and the problem must be readdressed.

APPROACHES TO CLASSROOM MANAGEMENT

There are essentially three general approaches to resolving behavioral problems in the classroom:

1. Consequence
2. Group-guidance
3. Guidance

The **consequence approach** (Canter and Canter, 2001; Jones, 1987) basically lays out consequences for bad behavior. The **group-guidance approach** involves the class in utilizing a judicial framework to adjudicate the infraction or violation in accordance with established class rules (Landau and Gathercoal, 2000; Gathercoal, 1993; Goldstein et al. 1988). In the **guidance approach**, the teacher talks privately with the misbehaving student and decides cooperatively on a resolution.

These three approaches provide the basis on which the management strategies discussed in Part II are developed. Together, the approaches and strategies can be used by teachers in developing their own case study approach to classroom management.

The following sample case studies provide examples of these three approaches.

■ ■ ■ ■ ■

SAMPLE CASE STUDY: CONSEQUENCE APPROACH

Billy Williams, a seventeen-year-old in your twelfth-grade mathematics class at Grover High, has been accused in an anonymous note of extorting lunch money from his classmates. Billy has a reputation as a bad kid, and he'd recently been blamed for a rash of drug activity outside school grounds, but there was no evidence of his being involved in any wrongdoing. Billy lives under a cloud of suspicion but his purported misdeeds have never been proven. Billy is physically large and has a menacing presence, and students and other teachers at your school have expressed to you their fear of him. It is rumored that he has been in fights after school, but no one has ever come forward to implicate him. A colleague, Ms. Kumar, recently had her tires slashed and has spoken to you of her suspicion that Billy slashed her tires in retaliation for the failing grade she gave him the previous semester. Ms. Kumar warns you that you should fear for your own safety as his teacher. You have spoken to Billy on numerous occasions about his poor participation in class, failure to do homework, and general deportment, without results. Billy resents people's judgment of him as a "criminal" and asserts that he's never done anything wrong. When you ask him about his homework he changes the subject, stating that even the principal, Mr. Wormock, has threatened him for no reason. He thinks that people are against him because he is African American. Billy is failing your class. This morning he came to you and explained that he had to pass your class in order to graduate, and that his parents had threatened that if he failed to graduate, they would kick him out of the house when he turned eighteen.

IOSIE Analysis Using a Consequence Approach

Identifying the Problem.   What exactly is the problem in this case? Is it the anonymous note? Billy's reputation as a bad kid? Billy's poor performance in class? His menacing demeanor and rumors that he gets into fights after school? Billy's charge that he is the victim of racial bias? Is it Ms. Kumar's slashed tires and her warning that Billy is dangerous? Or is the problem that Billy may be thrown out of the house if he does not graduate?

Clearly, it is not easy to determine the problem in a complex situation such as this. First it is necessary to prioritize the problems according to creditability and seriousness. Allegations made in an unsigned note, Billy's reputation as a bad kid, your colleague's suspicion that Billy slashed her tires, and rumors surrounding his aggressiveness, while troubling, deal with actions that are unsubstantiated. Billy's belief that he is the victim of racial bias is certainly a concern that must be addressed. But it is Billy's academic performance that is the most pressing problem here. If he fails he will not graduate, and this will, according to him, lead to serious problems at home.

Determining Objectives.   What is the desired outcome in this case? Based on your identification of the problem, your expectation would be that Billy will improve his performance in your class and achieve a passing grade. Since Billy's feelings regarding racial bias may be affecting his academic performance, you would want him to obtain appropriate support to deal with this issue. Your objective includes the expectation that over the long term Billy will become more disciplined in his studies (exercise self-discipline).

Proposing Solutions.   In this approach, solutions are crafted around consequences. Billy has divulged to you the consequence he faces if he does not graduate: he will be thrown out of the house. It is important that you corroborate this information with his parents, to ensure that the consequence Billy faces is real. The solution to the problem is for Billy to improve his performance in class. This would result in a positive consequence of a passing grade and graduation.

Implementation.   After talking with Billy's parents about the consequence to Billy of not graduating (being thrown out of the house), clearly lay out for Billy the expectations he must meet in order to receive a passing grade in your class. Provide tutorial assistance and counsel him on proper classroom deportment and participation. Arrange for Billy to get counseling to deal with his feelings about being the victim of racial prejudice.

Evaluation.   Assessing the results is easily achieved in this case. Were your objectives met within the established time frame? Did Billy's academic performance improve? Evaluation in this situation would need to be done on an ongoing basis to ensure that incremental progress was being made. If it were not, the solution might need fine-tuning or a different approach might have to be sought. Obviously, if Billy's academic performance improved enough for him to receive a passing grade and graduate, your solution was successful.

SAMPLE CASE STUDY: GUIDANCE APPROACH

Sara Ramirez, a thirteen-year-old in your eighth-grade social studies class, often behaves in ways that are inconsiderate of her classmates. She does not respect the personal space of others, often depositing her own wastepaper on a neighbor's desk or placing her personal belongings on another's chair. She has been caught throwing refuse on the floor instead of using the trashcan. She removes students' chairs to create obstructions or so that fellow students have difficulty finding their seats. She rudely pushes other students out of the way to be first out the door at dismissal. Sara often expresses amusement at the discomfort she causes others. She teases the boys and then complains that *they* are bothering *her*. She calls out in class and becomes angry when she is not recognized. You have spoken to Sara and warned her that her grade would suffer if she continued to be disruptive in class. She listens and promises to do better, but quickly lapses back into the bad behavior.

Sara is an average student with definite adolescent tendencies. She is physically mature for her age and dresses beyond her years, yet her behavior is typically child-ish. Students have complained to you about her actions but seem disinclined to con-front Sara directly. Sara comes from a privileged one-parent family, but her father is frequently away on business trips, during which time she stays with her elderly grand-mother. Sara boasts that at her grandmother's she can come and go as she pleases. Sara's mother is fighting for custody but has a history of drug abuse and mental health issues.

IOSIE Analysis Using a Guidance Approach

Identifying the Problem.   Is the problem Sara's lack of social skills? Is it her phys-ical development and inadequate supervision? Is her grandmother too elderly to properly care for her, and her father too distant? Is she acting out over her mother's attempt to gain custody?

As in the previous example, this case study is overburdened with potential problems. Remember, this child's specific actions—lack of regard for others' per-sonal space, rudeness, teasing, expressing amusement at others' distress, calling out in class—are not the problem, but rather indications that there is a problem. The first role of the teacher is to ensure that her students are learning. Sara's be-havior negatively impacts the learning environment and her own class work is suf-fering. The problem to be addressed is Sara's poor academic performance, but the solution might entail helping Sara to deal with her emotional issues.

Determining Objectives.   Your objectives in this case concern two interrelated areas: academic performance and emotional well-being. Your aim is for Sara to im-prove her performance before the end of the marking period. A second and con-comitant objective is for Sara to be more considerate of others in the classroom. Both objectives involve helping Sara to build self-discipline.

Proposing Solutions.   A guidance approach to this problem depends upon a car-ing, positive relationship with the child. Resolution involves having a private heart-to-heart with Sara, in which you encourage her to open up about her situa-tion. The information she divulges can assist you in deciding on the appropriate actions to take. Often, teachers will need the support of family members and car-ing professionals to get students like Sara the help that they need. Empathize with Sara, emphasize the importance of education, and express concern that her per-formance is suffering. Explain to her that you will do your best to get her the sup-port that she needs, but that she must acknowledge that there is a problem and take responsibility for helping to correct it. Encourage her to acknowledge that her behavior in the classroom is disruptive and hurtful to others. Emphasize that tak-ing responsibility for one's actions is empowering; that she may not be able to change others' behavior, but she has the power to change her own. The opportu-nity to talk openly with a caring adult might immediately change the situation for

Sara. Once she accepts responsibility for her actions, she is on the path to emotional health and self-discipline.

Implementation.   Implementation is difficult in this situation because the teacher is expected to assume the role of counselor and guide. Teachers are comfortable in the role of mentor, in the sense of being role models, but they are typically not trained therapists, and emotional/behavioral counseling can easily lead them into uncharted terrain. Often, implementation in such cases involves referring the student to someone trained to deal with the problem. You might involve the guidance counselor, who would seek to involve the family members involved in Sara's care. Most likely the counselor would advise family counseling and perhaps individual counseling for Sara.

Evaluation.   As with the consequence approach, assessment in this case is ongoing. There would likely be setbacks in Sara's case, as her home situation is in flux, given the custody battle. Assessment should focus on classroom performance and Sara's behavior toward classmates. Private consultations with Sara might give you a sense of her emotional development during this process. Observing how she interacts with classmates will also help you gauge the progress being made. Improvement in her class work would certainly be evidence of success.

SAMPLE CASE STUDY: GROUP-GUIDANCE APPROACH

Third grader Abdul Hussein habitually cries while in class. He complains that his classmates pick on him because of his ancestry and religious beliefs (he is Arab and a Muslim). Abdul's behavior has deteriorated over the past several months; he has gone from being an almost docile student to an uncooperative member of the class, and his class work has gone from exceptional to abysmal. You have not been a witness to the incidents that Abdul has described, which have been denied by his classmates. He has claimed that his lunches have been stolen, that his textbooks and notebooks have been defaced, that his homework has been destroyed. He has told you that children blame him for the 9/11 terrorist attacks. He gets emotional when he tells you that his uncle was killed in the World Trade Center attack. He complains that his fellow students think he is a liar and blaspheme his faith. Abdul's parents have requested that you address the harassment of their son. The president of the Parents' Association, whose son is a student in your class, has expressed to you her belief that Abdul is a compulsive liar and acts out in class to get attention. She thinks that Abdul is responsible for intimidating students and defacing student property. The situation comes to a head when you see Abdul fighting with a group of students in the schoolyard at lunchtime. When you intervene to stop the fight, the children claim that Abdul attacked them when they said they would not play with him. He spit at them and called them dirty names.

IOSIE Analysis Using a Group-Guidance Approach

Identifying the Problem.   Is the problem Abdul's frequent crying in class? Is it Abdul's charge that he is a victim of racial and religious bias? Is it Abdul's deteriorating academic performance? In this example, there seems to be a clear link between Abdul's academic performance and the incidents, real or imaginary, that he claims are occurring in the classroom because of racial and religious prejudice against him. In this case, there are three interrelated problems that must be addressed: Abdul's poor academic performance, his charges of racial bias, and his lack of emotional control in the classroom.

Determining Objectives.   Your first objective is for Abdul to turn his academic performance around and regain his superior academic standing in the class. A concomitant objective is to resolve the issues surrounding Abdul's belief that he is the victim of racial and religious bias. The cultural context of 9/11 demands group involvement in these objectives. The culture at large is inundated with terrorist imagery, so it makes sense to approach this problem in a cultural manner (i.e., one that addresses the class as a whole and its surrounding cultural issues).

Proposing Solutions.   As a Muslim of Arabic descent, Abdul is insecure, post-9/11, about his place in American society. You have no evidence to conclude that the students are singling out Abdul because of his ancestry or religious beliefs, but the political/cultural context of the time leads you to be concerned. Intervention in this case provides the teacher with an opportunity to address an individual student's problem while educating the class on a matter of primary importance: cultural and religious tolerance. You decide to have the members of the class read the children's version of *The Diary of Anne Frank* at home, with their parents. The text is then read in class. Then a class project is proposed: the class will be divided into two groups, a red group and a green group, based on colored strips drawn from a hat. Students each draw a strip, which is clipped to their clothing in a visible place. The teacher then explains the rules for each group:

1. Green-group children must line up behind red-group children at entrance, dismissal, and lunchtime.
2. Green-group children must keep their heads bowed when speaking to red-group children and cannot look them in the eyes.
3. In any discussion between green children and red children, the red children will always be considered to be right.

At the end of this project (no more than two class sessions) the class evaluates the impact of dividing the class between green and red, where one group has rights and privileges over the other. The green children discuss what it was like being "ruled" by the red children. The class discusses societies in which there are ruling classes and second-class citizens. The injustice and intolerance of such a system are explored.

Implementation.   A class activity such as the one described here requires the co-operation and support of parents and administration. Other members of the community such as the school guidance counselor, school psychologist, and outside human rights organizations can also be involved.

Evaluation.   In evaluating the solution in this case, you would want to see that the class's consciousness has been raised about the nature of intolerance. Did the children engage the issues of injustice and intolerance? Were they able to openly express their feelings? Did Abdul participate in the discussion? Were the children able to connect the red/green project with Abdul's situation? Are the children more sensitive to Abdul's concerns and feelings as a result of the project? Has Abdul's emotional state and class work improved as a result?

One potential problem with the group-guidance approach is that it may pit an individual against the group, putting one child on trial for creating a problem. Teachers must ensure that a group-guidance intervention does not deteriorate into a punishment session or an airing of grievances against an individual. Students should be encouraged to participate freely and to develop critical thinking during such discussions, but teachers must be active moderators, ensuring that the process is fair, empathetic, and inclusive. It should be a democratic process, as democratic classrooms perpetuate free and democratic nations.

PRACTICE EXERCISE
MINI CASES FROM THE FIELD

Analyze the following "mini" case studies using the IOSIE method. Reflect upon how you as the teacher might act in each situation. Be sure to follow all five steps of the IOSIE process:

1. *Identify* the problem.
2. Determine the *objectives* that you want to achieve.
3. Propose a *solution.*
4. *Implement* the solution.
5. *Evaluate* results.

In devising a solution, or behavior-management plan for these cases, utilize one of the four theoretical models of human behavior discussed previously (behavioral, psychodynamic, environmental, and constructivist).

1. John Paladino, a tenth-grade student with a reputation as a troublemaker, habitually disrupts your classroom presentations. He makes obtrusive sounds, clicking his tongue or tapping the underside of his seat. When you ask him to desist he denies responsibility or blames another student, which leads to protestations of innocence from other students and often provokes an argument. Your inclination is to have John removed from your class. Upon reflection, however, you decide to analyze this case using the IOSIE method. How might the behavioral model guide you? Describe the steps you would take toward resolution.

2. Tamara Jones is an emotional fourth grader. She often cries in class without apparent provocation. You are aware that her parents have recently separated and are

battling over custody of Tamara. You have spoken to the parents, who both blame the other for Tamara's emotional distress. When you ask Tamara about the problem she says, through her tears, that nothing is wrong. Upon reflection you decide to use your understanding of the psychodynamic model and the IOSIE method to address Tamara's situation. What are the steps that you would take?

3. Billy Marchica, in your seventh-grade English class, often bewilders you with his comments and questions, which are typically original but off-point. For example, on one occasion you were discussing with the class a song about a coal miner's daughter and Billy shouted out that anthracite is no longer mined in Wales. Is he being a wise guy? Are his comments an attempt to participate in the discussion or a deliberate effort to disrupt the class? Upon reflection you decide to use the constructivist model as a guide in assessing Billy's behavior. How would you address this case using the IOSIE method?

4. Susan Ramos, a ten-year-old in your mainstream fifth-grade class, struggles with reading. After administering the Woodcock Reading Mastery Test to your class, you have determined that Susan reads at a first-grade level. Susan's mother is in the military, and Susan has moved often; she has only been in your class two months. Your colleague questions your assessment of Susan and has suggested that your standards for reading might be too high, owing to your past experience teaching in a secondary school. How would you address this case using the IOSIE method, as well as from the perspective of performance discrepancy versus inadequate performance?

Addressing Emotional Problems

Spotting the Warning Signs.   One of the most difficult problems facing teachers is in identifying and addressing student emotional problems before they develop into serious behavioral issues. Unfortunately, emotional problems often go undetected by teachers and other adults; behaviors that are not overt (acting-out behaviors) are much more difficult to recognize and address. It is important that teachers attend to the warning signs, notify parents and other primary caregiver(s) when a problem is suspected, and seek appropriate intervention (referral to counseling) when necessary. According to Graham, MacMillan, and Bocian (1996), the following are warning signs one should watch for.

Warning Signs of Emotional Problems

Students may have externalized emotional problems if they

- Become a chronic discipline problem
- Lack empathy or compassion
- Have temper tantrums
- Are often truant
- Experience poor academic performance
- Have conflicts with authority figures

- Bully others
- Damage the property of others
- Become noncompliant
- Become impulsive
- Become aggressive

Students may have internalized emotional problems if they

- Appear isolated from peers
- Seem overly dependent on others
- Are moody
- Exhibit feelings of helplessness
- Show an interest in cults
- Have an inordinate attraction to fantasy
- Are apathetic
- Are a bully victim
- Are frequently absent because of illness
- Cry inappropriately and too often
- Abuse themselves

The Classroom as a Preventative Space

Teachers have limitations in dealing with emotional problems in the classroom, because they are trained as educators, not psychologists. But classrooms that meet the emotional needs of their students can go a long way toward ensuring that emotional problems do not become serious behavioral problems.

The key here is for teachers to engage students in meaningful learning while modeling appropriate behavior. Again, the goal of all efforts toward discipline is the building of self-discipline in students. Children naturally respond to teachers who seek to understand and support them. Behavioral problems can be minimized in classrooms led by teachers who bring effective management strategies and personal commitment to their classrooms. When students' emotional/psychological needs are met, the classroom becomes a preventive space, discouraging misbehavior and enhancing learning and personal development. Teachers can take the following steps (Henley and Long, 2003) to ensure that their classrooms meet their students' emotional/psychological needs:

1. *Make learning relevant.* Establish links between curriculum and students' lives.
2. *Foster positive peer relationships.* Help students develop interpersonal skills through peer tutoring and cooperative learning activities (see Goldstein et al. 1988).
3. *Teach behavior-management skills.* Help students develop self-discipline and utilize effective conflict-resolution strategies.
4. *Make the classroom a supportive environment.* Stress tolerance and empathy as expectations are set for student behavior. Ensure that classroom activities are

inclusive, build self-confidence in students, strengthen social relationships, and bolster self-efficacy.

5. *Help students cope with stress.* Assist students in keeping a proper perspective on individual and community/global problems.

6. *Instill hope.* Have a positive attitude. Contextualize problems so that students can be assured of a potential resolution.

KEY TERMS TO FOCUS ON

performance discrepancy/inadequate
   performance
behavioral model
psychodynamic model
environmental model

constructivist model
IOSIE method
consequence approach
group-guidance approach
guidance approach

DISCUSSION QUESTIONS

1. Define the five core types of classroom misbehavior: moral; personal; legal; safety; and educational.

2. Describe the four basic theoretical models of human behavior (behavioral, psychodynamic, environmental, constructivist), identified by Danforth and Boyle, that can be used with case analysis.

3. Describe the case study analysis of misbehavior using the four models of human behavior and the IOSIE method.

4. Write a critical appraisal of approaches to managing children's behavior and the practices you believe best facilitate instruction.

FIELD EXPERIENCE ACTIVITIES AND CASES FROM THE FIELD

Develop a behavior-management plan in response to the following situations. If possible, interview a practicing teacher about approaches he or she would use, and compare your responses. The cases can also be used in teacher-education classrooms, as a basis for role-playing behavior problems and possible interventions.

1. Billy is a second grader who constantly asks to leave the room to go to the bathroom.

2. Sammy is a fifth grader who makes fun of smaller classmates. His name-calling frequently provokes fights.

3. Mary, a sixth grader, claims that Betty took her pen from her desk and refuses to give it back.

4. Jane, a quiet fourth grader, sits crying in the back of the classroom. When you ask her what the trouble is she tells you that nobody likes her.

5. Richard, a bright tenth grader, is always late to class, and does not complete assignments on time.

6. You see students smoking on school grounds, in direct violation of school rules.

7. John is absent from your class two or three times a week.

8. A child in your kindergarten class cries often, disrupting lessons.

9. You've had frequent complaints from students in your fifth-grade class that personal items are missing from the student wardrobe.

10. A child in your second-grade class is lagging academically. The parent refuses to have her tested by the school-based support team.

11. A child in your sixth-grade class seems to be deliberately failing tests to avoid being promoted to the new junior high school.

12. A student in your tenth-grade math class begins to fail, and acts out in your class. When you speak to her privately she claims to be in love with an older man.

13. A student in your third-grade class seems inordinately fearful of adult strangers.

14. A colleague who uses your classroom in the period after your class blames your students for writing on the desks, and implies that you cannot control your students.

15. One of your students, Jamie, is struggling in class, and has told his parents that you are not explaining the work to him. You know Jamie as someone who has trouble taking responsibility for his actions; his parents tell you that their son never lies.

REFERENCES

Albert, L. 1996. *Cooperative discipline: How to manage your classroom and promote self-esteem.* Circle Pines, MN: American Guidance Service.

A Public Agenda Report. 2004. *Teaching interrupted.* New York: Public Agenda (May). www.public agenda.org/research/research_reports.cfm.

Canter, L., and M. Canter. 2001. *Assertive discipline: Positive behavior management for today's classrooms.* 3rd ed. Los Angeles: Canter and Associates.

Canter, L., and M. Canter. 1976. *Assertive discipline: A take-charge approach for today's educator.* Seal Beach, CA: Canter and Associates.

Curwin, R. 1997. Discipline with dignity: Beyond obedience. *Education Digest* (December), 11–14.

Curwin, R. 1992. *Rediscovering hope: Our greatest teaching strategy.* Bloomington, IN: National Education Service.

Curwin, R. L., and A. N. Mendler. 1999. Zero tolerance for zero tolerance. *Kappan* 81 (2), 119–20.

Curwin, R. L., and A. N. Mendler. 1988. Packaged discipline programs: Let the buyer beware. *Educational Leadership* 46 (2), 68–71.

Cooper, J. M., ed. 1999. *Classroom teaching skills.* 6th ed. Boston: Houghton Mifflin.

Danforth, S., and J. R. Boyle. 2000. *Cases in behavior management.* Upper Saddle River, NJ: Merrill/Prentice Hall.

Dohrn, B. 1997. Youth violence: False fears and hard truths. *Educational Leadership* 55 (2), 45–47.

Dreikurs, R. 1968. *Psychology in the classroom.* 2nd ed. New York: Harper and Row.

Gathercoal, P. 1993. *Judicious discipline.* 3rd ed. San Francisco: Caddo Gap Press.

Ginott, H. 1976. *Teacher and child.* New York: Avon.

Glasser, W. 1998. *Choice theory: A new psychology of personal freedom.* New York: Harper Collins.

Glasser, W. 1997. A new look at school failure and school success. *Phi Delta Kappan* 78, 596–602.

Glasser, W. 1990. *The quality school.* New York: Harper and Row.

Glasser, W. 1986. *Control therapy in the classroom.* New York: Harper and Row.

Glasser, W. 1969. *Schools without failure.* New York: Harper and Row.

Glasser, W. 1965. *Reality therapy.* New York: Harper and Row.

Goldstein, A. P. et al. 1988. *How to teach children prosocial skills.* Champaign, IL: Research Press.

Goldstein, A. P. et al. 1980. *Skillstreaming the adolescent.* Champaign, IL: Research Press.

Goodlad, J. 1983. *A place called school.* New York: McGraw-Hill.

Goodman, J. F. 2003. Is punishment passé? Or does it have a role to play in moral education? *Education Week* (November 5), 40, 42.

Gordon, T. 1975. *TET: Teacher effectiveness training.* New York: Peter H. Wyden.

Gossen, D. C. 1993. *Restitution: Restructuring school discipline.* Chapel Hill, NC: New View Publications.

Graham, F. M., D. C. MacMillan, and K. Bocian. 1996. "Behavioral earthquakes": Low-frequency salient behavioral events that differentiate students at risk of behavior disorders. *Behavioral Disorders* 21 (4), 277–92.

Henley, M., and N. Long. 2003. Helping students with emotional problems succeed. *Classroom Leadership* 7 (3), 1–4.

Jones, F. 1987. *Positive classroom discipline.* New York: McGraw-Hill.

Kounin, J. 1977. *Discipline and group management in classrooms.* Rev. ed. New York: Rinehart and Winston.

Landau, B., and P. Gathercoal. 2000. Creating peaceful classrooms: Judicious discipline and class meetings. *Phi Delta Kappan* 81, 450–54.

Mager, F. R., and P. Pipe. 1997. *Analyzing performance problems: Or you really oughta wanna.* 3rd ed. Atlanta, GA: Center for Effective Performance.

CHAPTER TWO

MANAGEMENT STYLES
What Teachers Bring to School

FOCUS POINTS

1. Management styles reflect a teacher's beliefs, skills, and practices.
2. Management styles can be developed, improved, and adapted; all teachers can become effective classroom managers.

As explained in Chapter 1, an effective teacher manages a classroom using "positive" disciplinary action (action aimed at building self-discipline); an ineffective teacher uses "negative" disciplinary action in an attempt to enforce control. Teachers' management styles determine how they run their classrooms and how learning takes place there. Management style is a reflection of teaching personality, which is influenced by a teacher's beliefs, skills, and practices. Peterson (1979) defined style as how teachers utilize space in the classroom, their choice of instructional activities and materials and their method of grouping students. One's life experiences and beliefs about how children learn make up an important component of teaching personality and contribute to the development of a management style. Management styles are as varied as the individual personalities that they reflect. Teachers put their own individual stamp on the management style they use. The wide assortment of management styles is a result of the fact that most teachers are eclectic in developing their own (Kellough and Roberts, 2002). Management styles are dynamic, and develop over a teacher's career. Teachers can work to improve their management styles to better meet the needs of their students and to enhance student learning, and teachers can adapt their management styles to fit particular situations.

An evaluation of management style would consider both process and product. Process refers to teacher intention, action, and input, and product refers to the result: the effect on children in the classroom. If the goal of a teacher's classroom-management style is to develop self-discipline in students, the success of that style depends on the extent to which self-discipline is present in students.

A classic study by Lippitt and White (1943) analyzed the effects on children of three different leadership styles, labeled authoritarian, democratic, and laissez-faire. The authoritarian leader issued orders and did not invite student questions or comments, and provided no guidance in doing the task, remaining separate from the activity. The democratic leader consulted with the children on the task, and guided students as well as participated in the activity. The laissez-faire leader gave the students some knowledge but was not a participant in the activity. The three styles resulted in different outcomes for the children with respect to both group morale and success of the end product. These styles can be understood as falling on the spectrum of management control that classifies management models as involving the most, a relative amount, or the least teacher control. The consequences, group guidance, and individual guidance method can also be seen as falling along this spectrum. Management approaches in general will fall somewhere along this control spectrum.

Emmer, Evertson, and Anderson (1980) examined how effective and less-effective teachers differ in behavior management. Those teachers with less-effective management styles tended to issue general rather than specific directives to their classes. Statements such as, "We will wait until all are sitting properly before we continue with this lesson," or "Are we ready to behave now?" are examples of general criticisms. In both of these examples it would have been much more appropriate to direct the criticism toward the individual(s) who were misbehaving.

Ineffective teachers were further found to have difficulty individualizing their instructional practices and tended to issue vague and unclear directions with regard to classroom assignments. Individualizing involves directing questions and assigning class work based on the individual student ability level or student input.

Ineffective teachers were also shown to do little monitoring of students' work. Also found to be limited was the students' understanding of teacher expectations. The most serious finding was that less-effective teachers were shown to spend less time actually teaching than did effective teachers. Instructional time can be curtailed for various reasons, all of which can be addressed by improvements in management style.

MANAGEMENT STYLE AND BELIEFS, SKILLS, AND PRACTICES

A teacher's management style can be determined through self-assessment that focuses on one's beliefs, skills, and practices. Beliefs refer to one's convictions with regard to classroom management and student learning, and the level of teacher control one feels is necessary in order to create a successful learning environment. All teachers have a particular comfort level when it comes to control of the classroom. This comfort level will also influence a teacher's management orientation. Those favoring a consequences approach to classroom management will tend to favor a high degree of teacher control, while those who are guidance oriented are more comfortable sharing control with their students.

The skills that teachers bring to class develop through instruction and experience. These skills involve pedagogy and curriculum, disciplinary measures, classroom organization, and presentation or teacher conduct. Teacher skills cover everything from employing the right tone of voice to determining the appropriate form of instruction for any particular lesson. The skills one brings to the classroom clearly affect one's management style; higher-skilled teachers tend to have more effective management styles and thus less behavior problems in their classrooms.

Practices are also important determinants of management style. Practices, routines, and procedures govern the day-to-day operation of a classroom. Practices that facilitate meaningful instructional transitions and the orderly entrance and dismissal of students from the classroom characterize well-run rooms. Procedures describe how classroom actions are properly carried out, and affect everything from a student's being excused to go to the bathroom, pencil sharpening, and garbage disposal to essential rules for conduct and deportment. In well-run classrooms, disciplinary rules are clearly understood by every student. The teacher's expectations are clearly defined and comprehended by each child. The mark of good classroom practices is their consistency. Consistent practice makes for good management; inconsistent practice is the mark of the less-well-managed room.

Ornstein (2002) understands teacher effectiveness to be commonsensical: organized teachers are better disciplinarians than disorganized teachers; friendly teachers are more effective at conveying meaning to students than unfriendly teachers. The same can be said of the beliefs, skills, and practices that make up one's management style: common sense dictates those elements that will have the most practical effectiveness in the classroom.

MANAGEMENT STYLE SELF-ASSESSMENT

Determining Beliefs

Teachers all hold convictions about how classrooms are properly managed and how much teacher control is needed in the classroom, as well as how students learn. Such beliefs can reveal the personal likes and dislikes of teachers as well as their biases, both realized and unrealized. Since beliefs influence management style, it should be possible, through a process of analysis and self-reflection on one's beliefs, to come to a deeper understanding of one's own style. The Teacher Inventory: Beliefs about Classroom Control (Figure 2.1) presents twelve sets of statements related to classroom managerial situations. Your response to the choices offered will enable you to assess your beliefs as they affect your management style. Your beliefs can be understood to fall somewhere on a continuum from least, to moderate, to most classroom-management control. The results may sur-

FIGURE 2.1 Teacher Inventory: Beliefs about Classroom Control

Instructions: Circle a or b to indicate the statement with which you identify the most. You must choose between the two statements for each item.

1. **a.** Students are immature and therefore limited. They need adults to establish rules of classroom governance for them.

   b. The emotional needs of individual students, rather than a scripted preestablished set of rules imposed indiscriminately on all.

2. **a.** Teachers should assign seating during the first class session of a new school year and require students to keep that seat unless they are reseated by the teacher.

   b. Student seating should be flexible, and students should be allowed to decide where they should sit through a class meeting discussions with the teacher.

3. **a.** Students should be given a choice of project topics and should be able to consult with the teacher in coming to a decision.

   b. The material students learn and the tasks they perform must be determined by the teacher, along with the sequence of instruction.

4. Classroom equipment and books are being misused, damaged, and even destroyed. I will most likely:

   a. Hold a class meeting, show the damaged materials to the class, and ask them how the problem is to be solved, including what action should be taken toward a student found to be misusing materials.

   b. Physically remove materials from the classroom, or limit the number of materials available and observe students closely to determine who is at fault. I will then deal with the behavior on an individual basis.

5. Two students of equal power and ability are engaged in a heated verbal conflict over classroom supplies. I would:

   a. Immediately intervene, demand that they desist, remind them of classroom rules about expected behavior, and threaten a sanction if they cannot behave.

   b. Avoid interfering in something that the students need to resolve themselves.

6. **a.** A student strongly requests not to work with the group during a class period. I would permit this, believing that the student has some emotional concerns related to the group experience.

   b. One student is being refused entry into group activities. I would raise this as an issue in a class meeting and ask for a discussion of the reasons for the exclusion and possible solutions from the student and the group.

7. The noise level in class is at an unacceptably high level. I would:

   a. Flick the lights to get everyone's attention, ask the students to be quiet, and later praise those who complied.

   b. Take aside those students making the most noise and ask them to reflect on their behavior and how it affects others. I would get an agreement from them to work quietly.

FIGURE 2.1 *(Cont.)*

8. During the first few days of class, I would:
   a. Permit the students to test their ability to get along as a new group and set no pre-determined rules, introducing only those rules that seem needed.
   b. Immediately establish class rules and consequences that would be applied if these rules were broken.

9. When I hear a student swear I:
   a. Assume that the student is frustrated and privately encourage him to talk about what is bothering him.
   b. Confront the student and counsel him about language expectations for the classroom.

10. If a student disrupts class while I am trying to lecture, I would:
    a. Ignore the disruption if possible and/or move the student to the back of the room as a consequence of this behavior.
    b. Express to the student my dismay at being disrupted in my task.

11. a. Students must accept that there are some school rules that need to be obeyed and that any student who breaks them will be subjected to the punishment that has been set for that infraction.
    b. Rules are not written in stone and can be renegotiated by the class, and sanctions will vary with each student.

12. A student refuses to put away her work or materials after using them. I would most likely:
    a. Express to the student how not putting things away will affect future activities in this space, and how frustrating this will be for other students. I would then leave the materials where they are for the remainder of the day.
    b. Ask the student to reflect on her behavior, think about how the noncompliance affects others, and tell her that if she cannot follow the rules, she will lose the privilege of using the materials in the future.

Scoring Key

Level of Teacher Control

1		2		3	
Least		Relative		Most	
Student Autonomy		*Confronting*		*Rules*	
Therapeutic		*Group Counseling*		*Strong Management*	
Listening, Relationship		*Leadership*		*Consequences*	
1b	4b	2b	3a	1a	2a
6a	5b	4a	6b	3b	5a
8a	9a	7b	9b	7a	8b
10a	12a	11b	12b	10b	11a

Source: Adapted from material in C. H. Wolfgang (1999). *Solving discipline problems: Methods and models for today's teachers.* 4th ed. Boston: Allyn & Bacon.

prise you or confirm what you already knew. Remember, one's management style can be developed to more closely reflect one's beliefs.

Determining Skills

Stronge (2002) developed a teacher skills checklist that can be used to evaluate a practitioner's skills as they relate to management style. The checklist includes the qualities that reinforce good classroom management, organization, and disciplinary practices for students. When used for the purposes of self-assessment, the checklist in Figure 2.2 can reveal an individual's strengths and weaknesses and identify those skills that may need to be developed in order for the practitioner to become a more-effective classroom manager.

Determining Practices

The checklist in Figure 2.3 should assist you in determining whether you are using practices that meet the basic needs of the children in your classes. By reflecting on and assessing your responses you should be able to determine if your current practices are negatively or positively impacting your management style. A practical exercise of this would be the example shown in Figure 2.4, which is adapted from the state of Florida's teacher program.

How Teachers Describe Their Management Styles

Coeyman (2002) interviewed teachers with longtime classroom experience and asked them to describe their management styles and what they believed to be the essentials of a well-run classroom. I posed the same question to teachers who were teaching special education and high school classes as well as to a high school principal.

> *John Johnson, eighth-grade teacher at PS 53 in New York*: In September, I size up the class and figure out who the leaders are. I write up rules and a syllabus and give it to the kids and send it home to parents so everyone knows exactly what to expect. I send letters home, with a copy to the assistant principal, if there is a serious problem. The classroom should be a safe environment. Students should feel comfortable, and the teacher should be in charge, but not a control freak. The teacher should exude confidence in himself and his subject matter, and make students feel he likes them. There is no one right way.

> *Jeanne Bustard, pre-kindergarten teacher at Friends Select School in Philadelphia*: The two overarching things are appropriateness for the age, and working on respect and learning—what that means and how we treat one another. These two things are primary and everything else falls under them. Talk to students about how to treat one another. Don't ask them to sit and listen or focus for too long, but at the same time expand their ability to do that. Much discipline is preventive, mak-

FIGURE 2.2   Teacher Skills Checklist

QUALITY	INDICATORS	NOT OBSERVED	INEFFECTIVE	APPRENTICE	PROFESSIONAL	MASTER
Classroom Management	■ Uses consistent and proactive discipline ■ Establishes routines for all daily tasks and needs ■ Orchestrates smooth transitions and continuity of classroom momentum ■ Balances variety and challenge in student activities ■ Multitasks ■ Is aware of all activities in the classroom ■ Anticipates potential problems ■ Uses space, efficiently, moves around the classroom to manage trouble spots and to encourage attention					
Organization	■ Handles routine tasks promptly, efficiently, and consistently ■ Prepares materials in advance; ready to use ■ Organizes classroom space efficiently					
Disciplining Students	■ Interprets and responds to inappropriate behavior promptly ■ Implements rules of behavior fairly and consistently ■ Reinforces and reiterates expectations for positive behavior ■ Uses appropriate disciplinary measures					

Scores should reflect which skills teachers need to develop in order to improve/enhance their management style.

Source: Strong, J. (2002). *Qualities of effective teachers.* Alexandria, VA: ASCD. Reprinted by Permission.

FIGURE 2.3   Meeting Basic Psychological Needs Checklist

The purpose of this checklist is to guide you in assessing whether or not you are using practices that attempt to meet the psychological needs of your students. Rate each of the items below by using the following scale:

1—Always Do   2—Sometimes Do   3—Rarely Do   4—Never Do

The higher your score, the greater is your utilization of practices that meet the psychological needs of your students.

The Need for Freedom to Make Choices

1. I provide opportunities for students to make choices that are meaningful to them.
2. I offer students a variety of ways and choices to demonstrate knowledge, intelligence, and mastery.
3. I attempt to accommodate for the choices of all learners, tactile, kinesthetic, global, visual, auditory, and verbal by creating assignments that meet these modalities.
4. I allow for ample opportunities for children to move about the room to make choices with regard to activities they wish to do.
5. I attempt to provide for a variety of interests, modality strengths, and learning preferences in my directions, instructions, and assignments.

The Need for Love and Belonging

1. I avoid using humiliation, sarcasm, ridicule, anger, and impatience when dealing with students.
2. I respect student needs for dignity, success, purpose, acceptance, and attention.
3. I attempt to be a model of a tender, caring person.
4. I work at eliminating prejudice with regard to race, sexual orientation, cultural background, and physical appearance, as well as academic or athletic competence.
5. I respond appropriately to any put-down or slur expressed by students or staff.

The Need for Power and Achievement

1. I encourage students to make decisions about their learning, such as what, where, with whom, and how or how much.
2. I provide opportunities for students to create, design, or renegotiate assignments in order to develop student competence.
3. I consult with students to make them aware of changes in their behavior or performance so that they can correct them.
4. I emphasize the positive consequences of cooperation and working to achieve your goals.
5. I explain how parents, teachers, and administrators can help students achieve rather than using threats and warnings to discomfort students.

The Need for Fun and Enjoyable Work

1. I attempt to meet student needs for fun in positive, constructive, and proactive ways.
2. I respect students' affective and emotional needs and am committed to listening and supporting their feelings in positive ways.
3. My use of humor is positive and never hurtful.
4. I ask students what activities make them happy and then plan accordingly.
5. I provide for breaks and limit the amount of time for stressful activities.

Source: Jane Bluestein, Ph.D., excerpts adapted from *Creating Emotionally Safe Schools: A Guide for Educators and Parents.* Copyright © 2001 by Jane Bluestein, Ph.D. Reprinted with the permission of the publishers, www.hcibooks.com.

ing sure things work, talking a lot before things happen, making things stop quickly.

Lynn Fuller, sixth-grade teacher at Indian Camp School in Pawhuska, Oklahoma: The main thing I do is to set my rules and consequences from Day 1. The key is consistency. I'm a little controlling, but I feel I have to have a safe environment for my kids to learn in. A lot of people say choose your battles, but if I let little things go by, they turn into big problems. If you ignore the little rules they break, they move on to the big things. If you're going to have a rule you don't enforce, don't have it. I had to figure this out and it was pretty hard. They tell you strategies you can use, but mostly you have to work it out for yourself.

Lucille Scarpaci, fifth-grade special education teacher at PS 163 in New York: A well-run classroom has a noise about it, a sound like spring rain falling on new leaves. It is alive with expectation of discovery. . . . The text around are the maps to this discovery, being worn, with corners turned up. Smells . . . the smell of bubble gum and lead from number two pencils . . . damp earth from plants on the windowsill . . . a fishy smell from the class pet, a turtle named Harry Potter. This is not the classroom of my youth, where the seats were bolted to the floor in neat rows, and children sat stiffly at attention hanging onto every word the unsmiling teacher lectured. . . .

Sidney Leibowiz, mathematics teacher at Pershing Junior High School in Brooklyn: As a retired junior high school math teacher who has taught in Brooklyn for over thirty years, I have found the following management techniques to be useful. The first is the student's need for routines. There should be a seating plan. When students come into the classroom, the room should be orderly. There should be an "aim" and a "do now," which reflect the skill taught in the previous lesson. Homework should be handed in at this time. From there we can proceed in teaching a new math skill. Here a well-thought-out lesson plan is essential. This must include motivation, procedure, practice, and a homework assignment based on the new skill as well as previous skills taught. The key, I believe, to classroom management is the establishment of routines.

Joseph S. Fusco, principal at Bergen Catholic High School, Oradell, New Jersey: The orderly classrooms in which I have witnessed good teaching and learning have clear expectations and a sense of concern for the student as an individual. Thirty years ago, as a young educator, I was faced with a situation that helped form my view with regard to what a well-run class was. I told my first class that I had one simple rule: I respect you and you respect me. The expectation was clear and it demonstrated concern for the individual. A few months into the term, a student, who was also a star football player, was having difficulty with a concept I was attempting to teach. Even though he didn't know the answers I kept pushing him to frustration. He finally said to me, you f——. I attempted to remain calm and said, "Rick, I didn't quite hear what you said, do you mind repeating it?" Rick said he was sorry. I also apologized to Rick because I, too, had violated the rule of mutual respect. I learned that day that concern, caring, and respect are the keys to an orderly class environment. Acknowledging the correlation between student academic success and the respect a teacher demonstrates makes for a successful career.

These observations show that teachers describe their management styles as issuing from their beliefs, skills, and practices. Teachers' beliefs about how students learn and what sort of leader and classroom they respond to determine the environments they create and the image they project. They have beliefs about how a classroom should be organized and how class time should be structured. Teachers also bring into the classroom beliefs about mutual respect and the need for consequences in developing self-discipline. Skills are spoken of with respect to how subject matter is presented and how curriculum supports social and emotional learning. Practices such as establishing rules, routines, and procedures are seen as paramount to the well-run classroom. The importance of communicating with parents is also seen as essential to well-functioning classrooms.

Survey of Beliefs, Skills, and Practices

To further your understanding of your personal management style, reflect on your own beliefs, skills, and practices. Review the following statements and mark them as a belief (b), skill (s), or practice (p) that you identify with as reflecting your management style. If you do not identify with a statement do not mark it. Reflect on your responses.

- I believe I establish clear rules of conduct for my students to follow.
- I have my class decide on the rules by which our class will function.
- I believe I never utilize harsh desists.
- I use mild desists.
- I believe in fostering interpersonal relations.
- I believe school is for learning, not socializing.
- I have the skills for resolving incidents of misconduct through discussion and negotiation.
- Effective classroom management results from teacher control, not discussion.
- I have the skills necessary to modify my classroom environment.
- I really don't know how to organize my class for learning.
- I have the skills to move my lessons effectively.
- My lessons at times lag and lose focus.
- I follow a practice with my students in that directions I give must be followed immediately.
- I practice the art of directing students without causing hard feelings.
- I have a practice of reprimanding all children who misbehave.
- I sometimes ignore misbehavior.
- A practice necessary for effective classroom management is clarifying expectations.
- I practice modeling to clarify expectations.
- I believe in a traditional, teacher-centered approach to classroom management.
- I believe in a progressive, student-centered approach to classroom management.

KEY TERMS TO FOCUS ON

management style
determining beliefs
determining skills
determining practices

authoritarian leadership style
democratic leadership style
laissez-faire leadership style

DISCUSSION QUESTIONS

1. What is meant by a teacher's "management style"?

2. What makes some management styles more effective than others?

3. How does a teacher's comfort level with respect to classroom control determine her management style?

4. Explain teaching beliefs, skills, and practices and how they contribute to management style.

5. Write a brief paragraph describing your personal management style, based on your beliefs, skills, and practices.

MINI CASES FROM THE FIELD

Analyze the following brief case studies utilizing the IOSIE method as explained in Chapter 1. Be sure to use commonsense understandings of what makes for good classroom management, and the information contained in this chapter, to assist you in resolving the problems presented.

1. Phil Cortez was a new teacher who wanted to meet the needs of his students but found little time to reflect on what he should do to gain control of his sixth-grade class, which had been misbehaving on a regular basis. He wanted to find an approach to classroom management that he could adopt and modify to suit his own teaching personality while also meeting the needs of his students. He knew he could determine his general beliefs by completing the Teacher Inventory: Beliefs about Classroom Control assessment contained in this chapter. Phil reasoned that once he was clear about his beliefs, he would be able to determine which approach (consequence, group guidance, or

guidance) was most in line with his teaching personality. He would thus be able to deal much more effectively with the misbehavior that occurred in his class. After analyzing this case using the IOSIE method, what advice would you give Phil with regard to developing a management style that reflects his beliefs?

2. Linder Tang could not come to grips with the procedures necessary to manage her tenth-grade biology class. She had few problems with her other four classes, which were made up of honors students who typically did exactly what they were told to do. She taught each of her five classes the same way. A "do now" was placed on the board and students were given five minutes to complete this task at the beginning of each class session. Then she lectured for exactly thirty minutes, allowing the remaining ten minutes of each instructional period for questions and a daily homework assignment. Her non-honors biology class seemed completely

unresponsive to this approach, which worked so well in her honors classes. These non-honors students seemed bored, and habitually talked during her lecture. Many ignored her directions entirely. Her supervisor told her that if she stressed procedures and worked on her teaching skills she would see an improvement. After analyzing this case using the IOSIE method, determine what teaching skills Ms. Tang should employ to better manage her non-honors class. Refer to the Teacher Skills Checklist, introduced in this chapter, to assist you in determining those skills that Ms. Tang would benefit from developing.

3. Yolanda Brown believed that if she could improve her management style, she would be a more effective teacher to her first-grade class, which seemed totally out of control. The children paid little if any attention to her calls for them to behave properly. Betty Sorkin, a veteran teacher whose class was next door, suggested that Yolanda focus on improving classroom practices. After analyzing this case using

the IOSIE method, draw up a list of practices, consistent procedures governing the day-to-day life of the classroom, that might help Yolanda become a more effective teacher.

4. Sal Verde knew he had to meet the basic psychological needs of his ninth-grade mathematics class if he was going to create an environment in which his students could learn. Adolescence was wreaking havoc on this classroom. On some occasions his students acted as if they knew it all and resented any direction offered by the teacher. At other times they seemed completely helpless and threw temper tantrums. The class as a whole refused to take responsibility for their actions. Sal knew he had to guide them along the path to maturity and hold them accountable for their actions, but the way to accomplish this eluded him. After analyzing this case using the IOSIE method and reviewing Figure 2.3, describe the actions that Sal could take to develop/adapt his management style to meet the needs of these particular students.

REFERENCES

Bluestein, J. 2001. *Creating emotionally safe schools.* Deerfield Beach, FL: Heath Communications.

Coeyman, M. 2002. It's 8 AM and everything is not under control. *Christian Science Monitor* (October 8).

Emmer, E. T., C. M. Evertson, and L. M. Anderson. 1980. Effective classroom management at the beginning of the school year. *Elementary School Journal* 80 (5), 219–31.

Kellough, R. D., and P. L. Roberts. 2002. *A resource guide for elementary school teaching.* 5th ed. Upper Saddle River, NJ: Merrill Prentice Hall.

Lippitt, R., and R. K. White. 1943. The social climate of children's groups. *Child Behavior and Develop-*

ment, ed. R. G. Barker and J. S. Kounin, 485–508. New York: McGraw Hill.

Ornstein, A. 2002. Interview with the author (September 29).

Peterson, P. L. 1979. Direct instruction reconsidered. *Research on teaching: Concepts, findings, and implications,* ed. P. L. Peterson and H. J. Walberg, 57–69. Berkeley, CA: McCutchan.

Strong, J. H. 2002. *Qualities of effective teachers.* Alexandria, VA: Association for Supervision and Curriculum Development.

Wolfgang, C. H. 1999. *Solving discipline problems: Methods and models for today's teachers.* Boston: Allyn & Bacon.

CHAPTER THREE

IDENTIFYING SUCCESSFUL TEACHERS

FOCUS POINTS

1. Successful teachers have in common personal attributes, pedalogical practices; and mastery over content while understanding the importance of classroom management. They possess the skills that enable them to meet the needs, both academic and psychological, of their students.

2. Successful teachers are engaging and well received by students.

3. Successful teachers are by definition effective classroom managers.

ATTRIBUTES OF SUCCESSFUL TEACHERS

Attributes are personal characteristics or qualities that are either inherent in an individual or acquired through experience or training. Successful teachers have been shown to share certain attributes that allow them to create classroom environments in which the needs of their students are met and learning is facilitated; successful teachers are by definition effective classroom managers.

Social and emotional characteristics shape pedagogical practice. Successful teachers take a "caring, sharing approach" to classroom management (Haberman, 2004); they are:

- Approachable
- Patient
- Truthful
- Warm
- Loving

Being *approachable* is an essential attribute of successful teachers. If children feel secure in your presence then you have succeeded in alleviating the biggest deterrent to learning, fear. Teachers can foster this quality in themselves by getting to know their students, making an effort to understand them as individuals. Ask focused questions and listen to the responses that your students give. Do they like sports? What sports? What kinds of lessons excite and engage them? Is the classroom an environment that stimulates their curiosity and reflects their world? Think about their responses and design-learning activities around them.

Patience is a necessary attribute when working with children, and successful teachers have this quality in abundance. One can focus their efforts on developing this quality by empathizing with students in their struggle to learn and develop as human beings. Patience issues naturally from a caring environment that values tolerance and respect.

Truthfulness is evidenced by a teacher's consistently following through on stated intentions. When you promise children that a week of good behavior will be rewarded with a special, fun activity and you do not deliver, you have forged your own classroom doom for the following week. Children are by nature understanding and forgiving, but they are also insightful. Teachers should ensure that their words match their actions.

The *warmth* that successful teachers exude extends to the social climate of their classrooms. Children thrive in warm, supportive learning environments. These environments also discourage misbehavior. A teacher who strives to be warm and supportive gains the trust and admiration of students, who respond by giving the teacher their best. How many times have children behaved well with one teacher only to turn into little demons with others?

Similarly, *loving* teachers tend to be loved in kind by their students. If the need for love, as Glasser (1998) claims, is genetic, and children require love for their emotional development, successful teachers are those who are able to create a classroom environment in which students feel loved.

PRACTICES OF SUCCESSFUL TEACHERS

Cotton (2000) identified the following ten contextual practices associated with successful teaching. These practices describe the context in which learning takes place.

1. *Academically heterogeneous class assignments.* Keeps student engagement high.
2. *Flexible in-class grouping.* Optimizes complementary learning styles.
3. *Maximized learning time.* Facilitates academic achievement.
4. *Monitoring student progress.* Allows for application of effective learning strategies.
5. *Parent and community involvement.* Supports student learning outside the classroom.
6. *Primary focus on learning.* Sets classroom priorities.
7. *Small class size.* Provides optimal attention to individual students.
8. *Safe and orderly school environment.* Foundational to learning.
9. *Strong administrative leadership.* Essential for teacher support and a successful academic program.
10. *Supportive classroom climate.* Meets the psychological needs of students.

Cotton also identified five instructional practices associated with student academic success.

1. *Careful orientation to lessons.* Focus is on learning.
2. *Clear and focused instruction.* Necessary for student engagement.
3. *Effective questioning techniques.* Supports understanding.
4. *Feedback and reinforcement.* Supports student engagement.
5. *Review/reteaching as needed.* Ensures successful outcome.

Teachers who come to class able to implement these positive instructional practices are able to create a learning environment that is focused on student achievement.

MASTERY OF CONTENT AS A MEASURE OF TEACHER SUCCESS

Teachers come to the classroom with varying levels of content expertise. Clearly, strong content knowledge, in addition to pedagogical knowledge, is an essential element for effective teaching. But mastery of content alone is insufficient. Teachers must be able to transmit this knowledge to students in an understandable, engaging, and accessible way. Teachers must also be able to contextualize content, to infuse it with real-world meaning for students. Successful teachers make it their practice to extend lessons to the level of higher-order comprehension by utilizing problem-solving strategies, direct and indirect instructional techniques, and inductive and deductive reasoning.

Ferguson and Womack (1993) indicated that alternatively prepared teachers have more problems in the daily operations of their classrooms than do traditionally prepared teachers. Traditionally prepared teachers are those who attended four-year colleges and completed pedagogical courses; alternatively prepared students are those who were not education majors as undergraduates and complete the necessary schooling, but are also given life experience credit by individual states (varies state to state). These researchers also found that certified teachers are more effective than teachers with less formal training. It has been noted that students perform better when their teachers have majored or minored in the subject areas in which they teach (Strong, 2002). In many instances students are delayed in their acquisition of knowledge as the result of inferior or poorly presented lessons. The educator Siegfried Engelmann (1969), in discussing direct instruction, commented, "If the student hasn't learned, then the teacher hasn't taught."

A teacher's content-area preparation has been shown to be positively related to student achievement. Goldhaber and Brewer (2000) indicate that students of teachers possessing emergency or probationary certification had lower scores than students of teachers with full or traditional certification, and teachers with higher scores on state certification examinations had students with higher test scores. Darling-Hammond, Berry, and Thoreson (2001) argue that certified teachers have a greater influence on student achievement than teachers with only a degree in their teaching field, suggesting that the preparation necessitated by state certification requirements is likely to increase subject matter competence. These researchers also indicate that pupils of experienced, certified teachers had significantly higher achievement than pupils of less-experienced teachers with alternative forms of certification.

Research supports the view that what teachers bring to school in the form of content mastery impacts the academic performance of pupils. A quantitative study by Harold Wenglinsky (2002) involving 7,146 eighth graders who took the 1996 mathematics assessment, and their teachers, claims that a significant relationship exists between a teacher's college-level coursework as measured by a teacher's major or minor in the relevant field and student test scores in those fields. The study further claims that the more professional development teachers received in hands-on learning and other topics, the less likely they were to engage in lower-order activities (referring here to Bloom's Taxonomy of Educational Objectives). Wenglinsky also reported that passive teachers demonstrated less of an impact on students' work ethic than active teachers. *Active teachers* engage students and evidence positive attributes; *passive teachers* do not engage students and do not evidence characteristics of successful teachers.

CHARACTERISTICS OF SUCCESSFUL TEACHERS

Successful teachers bring the following characteristics to their practice:

- They are effective classroom managers.
- They demonstrate mastery of subject area and content.
- They have high expectations that all of their students will succeed.
- Their methods and approaches are based on their beliefs and understandings about how children learn.
- Their teaching personality facilitates student learning.

There is no specific order of importance for these characteristics; each is important in its own right and together they define the successful teacher. One's teaching personality, which reflects one's personal attributes as well as one's beliefs, skills, and practices, can be understood as the foundation of the other elements listed here. One's teaching personality shapes one's expectations of student success as well as the methods one utilizes to ensure that expectations are met. The degree to which a teacher has mastered her subject is also a definitive factor in teaching personality. Self-actualization occurs when a teacher achieves mastery of subject matter and is effectively able to transmit content knowledge to students. Teaching personality also affects one's management style; as previously stated, successful teachers are by definition effective classroom managers.

Research has demonstrated that effective teachers influence a student's willingness to focus on subject matter while ineffective teachers discourage student interest (Monk and King, 1994). McBer (2000), researching the characteristics of effective teaching and the effect on student achievement, described three primary elements, all of which are in the teacher's control: teaching skills, professionalism, and classroom climate. Teaching skills and professionalism, associated with a teacher's individual attributes, are what teachers bring into their classrooms. The climate they create is a result of their skills and professionalism.

Teacher Qualities and Practices Favored by Students

Corbett and Wilson (2002) interviewed four hundred pupils from inner-city, low-income middle and senior high schools to identify those things that students feel their schools can do to encourage students and enhance learning. Teachers were identified as the main factor in determining the quality of students' educational experience. Students viewed sense of humor and charisma as among the qualities admired in good teachers. Good teachers were also said to:

- Be involved in students' progress by checking homework, providing individual reminders and feedback, giving rewards when appropriate, and keeping parents informed.
- Invite students to be involved in the learning process.
- Create a classroom environment that allows students to learn.
- Be willing to help students in accordance with how and when individual students wanted help.
- Explain content and assignments clearly, making information accessible to all.
- Vary classroom routines to keep class work interesting and engaging.
- Take time to get to know students.

Interestingly, students did not confuse professional behaviors and personal qualities. Sense of humor was valued in good teachers, but sense of humor alone was not seen as making for a good teacher. The study clearly indicates that good teaching equals successful learning on the part of students.

Characteristics of the Best and Worst Teachers

The National Association of Secondary School Principals (1997) surveyed one thousand students between the ages of thirteen and seventeen to determine those qualities students most associated with the "best" and the "worst" teachers. Their responses show the top five characteristics of each (see Figures 3.1 and 3.2).

It's safe to conclude from this survey that teachers described by students as the "best" are also the most effective. Since teachers are of primary importance to student achievement (Strong, 2002), the characteristics identified by students as the best in teachers should be carefully considered by all classroom practitioners.

FIGURE 3.1   **Top Five Characteristics of the Best Teachers**

1. They have a sense of humor.
2. They make the class interesting.
3. They have knowledge of their subjects.
4. They explain things clearly.
5. They spend time helping students.

FIGURE 3.2   **Top Five Characteristics of the Worst Teachers**

1. They are dull and have boring classes.
2. They do not explain things clearly.
3. They show favoritism toward students.
4. They have a poor attitude.
5. They expect too much from students.

CLASSROOM MANAGEMENT AND TEACHER SUCCESS

As stated repeatedly in this chapter, successful teachers are by definition effective classroom managers. Procedures are key to classroom management, and successful teachers bring to their classrooms an awareness of the importance of procedures, as well as the ability to develop and implement procedures from the first day of school.

Effective Classroom Management Begins on Day 1

The key to classroom management is to establish procedures on the first day, and reinforce them until they become accepted and established class routines. It has been noted that the primary problem in managing classrooms is not the lack of discipline but the lack of procedures. Procedures begin with the basics. Generally, students want the following information when they enter a class on the first day of school.

- Am I in the right classroom?
  The classroom should be clearly identified; for example, hang a sign on the door.
- Where am I supposed to sit?
  The students should be clearly informed about assigned seating or other seating arrangement; for example, place nametags on desks.

- How can I expect to be treated here?
  Immediately set the tone for your classroom; for example, write the word Respect *on the board to establish the principle that will govern classroom interaction.*
- What will I learn in this class?
  The syllabus and how it will be covered should be explained on Day 1.
- How will I be graded?
  Procedures for formative assessment and final grade should be clearly communicated to students.
- What sort of person is the teacher?
  Your expectations for the class, and with respect to learning in general, should be made known to students from the outset.

Teachers are of primary importance in creating an environment that facilitates learning. On the first day of class students will want to see what you are made of. The first thing you should do is introduce yourself. Students may know your name but they probably don't know anything else about you. Give them some idea of your background, including how you came to be a teacher. Let them know something about your home life, if you are married, have children, have pets, have hobbies. Be honest, but use good judgment about what you reveal. The information you divulge should be appropriate for the age group that you are teaching. Informing first graders about a recent divorce is unnecessary and inappropriate, but letting them know that you love toys and have a collection of glass rabbits will be much appreciated by them. Similarly, confessing to a group of rambunctious middle-school kids that this is your first day on the job is not advisable. But no harm will come from telling them about your love of sports.

Students will want to know what they can expect from you as a teacher and as an individual. What kind of person are you? How will you run the classroom? Will students' participation be invited, respected, valued? What expectations do you have for them as individuals and as a class?

Your primary goal on the first day of school is to establish classroom management procedures and set down your expectations for student learning. How procedures are introduced will vary depending on the age and maturity of your students. Procedures should in all cases be reasonable and fair. Keep in mind that a democratic process in establishing procedures sets the foundation for a democratic classroom. From a procedural standpoint, Day 1 activities should include:

1. *Seat assignments.* Have a seating chart made up for use on Day 1 and subsequent days. This will facilitate roll call and aid you in remembering names. As the term progresses you may wish to reseat students for various reasons (disciplinary or otherwise), or students may request that they be moved. The chart will become less important to you over time, but early on in a class, it is an important tool for getting to know students and how the classroom functions.
2. *Introductions.* Introduce yourself and have students introduce themselves. This lets the students see that you value them as individuals as well as a class.

3. *Icebreaker activities.* Develop activities that will help you get a sense of the different personalities in your class and how they work together. For example, you might ask students to each write one word on an index card describing how they feel on this, the first day of school. List the responses on the board and discuss them as a group. Your icebreaker activities should provide a natural segue into a discussion of classroom procedures.

4. *Establishment of classroom procedures.* This essential activity could be done in a variety of ways. Since successful procedures depend on student support, high student engagement is paramount. Procedures can be understood as a contract signed by both teacher and students as to how the classroom functions. Both parties must be in agreement. Procedures cover all aspects of classroom activity, from students entering the room to their exiting it and everything in between. Effective classroom management depends on students taking responsibility for their actions. If they "sign on" to classroom procedures, then any failure to comply with those procedures must be accounted for. This is why it makes sense to involve students in the development of procedures: student involvement ensures that they will perceive the procedures as fair and the process as democratic. Similarly, if they have signed on to established consequences for noncompliance, then disciplinary measures are also perceived as fair. Students are thus encouraged to practice self-discipline in the classroom. For example, you could write questions on one set of white index cards and answers on another set of blue index cards, then have students attempt to match the questions and answers. An example of a question might be, "What do I do when I first enter the class?" The answer card response could be, "When first entering the class take your seat and open your notebook to copy and complete the do now exercise." This particular icebreaker is effective in three ways it allows students to become familiar with class procedures and rules as well as get to know and interact with their classmates. It also allows you to see which students do not participate. You should let students know that you will start classes by having assignments labeled as do now on the board or overhead projector. This should become a routine way for your starting each class. It will assist you in having students start work immediately with no waste of instructional time. While students are working you can check attendance, collect money, and so on. Assignments should be posted before students walk in. Don't waste time calling the roll just check your seating plan. Always post your assignments in the same place. Consistency is a part of good classroom management. It will also add a sense of professionalism to your teaching. Remember, students should always come in, sit down, and get to work. There is no better procedure for maintaining effective learning momentum in a classroom. Discussion of procedures must not be limited to the first day of class. Be sure to revisit procedures throughout the term. Teachers should discuss, model, and define procedures until they become routine.

5. *Distribute and preview class textbooks.* Cover the syllabus as the textbook(s) is introduced. Go over the table of contents, glossary, and subject index. Discuss how the book will be used.
6. *Discuss classroom supplies available to students.* Expectations for how supplies are treated should be clearly addressed in classroom procedures.
7. *Clarify expectations.* Convey your excitement to students about the learning opportunities that your class makes available to them. Ensure students of your confidence in their success. Remember, children have a right to expect that their teachers will make a positive impact on their lives. Don't disappoint them.

Although these are described as first-day activities, don't rush them. Depending on student response and class time, these activities could take one to three sessions to adequately cover.

Establishing Democratic Classroom Procedures

Dreikurs and Grey (1968) proposed that both punishment and positive and negative reinforcement, as utilized in behaviorist theory, be rejected, because they create dependency and do not allow for personal growth and self-discipline. Dreikurs and Grey suggested that encouragement produces success, by allowing for non-competitive, supportive learning environments. Classroom procedures must be evaluated by analyzing the extent to which they embrace respect for all classroom members, and are reasonable; and by the extend to which all behaviors, including misbehavior, have expected outcomes, or consequences. Misbehavior typically results from a child's mistaken assumption about how identity is determined and status gained. Classroom procedures should make clear how a student is expected to contribute to classroom discussions, and teacher expectations should firmly establish those student behaviors that are considered valuable to the class as a whole.

Culturally Responsive Classroom Management

Given the increasing diversity of the classroom, a lack of multicultural sensitivity can exacerbate the difficulties that teachers have with classroom management. In order to address this situation Weinstein and colleagues (2004) proposed a theoretical conception, culturally responsive classroom management (CRCM). CRCM includes five essential components:

1. Recognition of one's own ethnocentrism.
2. Knowledge of students' cultural backgrounds.
3. Understanding of the broader social, economic, and political context.
4. Ability and willingness to use culturally appropriate management strategies.
5. Commitment to building caring classrooms.

Since its earliest conceptualizations in the 1960s, multicultural education has been in a state of evolution in terms of both theory and practice. Multicultural education has been discussed as a practical shift in curriculum designed to reflect a culturally divergent student (and teacher) population, and as a re-examination of educational practices that are Eurocentric and exclusionary.

Banks (1994), proposed a "notion of multiple identities," according to which all children are understood as coming to school with an ethnic identity, whether these identities are conscious or unconscious. When recognized and respected by teachers, these identities can become the basis for important learning activities. The idea is to acknowledge differences rather than ignore them. Children should recognize and appreciate their own ethnicity as well as that of their classmates.

Insufficient multicultural awareness and sensitivity can increase the difficulties that teachers have with classroom management. Appropriate behavior is culturally influenced, and conflicts can occur when teachers and students have different expectations of appropriate behavior based on culture. Americans of European ancestry, for example, are traditionally accustomed to a "passive-receptive" discourse pattern; they expect students to listen quietly while the teacher is speaking and then respond individually to teacher-initiated questions (Gay, 2000). African Americans, in contrast, may be traditionally accustomed to a more active, participatory pattern ("call-response"), and will demonstrate their engagement by providing comments and reactions that some teachers may interpret as rude and disruptive.

Many minority communities focus less on individual than on collaborative achievement. Disciplinary measures designed to "correct" for behaviors considered by the teacher as an infraction, such as a child talking to her neighbor, can create a cultural rift between the student and the teacher, especially if the student feels that the teacher makes no effort to understand or respect the intention of the action in question (Franklin, 2005).

Teachers ignorant of Southeast Asian culture may take it as a sign of disrespect when their student smiles while being scolded; but in the student's culture, this expression is an admission of guilt and an effort to show that there are no hard feelings. Similarly, Chinese American students who are unwilling to express their opinions may simply be following their parents' directive to listen and learn what the teacher tells them (Weinstein, Tomlinson-Clark, and Curran, 2004).

Valenzuela (1999) observes that Mexican American students must feel "cared for" before they can "care about" school. Withdrawal behaviors might be symptomatic of these students' rejection of an educational system that dismisses or derogates their language, culture, and community. Greeting students at the door with a smile and welcoming comment can set the tone for a positive school day. When teachers express admiration for a student's bilingual ability and comment enthusiastically about the number of different languages that are represented in class they are creating identity and building community. Cultural characteristics are also influenced by variables such as gender, education, social class, and degrees of cultural affiliation.

Teachers have to ask some basic questions like, does diversity require different approaches to classroom management? Should we examine the kinds of cultural conflicts that can arise in ethnically diverse classrooms? How can we as teachers become multiculturally sensitive? It should be understood that CRCM is not a discrete solution but a frame of mind, more a set of strategies or practices that guide the management decisions that teachers make. Teachers should reflect on how their culture influences their expectations for behavior and their interactions with students. Teachers must recognize that the ultimate goal of classroom management is not to achieve compliance or control but to provide all students with equitable opportunities for learning and to guide children in becoming self-disciplined. The goal of classroom management is to create an environment in which students behave appropriately, not out of fear of punishment or desire for reward, but out of a sense of personal responsibility.

In order to create a culturally responsive environment teachers should make an effort to learn their students' family backgrounds and cultural norms and values. They should ask questions about countries of origin and what languages are spoken at home. Teachers should also discover what type of discipline is used at home. Is it permissive or authoritative? What kinds of praise, rewards, criticism, and punishment are practiced at home?

Deciding when to accommodate a student's cultural preference and when to push the child toward assimilation into the larger community is a decision that teachers must make with the utmost care.

KEY TERM TO FOCUS ON

culturally responsive classroom management
   (CRCM)

DISCUSSION QUESTIONS

1. What personal attributes are most associated with successful teachers?

2. Describe the contextual and instructional practices associated with successful teachers.

3. How necessary is content mastery to success in teaching?

4. What things can teachers do on the very first day of school to ensure the successful management of their classrooms?

5. Why is it important that classroom procedures be "democratic"?

6. How do successful teachers deal with a culturally diverse student body?

MINI CASES FROM THE FIELD

Analyze the following brief case studies using the IOSIE method. Be sure to reflect upon the attributes and practices teachers need to develop in order to be successful.

1. Carl Warner wondered why his observation report was unsatisfactory. Carl's background in fine arts and European literature had certainly prepared him to be a successful high school teacher. Unfortunately, all his classes behaved poorly during his lectures. Most students stared into space bored or were outright rude and talked to their classmates. Carl felt the reason for the poor behavior was the ethnic diversity of his classes that he doubted anyone could teach. Was he supposed to lecture in different languages? Analyze this case using the IOSIE method and determine the contextual practices that Carl appears not to be using. Explain how you would improve instructional practice to avoid boredom and misbehavior. How could Carl become more culturally responsive to the needs of his students?

2. George Petrides had always wanted to be a middle school mathematics teacher. He knew his strengths as a teacher. He had won honors as a mathematician and considered himself excellently prepared to face adolescent children. He would not make the same mistakes his teachers had made. He would demand obedience, be stern, and demand respect. If any child wished to speak with him outside of class they would have to make an appointment with the school secretary. Caring and sharing would not occur in his classes—only learning. Analyze this case using the IOSIE method and decide if George is implementing a strategy for success based on positive attributes of successful teachers.

3. Lucille Bonnet, a first year teacher at Marcus Elementary School, had just read an article on the five characteristics of successful teachers. The article said a successful teacher has mastery of content, knows instructional methods, has high expectations, can manage a class, and has a teaching personality. Lucille believes she possesses what it takes to be a successful teacher. She knows the content and figured anyone could teach little children, especially the second-grade class she had been assigned. Management wasn't a problem, she thought, children would listen to her as long as she demanded good behavior and expected that all learned. Personality had little relevance; teaching certainly is not a personality contest. Analyze this case using the IOSIE method. Reflect on Lucille's interpretation of the article. How would you have interpreted this article?

4. Donna Fontanez is a student teacher at Gunning Elementary School. Her university supervisor has given her an assignment to prepare a list of icebreaker activities that a successful teacher would prepare for the first day of school. Donna wrote that each child in her first-grade class would be given a colored index card and asked to find other children with the same colored card. This would help them socially to become a part of their new class. She would also have children draw a picture that best reflected their summer vacation and have them describe it to their classmates. She would seat all the non-English speaking children at the same table so they would feel comfortable. Analyze this case using the IOSIE method and evaluate the potential for success with Donna's icebreakers. How would you prepare for your first class session of the year?

REFERENCES

Banks, J. A. 1994. *An introduction to multicultural education.* Boston: Allyn & Bacon.

Corbett, D., and B. Wilson. 2002. What urban students say about good teaching. *Educational Leadership* 60 (1), 18–22.

Cotton, K. 2000. *The schooling practices that matter most.* Alexandria, VA: Association for Supervision and Curriculum Development.

Darling-Hammond, L., B. Berry, and S. Thoreson. 2001. Does teacher certification matter? Evaluating the evidence. *Educational Evaluation and Policy Analysis* 23 (1), 57–77.

Dreikurs, R., and L. Grey. 1968. *A new approach to discipline: Logical consequences.* New York: Hawthorne.

Engelmann, S. 1969. *Preventing failure in the primary grades.* Chicago: Science Research Associates.

Ferguson, P., and S. T. Womack. 1993. The impact of subject matter and education coursework on teaching performance. *Journal of Teacher Education* 44 (1), 55–63.

Franklin, J. 2005. Managing the multicultural classroom: Effective learning communities are built on understanding. *Education Update* 47 (5).

Gay, G. 2000. *Culturally responsive teaching: Theory, research, and practice.* New York: Teachers Press.

Glasser, W. 1998. *Choice theory: A new psychology of personal freedom.* New York: Harper Collins.

Goldhaber, D. D., and D. J. Brewer. 2000. Does teacher certification matter? High school teacher certification status and student achievement. *Educational Evaluation and Policy Analysis* 22 (2), 129–45.

Haberman, M. 2004. *Creating effective schools in failed urban districts.* Myriad: University of Wisconsin in Milwaukee.

McBer, H. 2000. *Research into teacher effectiveness: A model of teacher effectiveness.* Research Report #216. Nottingham, England: Department of Education and Employment.

Monk, D. H., and J. A. King. 1994. Multilevel teacher resource effects on pupil performance in secondary mathematics and science: The case of teacher subject matter preparation. *Choices and Consequences: Contemporary Policy Issues in Education,* 29–58. Ithaca, NY: ILR Press.

National Association of Secondary School Principals (NASSP). 1997. Students say: What makes a good teacher? *Schools in the middle* 6 (5): 15–17.

Strong, J. H. 2002. *Qualities of effective teachers.* Alexandria, VA: Association for Supervision and Curriculum Development.

Valenzuela, A. 1999. *Subtractive schooling: U.S.-Mexican youth and politics of caring.* Albany: State University of New York Press.

Weinstein, C., S. Tomlinson-Clark, and M. Curran. 2004. Toward a conception of a culturally responsive classroom management. *Journal of Teacher Education* 55 (1), 25–38.

Wenglinsky, H. 2002. How schools matter: The link between teacher classroom practices and student academic performance. *Education Policy Analysis Archives* 10 (12). http://epaa/v10n12/.

PART II

MANAGEMENT APPROACHES AND MODELS

Management approaches and models can be arranged on a spectrum from least to most teacher control. They can be further categorized in terms of basic focus; that is, whether they fall under a consequences, individual-guidance, or group-guidance management approach. When organized in this fashion they comprise a matrix of management strategies that can be fitted to individual situations and individual management styles.

The discussion of management approaches and models rests on the belief that management style reflects one's teaching personality. A practitioner whose style is primarily teacher-dominant might choose to use a consequences approach to management, with a strong level of teacher control, while a teacher comfortable sharing control with her students might tend to focus on a group-guidance approach, utilizing a low level of teacher control. Each approach has as its goal the maximization of learning in the classroom as well as the development of self-discipline; success is achieved when students are able to take responsibility for their actions. Each approach has inherent strengths and weaknesses, which should be understood before utilization. The strategies can be used separately or together as the teacher sees fit. Most teachers will find it beneficial to use a trial-and-error, eclectic approach; if one strategy fails, another takes its place; and the process continues until positive development is recorded.

Chapter 4 describes the control spectrum and the models and strategies that can be understood as falling along this spectrum. It also discusses character development in children and how that relates to behavior management. Chapters 5 through 7 provide an in-depth look at consequences, group-guidance, and individual-guidance models.

MANAGEMENT STRATEGIES AND PRACTICES

FOCUS POINTS

1. Teachers select management tools based on their teaching personality, the needs of their students, as well as the demands of the behavioral situation.

2. Effectiveness of the three approaches to classroom management—consequences, group guidance, and individual guidance—depends on the quality of teacher application.

3. Character education supports both good behavior and academic learning.

Management strategies and practices are the tools that teachers use in resolving individual behavior and classroom management problems. Teachers select management tools based on their teaching personality and the needs of their students, as well as the demands of the behavioral situation. The three general approaches to classroom management—consequences, group guidance, and individual guidance—are effective only if properly applied by the teacher. A consequences approach can be misused as punishment, a group-guidance approach can unfairly pit groups against an individual, and an individual-guidance approach might require skills that the teacher does not possess. The teacher must evaluate the process at every stage, to ensure that it is leading to the goal of student self-discipline, and address skill deficits before implementing a plan.

Classroom management has been described as a four-stage process, in which the teacher (1) specifies desirable conditions, (2) analyzes existing conditions, (3) uses management strategies, and (4) assesses effectiveness (Cooper, 1999). Management can be viewed from two perspectives, one centered on consequences imposed by the teacher and the other focused on guiding individuals to make their own choices. The desired end result is in all cases an enviornment that facilitates learning on the part of the individual and the group. The strategies that fall under these approaches range from authoritarian on one end to permissive on the other. The center or middle ground is held by strategies allowing teachers to initiate group- and individual-guidance solutions. The classroom management control

FIGURE 4.1   Classroom Management Control Spectrum

Most Control $\longrightarrow$	Moderate Control $\longrightarrow$	Least Control
Consequences Approach	*Group-Guidance Approach*	*Individual-Guidance Approach*
• Assertive discipline	• Efficacy in action	• Ginott model
• Jones model	• Cooperative discipline	• Reality therapy and choice therapy
• Kounin effective momentum model	• Judicious discipline	• Restitution model
• Logical consequences	• Skillstreaming	• Curwin Mendler model
• Traditional model	• Peer mediation	• Teacher effectiveness training: Gordon model
• Behavior modification	• Positive action	• Transactional Analysis

continuum could also be seen as running from teacher-centered to student-centered and from consequences, to group-guidance, to individual-guidance models.

CLASSROOM MANAGEMENT CONTROL SPECTRUM

Most Teacher Control

At the extreme end of the management spectrum is the authoritarian approach, which gives teachers the maximum degree of control in the classroom. Authoritarian practice is teacher centered and emphasizes total control on the part of the teacher and obedience on the part of the student. The teacher establishes the rules that govern the classroom, and enforces those rules to maintain control. The quality of these rules and their enforcement can differ from teacher to teacher, in terms of degree of strictness, for example. Because the authoritarian approach relies on external control, actions associated with this approach could engender a negative response. The word *authoritarian* carries a pejorative connotation (repressive, tyrannical), and some practitioners and authors of behavior models that the term has been applied to balk at the label, since it suggests an ethos contrary to a democratic society. We tend to see an authoritarian mode of control as based on fear and punishment such as that employed by dictatorial regimes.

Douglas McGregor, in his classic work *The Human Side of Enterprise* (1960), promoted the application of behavioral science to the improvement of productivity in business organizations. His basic premise was that the thinking and actions of those in authority are based on two different sets of assumptions, called Theory X and Theory Y. Theory X represented authoritarian views, and Theory Y democratic leadership. The Theory X beliefs were that

1. people tend to dislike work and will avoid it if they can get away with it;
2. the best way to get people to work is to coerce, threaten, or punish them;

3. the average person dislikes responsibility and prefers to be directed, while desiring security above everything else. (Accel-Team, 2005)

Theory X business-model assumptions have been used as a rationale for educational models that advocate authoritarian approaches to classroom management. There are three basic assumptions of authoritarian classroom management:

1. Classroom management depends on total teacher control.
2. Students do not behave without strict discipline enforced by the teacher.
3. Student learning is facilitated in an environment of strong teacher control.

Intimidation practice might be seen as consistent with authoritarian practice, although educators are in general agreement that intimidation is both inappropriate and ineffective in most classroom situations. An exception might be made for using intimidation to prevent physical violence in schools. Intimidation with regard to management connotes an undemocratic, anti-American image in the minds of most. The basic assumption of intimidation practice is that fear of the teacher motivates students both to learn and to behave. The Jones model, discussed in Chapter 5, has been described as advocating intimidation on the part of teachers. But Jones and others have observed that *intimidation* is too strong a word for the practices that the Jones model supports.

Behavior modification practice falls farther along the spectrum, and is based on the belief that all behaviors, including misbehavior, are learned. Children are understood to misbehave because they have not learned appropriate behavior. Teachers are seen as central in correcting student behaviors. Learning is understood to be influenced by the environment, which can be regulated by an effective (controlling) teacher. To modify behavior, strategies such as modeling and demonstration are used. A classic example is the creation of a "token economy" system, where rewards for good behavior are combined with self-monitoring and behavioral counseling. Children are given tokens in the form of plus marks or smiley faces for good behavior, and they are encouraged to act as monitors of behavior while the teacher intervenes with offending students. Another example of behavior modification, called red light, green light, teaches children to monitor their own actions by visualizing a red light, which implies "stop" and "don't do" or a green light, for "go" and "do." Cues and prompts such as these give signals to children to be responsible for their own behavior. Privileges are taken away as a consequence of bad behavior; rewards are given for good behavior (behavior modification and other "consequences" models are discussed in more depth in Chapter 5). Rewards (reinforcers) are used as a stimulus to increase the frequency of desirable behavior. Negative reinforcers (punishment) decrease the frequency of inappropriate behavior.

The basic premises of behavior modification are that

- all behavior is learned and a few basic processes account for all learning;
- the role of the teacher is to promote appropriate student behavior by rewarding it and to eliminate inappropriate behavior by not rewarding it;

- the four major teacher actions teachers can use are positive reinforcement, punishment, negative reinforcement, and extinction, or time-out.

The rationale behind maximizing teacher control is that good lessons prevent management problems. Effective momentum management theory provides the theoretical rationale for this approach. It concludes that interesting, relevant, appropriate curriculum and instruction allow lessons to be conducted smoothly while avoiding management problems. By establishing effective classroom routines and giving clear directions you create a positive class environment. Showing interest in students and being sensitive to student needs makes for a positive learning environment, which by definition is misbehavior-free. In some classrooms misbehavior seems inconceivable, because the teacher's enthusiasm, pedagogical skills, content mastery, winning personality, and attentiveness to student needs yield a positive instructional approach that commands good behavior on the part of all students.

Instructional-eclectic, also called traditional, teacher practice, has no specific theoretical rationale; it is comprised of individual strategies that have proven effective in the past. The practice has been described as a "cookbook" approach of do's and don'ts that teachers have traditionally practiced. The approach is reactive rather than proactive and thus also falls on the most-teacher-control end of the spectrum. Goodlad (1983) describes the basic strategies of the traditional approach as positive reinforcement, rewards, honor rolls, and special privileges for well-performing students. He favors controlling misbehavior such as restlessness, giggling, disruptions, and stubbornness by ignoring the behavior, reminders, eye contact, commands and direct orders, verbal threats, separating students from the site of the behavior infraction, and sending offenders to the principal. The approach includes both positive reinforcement and intervention strategies including punishment.

Ornstein and Lasley (2004) relates traditional instructional practice to the business-academic approach developed by Emmer and Evertson (1981). The strategy stresses procedures that allow for a well-functioning classroom, in which an effective instructional pace is maintained. Procedures in the classroom are similar to those that are understood to govern profitable businesses and should be clear and well defined. Ornstein claims that eleven managerial methods taken from Emmer and Evertson, when applied to the classroom, lead to improvement in student achievement and behavior. Classroom management is understood not as one-dimensional—not concerned only with student behavior—but as assisting teachers in organizing their classes to create a learning environment conducive to student achievement. Traditional methods of classroom management continue to aid teachers in facilitating learning.

Carolyn Evertson and her colleagues have done work on a highly regarded classroom organization and management program (COMP), which emphasizes procedures and strong rules in order to facilitate learning (Evertson and Harris, 1999; Evertson, Emmer, and Worsham, 2003). COMP was designed as an approach to staff development in which teachers analyze their own practice by using various checklists and through an in-service training course. The essential premise is that

FIGURE 4.2   Traditional Methods of Classroom Management

1. *Readying the classroom.* Classroom space, materials, and equipment are organized by Day 1. Effective managers arrange their rooms to maximize learning and compensate for potential learning constraints.

2. *Establishing rules and procedures.* Teachers make sure students understand expectations and know what it takes to follow rules and procedures; they spend the necessary time at the beginning of the year explaining and reiterating rules and expectations.

3. *Reinforcing rules and procedures.* Rules and procedures are systematically reinforced. Teachers have incorporated into classroom practice cues or signals that demand student action or attention.

4. *Establishing/enforcing consequences.* Consequences of inappropriate behavior are clearly established; teachers practice consistent follow-through in applying consequences.

5. *Whole-group focus.* Students are expected to perceive themselves as a coherent and cooperative group.

6. *Strategies for potential problems.* Strategies for dealing with potential problems are laid out in advance. With these strategies teachers can deal with misbehavior on an as-needed basis.

7. *Monitoring.* Student behavior is closely monitored; the teacher does not lose audience contact; student academic work is also monitored.

8. *Stopping inappropriate behavior.* Inappropriate or disruptive behavior is handled promptly and consistently before it worsens or spreads.

9. *Organizing instruction.* Teachers organize instructional activities based on student maturity levels and achievement, as well as student interests.

10. *Student accountability.* Procedures emphasize student accountability for quality of work and behavior.

11. *Instructional clarity.* Teachers provide instruction intended to keep students on task and maximize learning; directions are clear, to minimize confusion and thus reduce discipline problems.

by teaching effective lessons, which by definition include effective pedagogical practices, teachers lessen the risk for classroom disruption while maximizing their classroom organizational skills.

Moderate Teacher Control

Group-guidance practice or group process is a sociopsychological approach based on group social psychology and group dynamics. Its primary focus is on orienting students toward behaving the way you expect them to behave. The discipline is achieved by working with the group or class within the confines of the classroom.

The approach is based on the assumptions that schooling takes place in a class-room group and it is the teacher's role to establish a productive group within the classroom social system. This social system needs clearly stated expectations, standards of conduct, democratic leadership, positive interpersonal relationships, and productive group norms that allow for open communication. Strategies revolve around group problem solving in which problems are identified, analyzed, and evaluated. Solutions are selected and the group reinforces solutions by giving feedback at classroom meetings that restore morale and focus the class. This practice takes credit for being one in which democratic practice is allowed to flourish, thus it is considered as residing in the middle of the teacher-control spectrum. (An in-depth discussion of group-guidance models can be found in Chapter 6.) Teachers find it consistent with the American ethos, in that

- it is founded on democratic principles;
- the primary role of the teacher is to create an environment where students can feel free to participate in the resolution of classroom managerial concerns in a democratic fashion.

The judicious discipline model of classroom management (Gathercoal, 1993; Landau and Gathercoal, 2000) is a prime example of positive group-process practice. The strategy calls for a democratic approach to classroom management in which children are encouraged and assisted in managing the behaviors of the group. Through the use of class consensus meetings that replicate early New England town hall meetings, the class is brought together to decide on the correctness or appropriateness of a specific rule or behavior. The focal point of the judicious discipline approach is the development of constitutional language that is used to discuss various issues as they arise in class. A central aim is to include the concepts of rights, liberty, equality, responsibilities, and freedom from coercion. One major caution with this strategy is that the teacher must be knowledgeable about group needs and not use group meetings as "trials" for student infractions. The danger is that an insufficiently trained teacher will take the role of grand inquisitor and prosecute a student in the guise of an impartial observer. Group guidance must not degenerate into a process in which the group is pitted against an individual. If used correctly, however, it can be a very effective tool in any teacher's arsenal of behavior-management techniques.

Least Teacher Control

Socio-emotional practice or individual-guidance process has its roots in counseling and clinical psychology. It advances the belief that positive teacher-student relationships are necessary if effective classroom management and instruction are to occur. The caring teacher's attitude helps to facilitate learning and foster trust, acceptance, and understanding, qualities associated with the successful teaching personality. The primary focus of socio-emotional practice is the positive interrelationship between teacher and student. Without this quality relationship, individual guidance cannot be purposefully practiced. (Individual-guidance models are discussed in more depth in Chapter 7.)

The teacher's understanding, warm, and caring attitude is seen as facilitating learning. Rodgers's theories of realness, acceptance, and empathy (1951); Ginott's (1976) ideas regarding effective communications; and Dreikurs and Grey's (1968) concepts concerning logical consequences and democratic process are the rationale for this practice. The goal of social and emotional learning is to develop children's emotional intelligence, so that they are able to show empathy for the feelings of others. Teaching social skills focuses on providing students with strategies for controlling how they react to their peers, so that they learn appropriate behavioral responses to typical basic social interactions. The less children understand their own feelings the more impulsively they will act. Children who do not have sufficient skills to deal with their own feelings will not be able to respond well to those of others. Eight areas need to be addressed before a child can function with empathy and caring for others.

1. Self-awareness
2. Awareness of others
3. Emotional self-regulation abilities
4. Communication abilities
5. Self-motivation
6. Problem-solving and decision-making abilities
7. Collaborative learning abilities
8. A realistic and positive sense of self

The work of Howard Gardner (1983) and Daniel Goleman (1998) has reinforced the idea that emotional intelligence and socio-emotional learning are keys to a person's success in school and on the job, and comprise the basis of satisfying relationships with others. Emotional maturity is as important to a child's growth as is the acquisition and development of literacy. Three essential aims of socio-emotional learning are (1) developing caring relationships as a foundation for learning, (2) understanding how emotions affect learning, and (3) the setting of goals for achievement. Students need to be taught to understand and manage both their positive and negative emotions, and use their emotions to impel learning. They have to be taught how to identify their dreams and how to work to achieve them. Only then will true emotional maturity be reached.

Tolerant/permissive practice is at the opposite extreme from authoritarianism on the teacher-control spectrum. It is essentially a student-centered approach that is focused on maximizing student freedom. The role of the teacher is not to interfere but to allow free student expression. In its pure form such an approach fails to recognize that socially acceptable behaviors are a basic requirement of civilized society. Few models utilize a permissive approach and those that do are generally considered to be on the cultural fringe.

One school gained notoriety in the 1960s for its tolerant-permissive approach to education. The Summerhill School **is** a progressive, coeducational residential school, founded by A. S. Neill in 1921; it continues to operate today in the United Kingdom and seven other nations. Neill claimed that Summerhill was a "free school," referring to the personal freedom of the children in his charge. The two nontraditional features of the school are: (1) all the lessons presented by the teachers are optional, which allows the children to decided whether to attend classes or not, and (2) all rules are made at a school meeting, where both pupils and staff have equal voting rights (Summerhill School, 2005). Summerhill was an experiment based on the premise that children, left to their own devices, would choose to behave positively and to pursue their education.

The basic premises of tolerant/permissive practice are that:

- the teacher is responsible for maximizing student freedom by interfering as little as possible;
- the role of the teacher is to promote the freedom of students, thereby fostering their natural development;
- students who are allowed to express themselves freely can reach their fullest potential.

CHARACTER DEVELOPMENT AND CLASSROOM MANAGEMENT

Character development is understood as furthering classroom management because children who are self-disciplined, respectful, and empathetic will be much less likely to misbehave. Managerial models that stress critical thinking, curriculum, discipline, guidance, and character education have as their goal improved student achievement and effective teaching.

Pantheon Program

The Pantheon Program is a management practice based on an instructional model that seeks to achieve academic excellence while developing good character in children. The program attempts to meet children's needs based on the premise that a rising tide (in this case academic excellence) lifts all ships. Pantheon philosophy celebrates the idea that to be fully educated is a lifelong adventure that begins with an individual's formal schooling and development of critical thinking skills. Herein lies the theoretical rational for the program: if children are able to develop their capacity for critical thinking, all else will fall into place. The first assumption regarding critical thinking is that human beings are by definition activist learners. The objective is to make the most of each student's academic and humanistic potential by stressing active learning and critical thinking. All children can learn when exposed to a quality education that provides coaching and advisement (Scarpaci, 2004).

Beliefs, Assumptions, and Components of the Pantheon Program

- All children can learn when exposed to a quality education.
- All genuine learning is active, not passive.
- Teaching children to think and not simply to recite or perform is a goal of education.
- Learning is a student's responsibility, while providing an enriching education for students is the role of the school and its teachers.
- The program is a one-track system of schooling where all children are exposed to the same quality education.
- The program stresses meeting and exceeding state educational standards.
- The program includes effective staff development, which involves the whole community.
- The program includes an advisor-advisee guidance component for every middle school child.

The program is devoted to the principles of democracy and equality based on a classical education that brings out the best in all children. The process employed in the program consists of identifying individual student abilities, interests, and learning-style preferences through the use of an advisor-advisee guidance program. The model further provides coaching, in and outside of the classroom,

---

FIGURE 4.3   Pantheon Program Model

Basic Assumption: All children can learn when exposed to a quality instructional program that encourages critical thinking.

Critical Thinking

Respect	+	Responsibility	+	Ethical Values	=	Good Character
Discipline Code				Guidance		Awards

Pantheon Teaching Practices

1. **Conventional Instruction**

   How is knowledge acquired? It is acquired by means of Conventional Developmental Lessons, Texts, Experience, Reason, Intuition, Authority, Active Construction

2. **Coaching Instruction**

   How do we develop Learning Skills? They are developed by means of Coaching Exercises, Guided Practice, Independent Study, Interest Groups, Problem Solving

3. **Seminar Instruction**

   How do we enrich our understanding of ideas and values? By means of Socratic Seminars, Enrichment Activities, and School and Community Service.

which focuses on solving problems, student interests, and guided independent learning. Teaching consists of rigorous classroom instruction made up of conventional developmental lessons, lectures, coaching, and seminar discussions. The practices of "gifted programs," traditionally applied to a select group of students, are in this program extended to all students (Adler, 1982).

"Teaching" Character

It is often claimed that there is a character crisis in our schools and communities, that values need clarification for both adults and children. The answer appears to be a return to traditional core values (caring, honesty, fairness, responsibility, respect for ourselves and others, forgiveness, hard work, and doing unto others as we would have them do unto ourselves). To achieve this, two pivotal questions have to be addressed: Is it really possible to teach young people good character? And if so, what is the best approach to take?

Character education generally is defined as promoting core ethical values as a basis for good character. Programs focus on teaching a recognized set of values, using interactive strategies that promote critical thinking skills. The goal is to clarify values and moral reasoning by establishing a set of agreed-upon values that are shared by all. The premise is that values can be taught and children can be guided in the development of good character.

A classic approach to character education is the Socratic approach. It holds that good character is best expressed in the types of choices one makes. Therefore, by teaching students how to make good choices we are educating for good character. This process consists of a teacher asking a series of questions that assist students in examining the validity of an opinion or belief they hold. The process actively engages the student and forces him to think critically.

Amitai Etzioni (1998) identifies two underlying skills, empathy and self-discipline, as prerequisites for character development. Empathy allows the child to appreciate the feelings of others, to sense violations of justice, and to better distinguish between right and wrong. Self-discipline allows one to take action and delay gratification in order to remain committed to a set of core values or goals. Empathy and self-discipline therefore provide a foundation for moral behavior and good character.

There are in fact no value-free schools or classrooms. All schools shape character for good or bad through the intrinsic values embedded in their makeup. As children learn to read they must also learn to be good. Parents and teachers must model virtuous behavior. Teachers should connect the curriculum content to character formation.

With all this said, the question becomes the selection of a program that reflects the philosophy of the school community and becomes the foundation for what happens at school and in life. Learning to read, write, and do math are positive actions as sure as is learning to be responsible and respectful. Feeling good about ourselves begins with identifying positive actions and taking them. The positive actions one takes are in the areas of the physical, the mental, and the emotional (body, mind, and feelings). Good character must be comprehensively defined to include thinking, feeling, and behavior. Any educational program must help the school community know what is good and to value it. The role of the school is to define the character qualities it values and admires while taking steps to practice them every day in the conduct of school activities. The school staff must become a learning and a moral community in which all share responsibility for character education and adhere to the same core values that guide the education of children.

Plato's *Meno,* a dialogue that involves whether virtue can be taught, concludes pessimistically that there are no genuine teachers of virtue. But positive actions that lead to good character *can* be taught. A character-education model based on a philosophy that "We feel good about ourselves when we do positive actions," can lead to genuine character development and school reform (Allred, 1996, 1998).

Pillars of Character

To evaluate the success of a school today one must consider academic success measured objectively, demonstrated effectiveness in developing children's social and emotional skills, as well as successful efforts toward parental and community involvement. The work of Gardner and Goleman has reinforced the idea that emotional intelligence and socio-emotional learning are keys to a person's success in school and on the job and the basis of satisfying relationships with others. My basic premise of Pillars of Character practice is that just as the acquisition and development of literacy is an essential ongoing process throughout a child's school career, so is the development of social and emotional maturity. This leads to the basic assumption that we feel good about ourselves when we make good choices, and if we are taught to think critically we will make good choices.

Pillars of Character practice addresses five areas:

1. *Beliefs.* We feel good about ourselves when we do positive actions. Our thoughts lead to actions, and those actions lead to feelings about ourselves, which lead to more thoughts both positive and negative. Learning to read is a positive action the same as learning to be responsible and respectful. When academics is considered positive action and the school community reinforces this by encouraging educational excellence and responsible citizenship, positive self-concept results.
2. *Goals and objectives.* In order to feel good about ourselves we must identify the actions that lead to good character and then do them. The model focuses on critical thinking and character development presented by teachers in their lessons.
3. *Classroom curriculum.* Teachers infuse character education concepts into lessons.
4. *School climate.* Climate ties together school activities and curriculum into a schoolwide program that creates many opportunities to practice lessons learned in class.

5. *Parent and community involvement.* The program encourages collaboration among school, home, businesses, and institutions.

Basic Components of the Pillars of Character Model

- It is a model that unites all program components into a comprehensive school improvement plan.
- Teachers stress good character based on the model's eight themes.
- The model involves parents in home teaching, mentoring, role modeling, and decision making.
- It includes a focus on increased academic achievement, attendance, and positive behaviors that evidence a strong moral character. Teachers and parents observe measurable results.

Eight themes (or topics) taught for a length of three to four weeks make up the Pillars of Character.

1. *Respect* is taught through utilizing classroom procedures that focus on modeling respectful behavior. A seminar is used to develop the meaning of respectful behavior by describing specific acts.
2. *Responsibility* is taught through the use of conventional instructional approach culminating in a seminar in which the meaning of responsibility is ascertained.
3. *Ethical moral education* is taught in conjunction with training seminars related to moral issues that are grade-appropriate.
4. *Honesty and truthfulness* and keeping one's word are core concepts in the model, which can be taught through modeling and seminars.
5. *Kindness, caring, and empathy* are also core values, which can be taught through modeling and seminars. Children are taught to treat others the way they would like to be treated, with kindness, and develop empathy for the needs of others. The four elements of caring are discussed: (1) warmth, (2) positive attention, (3) respectful communication, and (4) trust.
6. *Fairness and anger management,* the importance of a positive self-concept, along with critical thinking skills and emotional supports are incorporated in understanding the true meaning of fairness and how to manage anger. Four steps to manage emotions are: (1) identify and acknowledge emotions, (2) determine emotional triggers, (3) stay calm, and (4) reflect.
7. *Civic and citizenship education,* the meaning of civic responsibility, and the meaning of good citizenship are integral to being an American.
8. *Social emotional learning* leads to anger management, and violence and gang prevention through the use of conflict-resolution skills. The goal of social emotional learning is to help develop the child's "emotional intelligence" while combining it with self-knowledge, self-acceptance, and self-management for the purpose of developing understanding and empathy for the feelings of others.

The Pillars of Character model is seen as a process that helps students both achieve academic excellence and develop good character. All children can learn when exposed to a quality education that encourages critical thinking. Critical thinking aids children in understanding and dealing with their feelings, which in turn helps them to develop empathy for others. Empathy is central to emotional intelligence and good character, and its development in children should be seen as an important goal of education.

KEY TERMS TO FOCUS ON

authoritarian practice

intimidation practice

instructional/eclectic practice

socio-emotional practice

tolerant/permissive practice

emotional intelligence

DISCUSSION QUESTIONS

1. Of the management strategies and practices presented in this chapter, which do you find most appealing? Why?

2. Describe the differences in the basic assumptions of these practices.

3. Can you think of a situation in which intimidation or permissiveness might be deemed acceptable?

4. Why is it important for schools to teach emotional intelligence and focus on character development in students?

MINI CASES FROM THE FIELD

Analyze the following brief case studies using the IOSIE method. Be sure to reflect upon the practices presented in this chapter as you devise possible solutions.

1. Jose Santos is a senior in your high school who has had a spotty record throughout his four years of high school, though he has never gotten into serious trouble. He is an average to below-average student. He is exceptionally popular with his peers due to his obvious leadership qualities and because he sings in a band. He is constantly singing to himself in class, behavior that you feel is inappropriate and disruptive. You have repeatedly asked him to stop, and he has responded by as-

suring you that he is not disturbing anyone. He has even gone so far as to tell you to ask the class if anyone is upset with his singing. What level of teacher control do you think is necessary in getting Jose to comply with your behavioral expectations?

2. Connie Polloway is an articulate ten-year-old child who takes a very cavalier approach to your instruction; she is constantly fidgeting about and talking and laughing with her classmates while you are attempting to instruct the class. Connie is a very bright student who you feel is a bit too precocious. Everyone else in this sixth-grade classroom seems to respond

positively to your instructional practice. When you speak to Connie privately she claims to know all the work you present and is bored with your slow pace. Analyze this case using the IOSIE method. Also consider how you could improve your instructional practice so that Connie will no longer be bored and a behavior problem.

3. As a new teacher in the Marion Middle School you are experiencing a great deal of disrespect leveled at you by an eighth-grade class. The students in the class seem to resent the fact that you are to replace their former English teacher for the remainder of the school year. A veteran teacher has told you that the only way to effectively control middle school children and especially this eighth-grade class is by using the carrot-and-stick approach. She suggests that you pile on homework and give them lengthy worksheets to complete during instructional periods. She further

adds that you should only reward children once during the awards assembly at the end of the school year. Analyze this case using the IOSIE method and determine if these suggestions are valid from your perspective. What socio-emotional practices would be effective in implementing a strategy to turn this class around? Could you use any other practice to moderate misconduct on the part of this class?

4. At lunchtime you observe a group of children, led by Jackie Patton in your third-grade class, tormenting Simon James, a child who has emotional and academic problems and who has not done well on your class tests. Jackie has demonstrated a sarcastic wit and an interpersonal intelligence far beyond her years in the way she manipulates children to follow her lead. Analyze this case using the IOSIE method and explain how you would use a combination of individual guidance and socio-emotional practice to resolve this situation.

REFERENCES

Accel-Team. 2005. Douglas McGregor: Theory X and theory Y. www.accel-team.com/human_relations/hrels_03_mcgregor.html.

Adler, M. 1982. *The Paideia proposal: An educational manifesto.* New York: Collier.

Allred, C. 1998. *Positive action model for comprehensive school reform.* Twin Falls, ID: Positive Action Company.

Allred, C. 1996. *Positive actions for living.* Twin Falls, ID: Positive Action Co.

Cooper, J. M., ed. 1999. *Classroom teaching skills.* 6th ed. Boston: Houghton Mifflin.

Dreikurs, R., and L. Grey. 1968. *A new approach to discipline: Logical consequences.* New York: Hawthorne.

Emmer, E. T., and C. M. Evertson. 1981. Synthesis of research on classroom management. *Educational Leadership* (January), 342–47.

Etzioni, A. 1998. How not to discuss character education. *Kappan* (February), 446–48.

Evertson, C. M., and A. Harris. 1999. Support for managing learning-centered classrooms: The classroom organization and management program. In *Beyond behaviorism: Changing the classroom management paradigm,* ed. H. J. Freiberg, 59–74. Boston: Allyn & Bacon.

Evertson, C. M., E. T. Emmer, and M. E. Worsham. 2003. *Classroom management for elementary teachers.* 6th ed. Boston: Allyn & Bacon.

Gardner, H. 1983. *Frames of mind: The theory of multiple intelligences.* New York: Basic Books.

Gathercoal, P. 1993. *Judicious discipline.* 3rd ed. San Francisco: Caddo Gap Press.

Ginott, H. 1976. *Teacher and child.* New York: Avon.

Goleman, D. 1998. *Emotional intelligence.* New York: Bantam.

Goodlad, J. 1983. *A place called school.* New York: McGraw-Hill.

Landau, B., and P. Gathercoal. 2000. Creating peaceful classrooms: Judicious discipline and class meetings. *Phi Delta Kappan* 81, 450–54.

McGregor, D. 1960. *The human side of enterprise.* New York: McGraw Hill.

Ornstein, A. C., and Lasley, T. J. 2004. *Strategies for effective teaching.* 4th ed. New York, McGraw Hill.

Rodgers, C. R. 1951. *Client-centered therapy: Its current practice, implications and theory.* Boston: Houghton Mifflin.

Scarpaci, R. T. 2004. Pantheon program at Soterios Ellenas Parochial School. *Kimisis Theotokou,* 31–27. See also www.soteriosellenas.org.

Summerhill School. 2005. A. S. Neill's Summerhill School. www.summerhillschool.co.uk/index .html.

CHAPTER FIVE

CONSEQUENCES MODELS

FOCUS POINT

1. A consequences approach to classroom management is based on the understanding that teachers must exert strong control over children to create an environment in which learning can occur.

All teachers need control within their classrooms. The question is how much teacher control benefits the classroom, and how is that control best achieved? This chapter discusses six classroom management models that are based on the understanding that teachers must exert strong control over children in order for learning to occur. The models have a behaviorist, consequences orientation that sees the teacher as facilitating all actions related to classroom management. Students are acted upon, not with. The models are labeled consequences models because they utilize, to varying degrees, teacher-initiated consequences for both negative and positive behavior. There is relatively little if any individual guidance advocated. All of the models can be effectively applied to a variety of classroom situations.

ASSERTIVE DISCIPLINE MODEL

Lee and Marlene Canter's assertive discipline model (1976, 2001) focuses on training parents and teachers in the use of assertive disciplinary techniques. Teachers insist on proper behavior from students, recognizing and supporting them when they practice such behavior and utilizing well-organized procedures for following through when they do not behave. Assertive discipline is a system in which negative consequences is consistently meted out for rule infractions. Rules are determined by the teacher or other school personnel and must be obeyed; they are nonnegotiable. Consequences increase in severity with repeated incidents of misbehavior. Teachers are encouraged to enlist the help of parents and principal in attempting behavior modification. Teachers use a system of positive reinforcements or rewards, such as praise and extra credit, to encourage good behavior.

The model is based on the understanding that successful learning depends on a suitable learning environment; positive behavior results in positive academic performance. Teachers cannot be effective in an undisciplined classroom.

The Canters claim their position centers around student and teacher rights. Teachers' rights include establishing an optimal learning environment and expecting appropriate behavior from students. Teachers also have the right to receive help from administrators and parents when it is needed. Students' rights include a safe and productive learning environment. Students have the right to a full understanding of the teacher's behavioral expectations, and the consequences that will follow good and bad choices. Critics claim that the approach fosters dependence on the teacher as a determiner of good and bad behavior, and is thus authoritarian, but the Canters give the counterargument that carefully defined limits and expectations free children to learn. The teacher is at all times attentive to what is in the best interests of the student, and is expected to take a systemic approach to behavior management based on the beliefs and skills most associated with effectiveness in the classroom. Marzano, Marzano, and Pickering (2003) argue that assertive discipline "employs a balance of negative and positive consequences as opposed to negative consequences only," which encourages children to choose appropriate behavior.

Assertive discipline utilizes five basic procedures:

1. Determine negative consequences for noncompliance and positive consequences for appropriate behavior.
2. Identify your expectations. Draw a clear line between appropriate and inappropriate behavior.
3. Stress why positive behavior is necessary.
4. Persist in reinforcing expectations, using a firm tone of voice and maintaining eye contact. Use nonverbal gestures to clearly convey intention.
5. Be assertive in confrontations with students over behavior, reminding them of expectations and consequences, without hostility or threats. Make sure the established consequences are consistently enforced.

The Canters advocate the use of teacher assertiveness in setting clear limits and determining consequences. An assertive discipline plan explicitly defines expectations. Nonassertive teachers take a passive approach to teaching in which expectations are unvoiced, and then become hostile when these expectations go unmet. Hostile teachers react to misbehavior in a counterproductive way, often blaming the students when the fault lies in their failure to effectively manage the class. A hostile teacher tends to be abrasive and sarcastic with students, alienating students and further eroding the learning process. The assertive teacher responds to misbehavior in a calm, firm manner. She has a discipline plan with clearly stated rules and consequences that provide positive recognition. Students who comply are positively reinforced, whereas those who disobey rules or directions receive negative reinforcement.

When to Use

Assertive discipline can be used at any time the teacher needs to gain control of the classroom. This method appeals most to teachers who believe that the classroom is their domain; students play by the teacher's rules. It supports the inherent beliefs of those who see classroom management as the job of the teacher alone. Uses of the strategy can be both interventionist and preventive.

Strengths

The strengths of this model are that it is simple to use and straightforward; the way the classroom is run reflects the beliefs of the teacher. Teachers have the power; this gives them a feeling of security in the classroom and instills in them a measure of confidence in their abilities, which aids their effectiveness in relating to students. They avoid the powerlessness of the nonassertive teacher and the accompanying potential for hostility. The involvement of parents and administrators in the discipline process allows for a team effort in directing children to conform to the norms of appropriate behavior. Student security is enhanced because expectations are clear and consequences are consistently applied.

Weaknesses

The weaknesses of this model stem from the power inequity it creates in the classroom. Students are not invited into the management process; the teacher sets the rules and the students are punished or rewarded depending on their ability to conform to these rules. The rules are nonnegotiable. Students may resent this approach, feeling disempowered and undervalued. The goal of self-discipline is secondary to the model's aims; control is externally imposed on students. It also fails to deal with the underlying causes of discipline problems, such as emotional distress, parental divorce, poverty, racism, and so on. For extreme misbehavior, the model advocates student suspension; for some critics, this is an admission of failure. Such punishment stimulates rebellion and promotes the very behavior it was designed to eliminate.

PRACTICE EXERCISE:

Do Mini Case Study number one at the end of this chapter. Be sure to use the IOSIE method to analyze the situation and the assertive discipline model as a possible solution.

JONES MODEL

Fredric Jones, a psychologist at UCLA, conducted research (1987) in which he found that teachers needed to utilize their physical presence in the classroom to ensure that students remained on task and did not disrupt the learning process. According to Jones, classroom management procedures must be positive. They must affirm students while setting limits and promoting cooperation. Discipline procedures must be practical, simple, easily mastered, and not coercive. Jones draws theoretically and conceptually from the knowledge base of behavior modification and from anthropological and neurobiological research on how the brain functions. His basic assumptions are that children need a controlled environment in order to behave properly and that teachers can attain control through nonverbal cues and movements calculated to bring them physically closer to students. Jones views misbehavior as taking time away from learning. Students lose learning time through inattention and talking without permission. They lose such time by moving about the room without permission. Incentives can prevent time lost to learning. Jones believes that teachers should offer incentives, such as "preferred activity time," to keep students on task. He believes that reinforcing good behaviors will lead to an increase in their frequency. Jones (1994) also promotes the involvement of parents and school administration to help gain control of student behavior. He believes that teachers should have procedures to deal with misbehavior that enable them to quickly get on with the lesson.

Many of the problems teachers experience result from their mismanagement of various routines. Rules must be clarified or students will determine their own limits. The teacher should spend the first two weeks of school reiterating the rules, standards, routines, and expectations of the classroom if needed. Rules must spell out exactly what is expected and how students can comply. They must be revisited periodically throughout the year, though they should be enforced through cooperation (i.e., good behavior is rewarded), not dictatorial means.

Jones has specific ideas about classroom organization. He insists that teachers provide for open and quick access to all students. This he claims will help teachers maintain control within the classroom. In monitoring what is acceptable and what is not acceptable behavior, teachers are directed to use effective body language and physical proximity. Acts such as placing yourself so that you can monitor the whole room are most effective. It gives the impression that you have eyes in back of your head. Jones says that the following steps can be used as the need dictates.

1. *Address misbehavior.* Discipline comes before instruction; children aren't on task if they're goofing off. Effective procedures can help teachers address misbehavior with minimal loss in teaching time. Teachers should stay calm and take two relaxing breaths before any action is taken.
2. *Turn, look, names, wait, and turn.* The second step requires you to slowly turn and face the misbehaving student(s), making direct eye contact. Say the name(s) of the student(s) in a nonthreatening manner.
3. *Walk.* If they do not respond to your initial effort to stop their behavior, move in their direction. Walk slowly, in a relaxed manner. Approach the biggest troublemaker first. Stand close to the student's desk and actually brush it with your leg.

4. *Prompt.* Lean in slowly while giving visual prompts such as turning papers and pointing to redirect them to work. Give a verbal prompt only if necessary. Keep it simple—no more than two declarative sentences. Speak calmly; do not raise your voice.

5. *Palms.* If the response is still insufficient, place your palms flat on the desk while maintaining eye contact. This will discomfort the offender, who should cease the objectionable action.

6. *Stand your ground.* Remain near the student until he is back on task.

7. *Move out.* When all is settled you can move away by quietly thanking the student for getting back to work.

Once this procedure has been undertaken it is unlikely that you will have to repeat it. A simple look may be all you need. The Jones model is very practical and offers specific procedures for the teacher to take when the situation arises. Many of these practices are easily interchanged with other practices. The key is being eclectic when dealing with management problems. If it works and helps you to achieve your educational objectives, do it. You can see in Table 5.1 that Jones is not shy

TABLE 5.1 The Jones Positive Discipline Model

PART	DEFINITION	KNOWLEDGE BASE	EXAMPLES
Responsibility Training	The use of an incentive system for obtaining new behaviors or increasing existing ones	Behavior modification	Group incentives Preferred activity time (PAT) Differential reinforcement
Omission	Getting a very difficult student to desist misbehavior	Behavior modification	Differential reinforcement, group incentives
Backup System	Three levels of intervention (warning, conference, suspension or expulsion from school) from private to public sanctions	Traditional school practice	Office referral, time-out, expulsion, suspension, staffing, parent conferencing
Classroom Structure	The arrangement of objects and furniture and the teaching of rules and procedures		Three-step lesson: say, show, do over practice
Limit Setting	Actions taken by the teacher to control students	Brain theory	Relaxed breathing, inhibit talking, eye contact, posture

Source: Adapted from Wolfgang, C. H. 1999. *Solving discipline problems.* 4th ed. Boston: Allyn and Bacon, p. 195.

about borrowing from a number of knowledge bases as long as his objective is achieved.

From this discussion and the table, we can see that the major strength of the Jones model is that it specifies a set of steps to follow in dealing with discipline problems. It tells exactly how far to go in applying discipline techniques and defines the role of the teacher as well as the role of administrators in discipline. The model's major weakness, as with most behaviorist approaches, is that it does not promote autonomy in students. It is also difficult for some teachers to apply techniques because they become uncomfortable getting close to students. Jones's insistence that discipline take precedence over instruction goes against standard theory by allowing the misbehavior of individual students to penalize the entire class. This strategy may cause some students to become submissive and others to rebel. The model also tends to encourage teachers to be aggressive and controlling instead of helpful and supportive.

Discipline, according to Jones, is creating time on task in the most unobtrusive fashion. As an example, Jones speaks of pheasant posturing which is what animals do to put on a great show without anything really happening. In birds it takes the form of flapping wings and squawking loudly. In humans it takes the form of body mannerisms such as looking intently at a student without anything really happening. The stakes are only raised if the student continues to misbehave. Jones suggests that classroom discipline be thought of as a card game in which every move ups the ante. A commitment to discipline must be shown. And it will take some time. Jones advocates four basic realities of learning, which he claims his model helps achieve.

1. We learn one step at a time.
2. We learn by doing.
3. We learn by teaching.
4. We improve through practice, practice, and practice.

If your objectives are achieved and children are learning, then your choice of this intervention approach to classroom management is the correct one. Jones's strategies can be used in combination with other approaches.

The Jones model is an example of a management strategy that could be criticized as utilizing intimidation in the classroom. The use of proximity and physical presence to convey nonvocal desists has been described as a strategy of intimidation under the guise of a positive discipline model. Jones argues that, rather than intimidating students, his program affirms a positive way of setting limits and promoting cooperation.

When to Use

The Jones model has practical application to discrete incidents of misbehavior. The quintessential interventionist model, it was developed to be used when your authority as the teacher is challenged. Jones emphasizes that incidents of misbehavior must be dealt with immediately. Infractions don't go away of their own accord. Because its primary tool is body language, the strategy can be implemented at a moment's notice. This approach can be used to supplement any preventive management strategy.

Strengths

The strength of this model is that it provides the user with a specific, detailed approach to handling discipline problems. It specifies a set of steps to follow in dealing with discipline problems. It tells exactly how far to go in applying discipline techniques and defines the role of the teacher as well as the role of administrators in discipline. Its positive approach avoids the teacher becoming frustrated and resorting to yelling, hostility, or sarcasm.

Weaknesses

The weakness of this model is that it does not attempt to understand the underlying causes of misconduct. The model encourages the teacher to be controlling and avoids a helpful, supportive guidance approach. As with most consequences approaches, it does not promote autonomy in students. Some teachers might not be comfortable with its emphasis on physical proximity. Jones's insistence that discipline take precedence over instruction can allow the misbehavior of individual students to penalize the entire class. The strategy may cause some students to become submissive and others to rebel.

KOUNIN EFFECTIVE MOMENTUM MODEL

This model is based on the work of the psychologist Jacob Kounin, who found that effective lesson management led to good behavior in the classroom. Kounin perceived a ripple effect occurring in the classroom when individual misbehavior was handled efficiently, with clarity and firmness and strong desists. Kounin's research shows that teacher intervention has an impact on those students not directly subjected to the behavioral directive. He came to the conclusion that teacher actions such as praise or encouragement or remarks intended to stop misbehavior (desists) influence the behavior of not just the intended recipient but students who witness the event. Kounin concluded that teacher behaviors clearly impact classroom discipline. His research (1977) found that the most effective teachers used preventive strategies rather than intervention to maintain classroom discipline. They made smooth transitions during lessons and maintained momentum through activities that engaged students. This momentum he viewed as essential to good classroom management. Teachers were found to be more effective when they demonstrated "with-it–ness," or an insightful awareness of what was going on in the classroom. "With-it–ness" is perhaps another way of describing Jones's monitoring of class behavior. It is the ability to communicate to students that you know what everybody in the classroom is up to. Teachers who are successful at this practice appear to have eyes in the back of their heads. Planning and presenting superior lessons, Kounin felt, avoided boredom and increased the alertness of students while preventing most discipline problems. The following behaviors are associated with the Kounin model:

- *With-it–ness.* Teachers have an instinctive feel for situations going on in their classrooms; they have eyes in the back of their heads when it comes to classroom management. They are able to nip behavioral problems in the bud.
- *Overlapping.* Teachers deal with disruptive behavior while lessons are ongoing. They demonstrate an ability to manage behavior while keeping a focus on the lesson.
- *Momentum.* Teachers' ability to pace lessons and keep students involved prevents boredom and management problems. Teachers are able to maintain a steady sense of progress and movement throughout a lesson.
- *Smoothness.* Teachers move lessons from activity to activity by providing sufficient variety at appropriate times. Activities are conducted at a brisk pace in a logical order without lengthy directions.

The basic assumptions of effective momentum are:

1. Negative or positive actions by teachers influence students around them. This is called the Ripple Effect.
2. Students cannot control their own behavior, they need to be controlled by their teachers.
3. By increasing the clarity and firmness of their interactions with students, the teacher's control of the class will improve.
4. Teachers who display with-it–ness in their classrooms improve their classroom management.
5. Avoiding jerky transitions in a lesson by providing a variety of activities avoids management problems.
6. Stopping lessons to deal with discipline problems only adds to the problem. (Note both the Canters and Jones would disagree with this statement.)
7. Effective control depends on the well-executed management of more than one activity simultaneously called overlapping or multitasking.

When to Use

Maintaining momentum in the classroom is key to successful teaching. Instructional momentum and student engagement tend to discourage misbehavior. This strategy allows the teacher to focus on classroom learning rather than disciplinary action. It can be applied to classroom lesson management. However, it should be combined with interventionist techniques such as traditional models, assertive discipline, or the Jones model if it is to be successful in dealing with infractions of classroom rules.

Strengths

Efficacy of the model was determined by empirical research. Kounin's work documented teacher behaviors that aided or interfered with learning. Teacher actions were seen as affecting the entire classroom, not just students singled out for behavioral directives. The model offers several procedures for making desists effective, such as targeting the proper students, timing of desists, overlapping, and "with-it–ness."

Weaknesses

The model has practical application only to classroom recitation sessions. The model is limited in that it is not readily adaptable to many classroom situations or teaching approaches. It is essentially preventive, and shows how to avoid discipline problems. It does not provide corrective measures to solve serious discipline problems. The model also does not assist students in developing self-discipline.

PRACTICE EXERCISE:

Do Mini Case Study number two at the end of this chapter. Be sure to use the IOSIE method to analyze the situation and attempt to combine the Jones model and the effective momentum model as a possible solution.

LOGICAL CONSEQUENCES

Logical consequences (Dreikurs and Soltz, 1964; Dreikurs and Cassel, 1972) is a management theory developed in Vienna by the psychiatrist Rudolf Dreikurs (1897–1972). Dreikurs's associate, the psychiatrist Alfred Adler, influenced his work. In this model, democratic principles are understood to be central to discipline, the basic premise being that children should be given a choice of consequences when they don't behave rather than being forced to behave as directed. Dreikurs felt that one's behavior was driven by one's biased interpretations of the world. He believed that people act according to their own subjective appraisal of the reality that surrounds them. He concluded that when an individual is able to assess the consequences associated with their behavior, their actions are more informed. Students misbehave because their needs are not met. When these needs are acknowledged behavior improves. Dreikurs asserted that misbehavior is due to the students' need for recognition, which can lead to behaviors involving (1) attention getting, (2) power seeking, (3) revenge seeking, and (4) displaying of inadequacy.

Dreikurs rejected the administration of both punishments and positive and negative reinforcements, because he considered them as inappropriate responses and as creators of dependency. Teachers, he said, should use encouragement as a means of allowing children to experience success in a supportive, noncompetitive environment. Dreikurs believed that the fostering of personal responsibility, which is fundamental to a democratic society, requires that children experience, understand, and accept the consequences of misbehavior. Standards of relatedness, respectfulness, and reasonableness must characterize potential consequences, so that they are perceived as logical and not arbitrary. All behaviors including misbehavior are purposeful and directed toward achieving social recognition. All misbehavior is the result of a child's mistaken assumption about how to find a place and gain status. When children solicit recognition without success, they usually misbehave to gain it. Children justify these mistaken goals because they have a limited conscious understanding of their real motives.

How do we address students' mistaken goals? Dreikurs's model claims that teachers must understand that discipline is not punishment; it is an attempt to instill in students self-control. Thus, the teacher's role in this process is to assist pupils in imposing limits on themselves. By modeling democratic behavior teachers provide guidance in assisting pupils to set goals and appropriate consequences. It must be understood that all students want to belong to the group and their behavior is directed at achieving that purpose. Misbehavior, according to Dreikurs, results from the mistaken belief that it will aid them in gaining recognition from their peer group (Charles, 1985). The teacher's objective is to identify the specific mistaken goal the pupil is seeking and then act in ways that do not reinforce that goal. The teacher should reinforce the concept that negative consequences result from inappropriate behavior. Logical consequences are commonsense results that follow such behavior. Examples might include:

1. A child who writes on the wall either cleans the wall or pays the custodian to do it.
2. A child who marks his desk either refinishes it or pays to have it done.
3. A child who initiates a fight during recess is banned from recess until he develops a plan to avoid fighting.
4. A child who turns in a sloppy assignment receives a grade of zero until a new paper is received.
5. A child who pushes another on the staircase is not allowed to walk with the class until she or he apologizes or everyone else has cleared the staircase.

This commonsense approach can be summarized by a list of do's and don'ts, which can be used as nonsequential steps to follow in implementing this strategy (Dreikurs, Grunwald, and Pepper, 1982).

- Do try to understand the purpose of children's misbehavior.
- Do give clear-cut directions for actions expected of children.
- Do focus on children's present, not past, behavior.
- Do give misbehaving students a choice to leave or remain without disturbing others.
- Do build on the positive; avoid the negative.
- Do discuss problems when not emotionally involved.

- Do use logical consequences instead of punishments, being kind yet firm.
- Don't be preoccupied with your own prestige and authority.
- Don't nag.
- Don't ask a child to promise anything.
- Don't give rewards for good behavior. It only conditions students to expect more rewards.
- Don't look to find fault.
- Don't hold your students and yourself to different standards.
- Don't use threats.
- Don't be vindictive.

Clearly, though this strategy has been categorized as behaviorist it overlaps with a guidance approach.

When to Use

Logical consequences, though listed as a strong teacher control model, can be utilized in practically any position on the control spectrum advanced in this text. It works extremely well in conjunction with most other classroom management techniques. As a preventive approach it allows the teacher to assist the student in developing understanding for their actions. When a child realizes that there is a price to pay for negative behavior the reward associated with this behavior tends to diminish.

Strengths

The primary strength of this model is that, unlike most consequences approaches, it promotes autonomy in students. It helps children both to understand and correct their behavior. It is considered an effective preventive approach to discipline. It relies on logical consequences instead of arbitrary punishment and promotes mutual respect. It assists teachers to focus on causes before they take action.

Weaknesses

The weakness of this model stems from the fact that teachers may have trouble determining students' actual motives, since students may be unable to understand or admit to those motives. Teachers may find it difficult to dialogue with students about consequences of misbehavior.

TRADITIONAL MODEL

The traditional model is sometimes described as a "cookbook approach" to classroom management. This strategy is based on a collection of practices that teachers have traditionally employed in their classrooms. Many teachers tout it for containing commonsense remedies for management ills. It tends to be interventionist rather than preventive, and reactive rather than proactive. The model includes both positive reinforcement and intervention strategies including punishment. Goodlad (1994) in his research includes characteristics such as positive reinforcement, rewards, honor roles, and privileges as suggested strategies. He also favors controlling misbehavior such as restlessness, giggling, disruptions, and stubbornness by ignoring, reminders, eye contact, commands and direct orders, verbal threats, separating students from the site of the infraction, and sending offenders to the principal. Essential practices involve having the teacher (1) develop classroom rules, (2) create classroom rewards, (3) devise classroom consequences, (4) establish routines and procedures, (5) organize the classroom space, and (6) practice effective communication.

The major assumption of the model is that tried-and-true measures exist for dealing with managerial problems. Teachers can address various problem situations utilizing the remedies that have been developed by a long line of teachers before them. The managerial strategies have a history of effective and logical application; they include such teacher directives as (1) Always be consistent in enforcing rules, and (2) Never play favorites when rewarding students.

When to Use

Traditional methods of classroom management are in most cases the easiest to use since by definition they are those that teachers have traditionally accepted as their modis operandi. Since the approach is based on tried-and-true procedures it is typically successful. Teachers are advised to use the strategy in combination with other strategies that have a specific sequential base.

Strengths

Teachers feel comfortable using familiar, reliable approaches to management problems, and this approach offers a variety of strategies for teachers to use.

Weaknesses

Teachers who rely on the traditional model tend to simply enforce rules without analyzing each situation individually. In many instances this method leads to using coercive forms of management, which is why it is considered a consequences model. Students can react to traditional, rote punishments in a negative fashion (for example, in a situation in which the entire class is punished for the infraction of one student). There is little evidence of long-term improvements in student behavior as a result of the traditional approach.

PRACTICE EXERCISE:

Do Mini Case Study number three at the end of this chapter. Be sure to use the IOSIE method to analyze the situation and attempt to combine the logical consequences model and the traditional model as a possible solution.

BEHAVIOR MODIFICATION

The psychologist B. F. Skinner (1904–1990) claimed that individual choices are determined by the environmental conditions under which people live. Skinner believed that students' behavior could be controlled through a program of reinforcement. His work led to the science of human behavior known as behavior modification. Skinner's claim that our minds are not our private preserve and could be controlled and shaped through science remains controversial. This reaction was similar to Copernicus, who said the earth was not the center of the universe, and Darwin, who said the human body is not so special because of evolution and natural selection. You can imagine the negative reactions to these beliefs at the time.

The following five historical figures led to the founding of behavioral psychology and eventually behavior modification. There is a clear line from the ancient Greeks through the Renaissance and the Victorian period that establishes the thought process that led to behavioral psychology.

1. Aristotle was the first to classify human behavior into five categories: sight, smell, hearing, appetite, and fashion.
2. Rene Descartes (1600s) viewed behavior as mechanical since the body was thought to be like a machine.
3. In the 1800s, Darwin's theory of evolution and natural selection was used as an explanation for human behavior.
4. Ivan Pavlov demonstrated behavior modification theory by getting dogs to salivate when a bell was rung.
5. John B. Watson formalized previous study into a field called behavioral psychology.

Skinner, following the work of Watson, isolated behavior as its own entity separate from all other aspects of life by disregarding the mind, soul, and human spirit.

Behaviorists do not explain human behavior in terms of will. They believe behavior is controlled by consequences and that any behavior can be reinforced if a sufficiently strong reward is associated with it. Behaviorists modify behavior utilizing both positive and negative reinforcement (punishment). Skinner claimed that aggression is not implicit in man's nature but taught through the culture. In his book *Walden Two* (1948) he claimed that society operated on the principle of self-interest and the rewarding of socially acceptable behaviors. This led to a theory called contingencies of reinforcement.

In *The Technology of Teaching* (1968) Skinner applied the principles of behavior modification to the classroom. "Education is a process where we arrange the educational environment to expedite learning," he wrote. His teaching system consists of lessons and rewards leading to self-control. "Positive reinforcement, not punishment, is the most effective consequence to human response." According to behavior modification theory, both appropriate and inappropriate behavior is learned, and a child misbehaves because he has not learned appropriately. Learning is influenced by events in the environment, which can be regulated by an effective teacher.

Skinner believed that a few basic processes account for all learning. The role of the teacher is to promote appropriate student behavior by rewarding it, and to eliminate inappropriate student behavior by not rewarding it. The principals of management that form the basis for behavior modification are positive reinforcement, punishment, negative reinforcement, and extinction, or time-out. To modify behavior, teachers are directed to use the following correction strategies.

1. *Extinction.* Inappropriate behavior is ignored until it disappears. Extinction is particularly effective when desired behaviors are reinforced at the same time.
2. *Reinforcement.* Reinforcers are stimuli used to produce certain behaviors. Negative reinforcement involves withdrawing stimuli. Positive reinforcement utilizes stimuli as rewards. An example of positive reinforcement would be to give points for good behavior, while an example of negative reinforcement would be to take points away if poor behavior is evidenced. The following is a list of the various types of reinforcers that can be used to modify behavior.
   - *Conditioned reinforcers* are reinforcers that are strengthened by association with another reinforcer. An example would be to give verbal praise for good behavior in conjunction with a material reward or special privilege.
   - *Edible reinforcers* are food treats such as candy or other goodies. (Not recommended today due to various state laws that prohibit their use.)
   - *Material reinforcers* are favored objects such as toys.
   - *Activity reinforcers* are pleasurable experiences such as playtime.
3. *Response-cost procedures.* These correction procedures involve the removal of desirable stimuli, such as taking a token away each time an infraction takes place.
4. *Time-out.* A time-out removes the student temporarily from the environment in which the misbehavior is being reinforced.
5. *Punishment.* Punishment can be used for bad behavior rather than ignoring it or reinforcing good behavior. It should be used only as a last resort when more positive approaches have failed. Fighting or threats of violence are behaviors that should be punished. Effective punishment is seen as decreasing the severity of, or eliminating, the objectionable behavior.

In modifying behavior, strategies such as modeling and demonstration are used. One example is the creation of a token economy system, which combines rewards with self-monitoring and behavioral counseling. Another example, red light, green light, teaches children to monitor their own actions by visualizing "stop" and "go" signals. Such cues and prompts help children to be responsible for their own behavior.

Skinner's followers applied his principles of reinforcement to the development of behavior modification, using it to shape desired behavior in the classroom. Skinner formulated principles for behavior shaping and his followers modified these principles to formulate strategies to control behavior in the classroom. The key elements in the behavior modification process revolve around behavior shaping, which is the systematic use of reinforcing stimuli to change behavior in desired directions. Operant behavior is understood to be any voluntary action performed by an individual. To reinforce a desired behavior, a process of reinforcement or the supplying of reinforcing stimuli such as rewards, is used. Various catchphrases and terms have been used over the years in describing the traditional approaches used for behavior modification in the classroom. These include:

- *Catch 'em being good.* Provide praise for good work and good behavior.
- *Rules-ignore-praise.* Make rules, ignore rule breakers, and praise rule followers.
- *Rules-reward-punishment.* Make rules, reward rule followers, and punish rule breakers.
- *Token economies.* A systematic use of tangible reinforcers such as candy, certificates, toys, and so on.
- *Contracting.* Formalized behavior agreements signed by teacher, student, and parents.

The main strength of the neo-Skinnerian model is that behavior modification works, and works well, especially in the short term. Without question it can promote better student behavior and more effective learning. Critics observe that the practice has been shown to be ineffective for changing behaviors over the long term (Brophy, 1998; Jensen, 1998; Kohn, 1993, 1996). All teachers use behavior modification to some extent, but few do so systematically, as advocated by Bandura (1969).

Bandura's behavior modification strategy utilizes the following procedures:

- *Analysis.* Determine your concerns, what is going wrong, and the desired behavior.
- *Develop a plan.* Identify rules, reinforcers, and consequences to achieve desired behavior.
- *Implement plan by:*
    - Correcting conditions that may be causing the problem (antecedents)
    - Reviewing and clarifying rules
    - Describing consequences
    - Tightening up lessons and making them as interesting as possible
    - Discussing the process with students as often as necessary

When to Use

Teachers who accept its underlying philosophy will have the most success utilizing behavior modification. Since behaviors are understood to be learned, the teacher's role is to provide instructional episodes combined with reinforcers in managing the classroom.

Strengths

The major strength of the model is that it is easy to use and results are seen almost immediately. The model gives teachers a comfortable level of control in their classrooms. The model combines feelings of success with obtaining rewards. Rules and standards are clear, consistent, and the same for all students. Class time is not lost discussing rules and conduct. It can be applied to children of all ages. It is well researched and works consistently with most students.

Weaknesses

The basic weakness with behavior modification strategy according to its critics is in its implementation. Most teachers resist its full application as overly manipulative or contrary to free will. Unless punishment is included, behavior modification is ineffective for dealing with blatant misbehavior. The model is most effective in its preventive and supportive aspects of discipline, while relatively weak in intervention and corrective discipline.

The results may not be long term; once positive or negative reinforcers are removed poor behavior may return. Students are not taught to take responsibility for their own behavior. To many this approach is unethical, in that its rewards for good behavior are akin to bribery. It ignores the underlying causes of misbehavior. The home environment and the larger society are not taken into account. Also, the model does not give students an opportunity to clarify emotions, weigh alternatives, decide on solutions, or develop self-discipline.

PRACTICE EXERCISE:

Do Mini Case Study number four at the end of this chapter. Be sure to use the IOSIE method to analyze the situation and attempt to combine the logical consequences model and the behavior modification model as a possible solution.

KEY TERMS TO FOCUS ON

assertive discipline	logical consequences
Jones model	traditional model
Kounin effective momentum model	behavior modification

DISCUSSION QUESTIONS

1. How do the strengths of assertive discipline outweigh the weaknesses?

2. How can the Jones model be used with the effective momentum model?

3. Why is logical consequences considered a positive discipline model?

4. In what ways did your former grade school teachers used the traditional model? Cite at least one example.

5. How can one justify the use of behavior modification in a democratic society?

MINI CASES FROM THE FIELD

Analyze the following mini case studies using the IOSIE method from the perspective of the consequences management models discussed in this chapter. Each study should be analyzed using the specific model suggested as a plausible solution.

1. Juan Camacho is frequently inattentive in your tenth-grade mathematics class. He talks to his neighbors during lessons and when directions are given. You have spoken to him about this behavior but he has quickly dismissed your requests. Juan's grades are not good; he is on the verge of failing the class. During the midterm examination you see Juan copying from Violet Carlson's paper. You swiftly approach his desk and attempt to pick up Juan's paper. He exclaims, "What the f— are you doing?" You motion for him to leave the classroom and angrily tell him not to come back unless he brings his parents with him. Upon reflection you realize you may have acted improperly with regard to this situation. Analyze this case study using the IOSIE method to determine how an assertive discipline strategy could have been used to help Juan become a productive participant in your class and resolve his misbehavior.

2. Kelly Yates is an energetic sixth grader who is seemingly unable to sit still in your class for more than two minutes. She is constantly bumping into or knocking over anything within a three-foot radius of her desk. She is a good student but often has a faraway look on her face during instruction. You have spoken to her on many occasions, attempting to focus her attention, without any positive results. Her incessant clumsiness and persistent daydreaming are interfering with her learning. She claims she is bored and that the work you provide is not challenging. After analyzing this case using the IOSIE method explain how you could combine the Jones model and the effective momentum model to help improve Kelly's performance in class.

3. Richard Spiro is a bright student who is scheduled to graduate this coming June from your middle school. Richard is a rambunctious, wisecracking child who is frequently disrespectful of your authority. One morning you see him writing profane graffiti on one of the walls in your eighth-grade science class. You approach him and ask, in a commanding voice, "Just what do you think you are doing, young man?" He calmly looks at you and says, "I am covering up the bad words that someone else wrote on the walls." Analyze this case using the IOSIE method and make clear how you would put Richard back on the proper road to graduation by utilizing the traditional model and logical

consequences. Which of the other models discussed in this chapter could also be used to resolve this situation?

4. Benjamin Chan is a handsome young boy of nine. He has a mild learning disability combined with attention deficit disorder, which makes it difficulty for you to engage him in meaningful instruction in your mainstream fourth-grade class. Lately Benjamin has been asking to go to the bathroom every time you begin an academic instructional period. If you refuse to let him leave the room, he sits in the corner and sulks. He refuses to do any work, claiming that his stomach hurts because you don't let him go to the toilet. You have spoken to his mother, who has confirmed that he doesn't have any health problems. She claims he is lazy, and she is ashamed of his inability to succeed in school. Analyze this mini case study using the IOSIE method and determine how this episode could be addressed using a behavior modification strategy.

REFERENCES

Bandura, A. 1969. *Principles of behavioral modification.* New York: Holt, Rinehart, and Winston.

Brophy, J. 1998. *Motivating students to learn.* Boston: McGraw.

Canter, L., and M. Canter. 2001. *Assertive discipline: Positive behavior management for today's classrooms.* 3rd ed. Los Angeles: Canter and Associates.

Canter, L., and M. Canter. 1976. *Assertive discipline: A take-charge approach for today's educator.* Seal Beach, CA: Canter and Associates.

Charles, C. M. 1985. *Building classroom discipline: From models to practice.* New York: Longman.

Dreikurs, R., and P. Cassel. 1972. *Discipline without tears.* New York: Hawthorne.

Dreikurs, R., and L. Grey. 1968. *A new approach to discipline: Logical consequences.* New York: Hawthorne.

Dreikurs, R., B. B. Grunwald, and F. C. Pepper. 1982. *Maintaining sanity in the classroom: Classroom management techniques.* 2nd ed. New York: Harper and Row.

Dreikurs, R., and V. Soltz. 1964. *The challenge.* New York: Dutton.

Goodlad, J. 1994. *Educational renewal: Better teachers, better schools.* San Francisco: Jossey-Bass.

Jensen, E. 1998. *Teaching with the brain in mind.* Alexandra, VA: Association for Supervision and Curriculum.

Jones, F. 1994. *Positive classroom discipline: A video course of study.* Santa Cruz, CA: Fredric H. Jones and Associates.

Jones, F. 1987. *Positive classroom discipline.* New York: McGraw-Hill.

Kohn, A. 1996. *Beyond discipline: From compliance to community.* Alexandra, VA: Association for Supervision and Curriculum.

Kohn, A. 1993. *Punished by rewards.* Boston: Houghton Mifflin.

Kounin, J. 1977. *Discipline and group management in classrooms.* Rev. ed. New York: Rinehart and Winston.

Marzano, R. J., J. S. Marzano, and D. J. Pickering. 2003. *Classroom management that works: Research-based strategies for every teacher.* Alexandria, VA: ASCD.

Skinner, B. F. 1968. *The technology of teaching.* New York: Appleton, Century, Crofts.

Skinner, B. F. 1948. *Walden two.* Upper Saddle River, NJ: Prentice Hall.

CHAPTER SIX

GROUP-GUIDANCE MODELS

FOCUS POINT

1. Group guidance can improve classroom behavior, as individuals seek to meet the expectations established by the group.

Most teachers describe themselves as taking a moderate approach to classroom management. *Moderate* is a relative term, however, and teacher actions that fall in the middle of the management spectrum will still evidence variations in quality of teacher control. The following models are designed to get students to take responsibility for their actions; this is seen as the best way to attain a positive classroom management environment. Most of these strategies are preventive rather than interventionist; they focus on preventing misbehavior before it can take root. Common to moderate control models is their emphasis on group effort as it relates to managerial success.

EFFICACY IN ACTION

The efficacy in action approach (Howard, 1998) is less a behavior management model than a model for effective learning. It can, however, be viewed as a moderate teacher-management method based on the assumption that when children are motivated to learn they tend not to misbehave. The approach is based on the belief that learners are in control of their success. The model is based on a key question: "Is smart something you just are, or is it something you can get?" What its developer, the psychologist Jeff Howard, is really asking is whether one believes that intelligence is fixed at birth or developed over time. Is it a product of heredity or environment, nature or nurture? According to Howard, the prevailing belief system is based on the conception that some have it and some do not. This conception leads to an operating principle that sorts and selects by ability. The efficacy operating principle is to accelerate *all* student development. The goal of schooling is to bring all students to the same level of achievement. "Smarts" is not something you're born with, it is something that you get through personal effort. Howard's maxims are "Learn to think and you can do it" and "Think you can—Work hard—Get smart."

Efficacy concepts recognize that excellence—and, by extension, good behavior—can be both taught and learned. This challenges the prevailing belief that talent is inherent, that there are gifted students who are by nature "special." According to this belief, art class will reveal a child's artistic ability or lack thereof. Efficacy models demonstrate that ability is achieved; an individual can *learn* how to draw well. This parallels understandings of self-discipline, which is achieved through individual student effort. The efficacy approach takes an "if at first you don't succeed, try, try again" approach. Howard's "learning zone concept" establishes a practical learning curve. According to this concept, there are three dimensions, or zones, in which learning occurs. The zones distinguish content as too easy, challenging, and too hard with respect to where children are in their learning "right now." Children are assessed in terms of where they are now and where they are expected to go. This understanding recalls Lev Vygotsky's (1896–1934) zone of proximal development (ZPD). According to Vygotsky (1930/1978), learning can only occur within the ZPD zone. Teachers must teach neither below nor above a student's learning zone, but in the area of intellectual challenge, where learning takes place. (See Figure 6.1.)

An example of the practical application of efficacy in action to the classroom would be an activity in which various levels of writing samples are viewed so that a student's present level can be identified and a goal set for improvement. Feedback about where students are now in their writing abilities and what expectations you have for their improvement is critical to this process. It is important to understand that feedback is offered to improve performance and not as a punishment. This technique is also applicable to behavior management, which can be utilized in teaching students to accept responsibility for their actions. Responsibility is inherent in the process because students take responsibility for level of work. The

---

FIGURE 6.1   Efficacy in Action Learning Zones

1. *The Unchallenging Zone* (too easy). The goals in this area are too easy given what the student already knows and can do. Goals set at this level leave the student feeling unchallenged, unsatisfied, and often bored.

2. *The Learning Zone* (challenging, yet realistic). Goals set in this area involve new challenges. As a student takes on one of these new tasks, he won't always be successful, but he will improve and learn something new. Achieving goals in the learning zone builds students' skills, and leaves them feeling confident and ready to take on the next challenge.

3. *The Unrealistic Zone* (too hard for now). Goals here are too difficult, given the student's current level of skills. Goals at this level leave students feeling disappointed and defeated when they fail and merely "lucky" when successful.

strength of this model is contained in the spirit generated by the group approach. Children are encouraged to feel that they are part of a team and share in a group effort focused on self-responsibility and self-esteem. The weakness, however, with efficacy in action is that it can be like a cheerleading session that raises self-esteem, which is not really earned. The emotional letdown that follows this could result in misbehavior.

When to Use

"Efficacy" implies that the model achieves results in guiding the group and individuals within the group to act appropriately. Group incentives and morale-building exercises are intrinsic to this strategy. Peer acceptance and objectives are focused on moving all members of the group to conform to expected behavior. The assumption is that individuals will bring their behavior in line with group expectations. The class is a team that works together to achieve results.

Strengths

Efficacy in action, with its group support structure, is a positive model that generally garners an enthusiastic response from children. The group is seen as reinforcing individuals' self-esteem.

Weaknesses

The stress on self-esteem may not be realistic. Expectations may be set too high and therefore goals can be unachievable; self-esteem is not earned.

PRACTICE EXERCISE:

Do Mini Case Study number one at the end of this chapter. Be sure to use the IOSIE method to analyze the situation and use the efficacy in action approach as a way to resolve the case problem.

COOPERATIVE DISCIPLINE

Linda Albert (1996) claims that her work is based on that of Rudolf Dreikurs, who was a proponent of group discussions, shared responsibility, and recognition of consequences as appropriate management techniques (refer back to Chapter 5). While advocating all of Dreikurs's techniques, Albert adds the importance of communication. She claims that the key element to her cooperative discipline management model is the quality of teacher-student interaction. Albert views interaction as being tri-modal and involving three specific approaches: a (1) hands off,

(2) hands on, and (3) hands-joined approach. Albert promotes a hands-joined approach, and places a strong emphasis on a concomitant, structured character-education program. Her program (available as a package) is representative of management strategies that combine group guidance with character building.

The Interaction in Cooperative Discipline

1. The *hands-off approach* implies that behavior is based on internal controls that help us eventually make the right decisions. The role of the teacher is that of the bystander who at most aids the child in clarifying what is happening. Any discipline program that utilizes communication skills only is based on this approach. It is similar to a values-clarification strategy in which the role of the teacher is to allow the students to reach their own conclusions based on rational group discussion. In effect it could be termed a permissive strategy.
2. The *hands-on approach* implies that external controls are needed to help a child make proper decisions. The role of the teacher is to take charge by demanding, commanding, and directing. Behavior modification and assertive discipline models are based on this approach.
3. Albert advocates a *hands-joined approach*, which assumes that a child's behavior is the product of both internal and external forces. The role of the teacher is to be a cooperative leader, guiding students by offering choices, setting limits, and involving students in the process. This strategy is intended to build self-esteem through encouragement and by building positive relationships.

The basic concept of cooperative discipline is that students choose their behavior to fulfill their need to belong. This need is preeminent in the social ecology in which children reside. Students need to feel capable of completing tasks in a manner that meets the standards of the school and expectations of their teachers and peers. Students need to know they contribute in a significant way to the group. Factors that influence student behavior are

- the quality of student-teacher relations;
- the strength of the classroom climate for success;
- the appropriateness of the classroom structure.

Albert, like Dreikurs, believes that students misbehave in order to achieve one of four immediate goals: (1) attention, (2) power, (3) revenge, and (4) avoidance of failure. (See Table 6.1.) She considers these goals as the primary basis for all misbehaviors that occur in schools and classrooms. Albert addresses these four goals of misbehavior with a summary chart for outlining proposed interventions, general strategies, and techniques that can be used to address each (see Table 6.2).

Albert's Summary Chart of Interventions (Table 6.2) explores each of the goals of misbehavior. Each section highlights a general strategy and specific technique for dealing with that individual misbehavior. The suggestions contained in these charts can be used to develop a cooperative discipline program in your classroom that is consistent with your personal management style.

TABLE 6.1 Cooperation Discipline: Four Goals of Misbehavior

	1-ATTENTION-SEEKING	2-POWER	3-REVENGE	4-AVOIDANCE OF FAILURE
Active Characteristics	Behavior that distracts teacher and class	Temper tantrums, confrontational/disruptive	Physical/psychological threats and attacks	Makes excuses, voices refusal
Passive Characteristics	Operates on slow speed	Quiet noncompliance	Sullen, withdrawn	Procrastinates, pretends to have a disability
Origins of Behavior	Misbehavior gets attention, not taught, needs	Stress, role clarification, dominant submissive	Violence in society and media	Society's emphasis on perfection and competition
Good Characteristics "Silver Lining"	Student wants positive relationships	Leadership, independent thinking	Student wants to protect self	Student wants to succeed
Principles of Prevention	Give attention for appropriate behavior, let student ask for extra attention	Defuse confrontations, give power through choices	Teach how to express hurt, talk, build relationship	Build self-esteem
Intervention Strategies	Minimize the attention, legitmize the behavior, do the unexpected, distract the student, notice appropriate behavior, move student	Use time-out, exit gracefully, use logical consequences (*Use the same strategies for revenge behavior*)		Modify instructional methods, provide tutoring, teach self-talk, build self-esteem, focus on successes, make learning concrete, recognize achievement

Note: This table describes the characteristics of active and passive misbehavior as they are related to the four goals of misbehavior. It further describes the origins of the misbehavior, while concluding with the good characteristics and the principles of prevention, with specific intervention strategies to use for each type of misbehavior.

Source: Adapted with permission from Appendix A in *Cooperative Discipline* by Linda Albert © 1989 American Guidance Service, Inc. 4201 Woodland Road, Circle Pines, MN 55014-1796. All rights reserved.

TABLE 6.2   Summary Chart of Interventions

GOAL	GENERAL STRATEGY	TECHNIQUES
Attention Seeking	Minimize the attention.	Ignore the behavior. Give "the eye." Stand close by. Mention student name. Send a secret signal. Give written notice. Give an I-message.
	Legitimize the behavior.	Make lesson out of behavior. Extend to most extreme form. Whole class does behavior. Use a diminishing quota.
	Do the unexpected.	Turn out lights. Play a musical sound. Lower your voice. Change your voice. Talk to the wall. Use one-liners. Temporarily cease teaching.
	Distract the student.	Ask a direct question. Ask a favor. Change the activity.
	Notice the appropriate behavior.	Thank students. Write well-behaved student names on the board.
	Move the student.	Change student's seat. Send to thinking "time-out" chair.
Power and Revenge	Make a graceful exit.	Acknowledge student power. Remove the audience. Table the matter. Change subject. Use a fogging technique: Agree with the student.
	Use time-out.	Time-out in classroom. Time-out in another class. Time-out in a special room. Time-out in the office. Time-out at home.
	Set the consequences.	Loss or delay of activity or materials. Loss or delay of access to school areas (gym). Denied interaction with other students. Required interactions with school personnel, parents, or police. Restitution: Repair of objects. Replacement or pay for.

TABLE 6.2 Continued

GOAL	GENERAL STRATEGY	TECHNIQUES
Avoidance of Failure	Modify instructional methods.	Use concrete learning materials, and computer-assisted instruction.
	Provide tutoring.	Get extra help from teachers. Remediation programs. Adult volunteers. Peer tutoring. Use learning centers.
	Teach positive self-talk.	Post positive classroom signs. Require two "put ups" for every put down. Encourage positive self-talk.
	Make mistakes okay.	Talk about mistakes. Equate mistakes with effort. Minimize effects of mistakes.
	Build confidence.	Focus on improvement. Notice contributions. Show faith in students. Build on strengths. Acknowledge difficulty. Set time limits on tasks. Focus on past success. Analyze and repeat past success.
	Make learning tangible.	Encourage "I-Can." Create Accomplishment albums. Create a checklist of skills. Talk about yesterday, today, tomorrow.
	Recognize achievement.	Give applause. Encourage clapping/ovations. Use stars and stickers. Host awards and assemblies. Display exhibits. Use positive time-outs.

Source: Adapted with permission from Appendix C in *Cooperative Discipline* by Linda Albert © 1989 American Guidance Service, Inc. 4201 Woodland Road, Circle Pines, MN 55014-1796. All rights reserved.

When to Use

Cooperative discipline can be used when the teacher wants to assume the role of cooperative leader. The teacher offers students choices to fulfill their needs, while also explaining the consequences of their choices. This group-guidance approach is essentially preventive in that students are taught to analyze their choices before they make final decisions. It also provides systematic procedures that can be used to deal with specific classroom situations. This strategy blends well with logical consequences (see Chapter 5) and judicious discipline, outlined later in this chapter.

Strengths

The cooperative discipline model blends well with cooperative learning strategies presently in vogue. The model stresses prevention but also offers specific actions to resolve misbehavior. It provides teachers with a comprehensive framework of management responses.

Weaknesses

Cooperative discipline is prescriptive, and does not allow for a great deal of teacher innovation. Its implementation requires conforming to an established framework. The model has also been criticized as a consequences model in the guise of group guidance. Some critics have labeled it repressive.

PRACTICE EXERCISE:

Do Mini Case Study number two at the end of this chapter. Be sure to use the IOSIE method to analyze the situation and explain how you would resolve the problem using the cooperative discipline model.

JUDICIOUS DISCIPLINE

Judicious discipline (Landau and Gathercoal, 2000) does not aid the teacher in dealing with particular instances of misbehavior, but it does present a model in which the conditions for misbehavior are minimized. It offers a framework by which teachers can create a climate, attitude, and set of procedures for effectively running a class. It is a comprehensive approach to democratic classroom management based on the constitutional principles of personal rights balanced against societal needs. Judicious discipline is predicated on the understanding that students have individual freedoms. Young children may simply be taught that they have the right to "be themselves." Older children can be taught their individual freedoms under the Bill of Rights. Democratic rights should always be understood as being balanced with responsibilities. The basis for all classroom rules are (1) health and safety of all, (2) protecting individual and school property, (3) facilitating/enhancing the educational experience, and (4) preventing disruption. That is, the classroom should enable students to: be safe; be protected; do their best work; have their needs respected. Students are taught to govern their own behaviors by assessing their actions in terms of time, place, and manner. (Is this the right time for this action? Is this the best manner? Is this the appropriate place?)

Class meetings are key to implementing this strategy. For this group-guidance approach to work there must be a commitment on the part of both students and teacher. The rules governing the process are best served when democratically agreed upon, not imposed by the teacher. If this is done properly it will provide student ownership and hence commitment. Students should participate in deciding how they are to be seated and who can call a meeting. It should also be established at the very start that individuals are not on trial, only issues and procedures. The process can evolve through trial and error. Students learn by their own mistakes.

Judicious discipline involves the following procedures:

- Determine who can call a class meeting and when such meetings should be held.
- Seat participants so that all can be seen.
- Do not discuss individuals; only issues and procedures.
- Ensure that meetings stay on topic.
- Avoid coercing anyone to participate.
- Have all group members keep a journal of the meeting.

The basic assumptions that support the judicial discipline model are the same as those that support the U.S. Constitution. Schools have traditionally been understood to operate in loco parentis (in place of the parent); in this model, students' individual constitutional rights are stressed. Judicious discipline suggests that core constitutional principles should be the basis for establishing school and classroom rules. The assumption is that students who understand and appreciate their constitutional rights will be better prepared and more involved citizens. Thus all discipline practices or sanctions are established as recognizing the student's due process rights, making this a commonsense approach to the democratic classroom.

Teachers in many instances have difficulty committing to the running of a democratic classroom as well as the teaching of principles associated with individual rights because of the accompanying trade-off in teacher control. Establishing class rules based on three core constitutional amendments—the First (right to free speech), Fourth (protection against unreasonable searches and seizures), and Fourteenth (due process rights)—can easily alleviate the possible management problems that might result from this approach. Teachers should follow some basic procedures in implementing the process.

1. Post and publish the classroom rules.
2. Be sure to establish standards to be used to justify the withdrawal of a personal right. The reasons used should be couched in terms of "compelling state interest."
3. Conduct preliminary lessons that foster a comparison between group rights versus individual rights.
4. Conduct lessons that explore judicious consequences for infractions of the laws. These should be explored in depth.

When to Use

Judicious discipline is best used as a strategy that helps to develop democratic procedures. By using this group-guidance approach you will be able to develop positive instruction in citizenship while also enhancing respect for the social order necessary to a democratic society. This strategy can effectively supplement other strategies if it is used as a rationale for democratic, not autocratic, action. Teachers *earn* respect with this approach, rather than demand it as a right of their position, which tends to foster an adversarial climate.

Strengths

Judicious discipline provides a historical and cultural (democratic) basis for establishing rules, procedures, and policies that govern classrooms. It teaches civic understanding and instills civic responsibility, educating students about due process and raising their consciousness about the rights and responsibilities of citizenship.

Weaknesses

Judicious discipline does not address teachers' needs to set limits on student behavior, and does not provide remedies to deal with students who misbehave. It can also require a great deal of time to implement. Teachers must reconsider the model of teacher control implied by the traditional legal guideline of in loco parentis. The judicious discipline model also requires the teacher and school to examine policies and procedures that affect traditional school practices such as absence, lateness, suspension, denial of privileges, dress, corporal punishment, and so on. The model, though consistent with the principles of a democratic society, goes against time-honored concepts of adult authority in schools and classrooms.

SKILLSTREAMING

Dr. Arnold P. Goldstein and Dr. Ellen McGinnis (1988; 1997a; 1997b) developed a model they termed *skillstreaming*. It is based on behavioral analysis stemming from an individual's psychology, education, and philosophy. The assumption of the model is that large numbers of children are growing up today without obtaining the basic social skills necessary to function in modern society. Goldstein and McGinnis's view advances the proposition that teaching social skills, if not done at home, must be done in school. Teachers must teach social skills so that children learn appropriate behavioral responses to typical basic social interactions. The model identifies sixty key skills and methods to use in teaching these social skills. It uses a procedure called "structured learning," which focuses on four steps: (1) modeling, or showing, (2) role-playing, or trying, (3) performance feedback, and (4) transference activities or practice such as homework. This instructional approach is based on reinforcement theory as defined in behavioral analysis. The philosophical position is that misbehaving students have skill deficits, and if taught the necessary skills, they will be able to transfer this training to school and daily life, thus becoming a socially skilled and well-behaved, productive person (see Figure 6.2).

In order to set up a skillstreaming program for your class or school, some basic procedures should be followed. First, space in the form of a classroom should be secured for instructional purposes and, if necessary, additional group leaders should be trained. You should also provide time for assessing student social skills through observation or from a prepared checklist. The program also calls for the use of motivational techniques in order to enlist the cooperation of the student participants. Homework, reports, group self-report cards, skill contracts, self-recording forms, and awards can all be used to provide motivation and structure to the program. Groups usually consist of six or more children that have a shared skill deficit. The children have to be taught to analyze situations that may occur, while thinking about alternatives and making decisions. The program's teaching strategy stresses modeling and includes techniques such as role-playing, performance feedback, and transfer, with the teacher as group leader. The process consists of an orderly program that involves the following nine steps:

1. *Define the skill.* Teacher engages student in discussion of skill.
2. *Model the skill.* Modeling is done, so student can learn through imitation.

FIGURE 6.2   Social Skill Categories Necessary for Effective Skillstreaming

- *Classroom survival skills.* Asking for help, saying thank you, listening, bringing materials to class, following instructions, completing assignments, contributing to discussions, asking questions, ignoring distractions, making corrections, deciding on goals.

- *Friendship-making skills.* Introducing yourself, beginning and ending a conversation, joining in, playing a game, asking a favor, offering help, giving a compliment, suggesting an activity, listening, apologizing.

- *Dealing with feelings.* Expressing your feelings, recognizing another's, dealing with feelings of anger, knowing your feelings, showing understanding, expressing concern, rewarding yourself.

- *Alternatives to aggression.* Maintaining self-control, responding to teasing, avoiding trouble, staying out of fights, problem solving, accepting consequences, dealing with an accusation, negotiating.

- *Dealing with stress.* Dealing with boredom, reacting to failure, saying no, accepting no, deciding what caused a problem, making and answering a complaint, dealing with losing, being a good sport, dealing with being left out, dealing with embarrassment, reacting to failure, accepting no, saying no, relaxing, dealing with group pressure, dealing with wanting something that isn't yours, making a decision, being honest.

3. *Establish student skill need.* Student is asked to explain why he might need this skill in the future.
4. *Select role players.* Particular students are asked to role-play the skill.
5. *Set up the role-play.*
6. *Conduct the role-play.*
7. *Provide performance feedback.*
8. *Assign skill homework.* Students are assigned homework in which they are required to practice skill at home or other authentic situation.
9. *Select next role players.*

When to Use

The process, though developed for small groups, can be adapted to regular classroom situations as the need arises. This method can be utilized as both a preventive procedure and an interventionist procedure. Teachers are required to demonstrate and model appropriate behavior through direct instructional techniques. The teacher's overt creativity is in handling the dynamic role-playing process necessary to implement the skillstreaming process. The teacher also must be able to evaluate the need for this group-guidance approach. Assessing students regarding their lack of social skills is performed via a clearly delineated checklist that Goldstein provides with the program. You could also use you own ingenuity and assess needs through observation and your own checklist. Organization of space and the training of group leaders should be done covertly in order to eliminate questions before you are ready to provide answers. If possible, have children and teacher aides act as assistants to help expedite the success of this strategy. This is an ideal approach to use when there is evidence of a deficiency in mutually-agreed-upon social skills. The skillstreaming curriculums of Goldstein and McGinnis contain a complete prosocial skills curriculum, which follows a direct-instruction approach.

Strengths

Skillstreaming is a proactive process based on well-established behavioral analysis theory. The program can be used on all levels. The prosocial skills taught should be considered as important as reading, writing, or arithmetic. For some children they may be even more important. Children who have well-developed social skills are more likely to be successful later in life.

Weaknesses

Such a program requires a commitment of time and personnel that some schools may be unwilling or unable to make, given the demands of the academic program. The success of skillstreaming can also require a schoolwide commitment by teachers and administrators, which may be difficult to achieve.

PEER MEDIATION

Schrumpf and Crawford (1992a; 1992b) worked on a peer mediation model based on the idea that behavioral change should not be based on a process of coercion. It should occur in an educational setting where students can reflect on their actions and negotiate alternative solutions using the skills of negotiation, reasoning, and compromise. This model draws heavily on a nonjudgmental response by peer mediators and on summary statements (much like active listening), as well as win-win discussions and negotiations. The model is proactive rather than reactive to specific discipline incidents. Detailed preparation to gain the acceptance of parents, teachers, and the community is necessary for the model to succeed. Mediators must be trained and the process must be actively monitored and administered.

The rationale for this model is that students coming into contact with the needs of others learn appropriate behavior. Students learn to understand individual relationships in order to live in a civilized society. The appropriate medium for such learning is communal; students benefit by proposing solutions that are acceptable to teachers and classmates and not wholly in their own self-interest. The teacher in this model becomes a judgmental facilitator who delineates boundaries of behaviors in which choices can be made. Overtly the teacher and school are not directly involved in mediation because the model is essentially a peer-to-peer process. The only covert teacher behaviors are those actions related to gaining acceptance for the program, selecting and training student mediators, and monitoring the process. The process consists of six steps in logical progression that develop negotiation skill-building:

1. Open the session (set up rules).
2. Gather the information (student tells his story, vents).
3. Ask, What do you want? (student expresses what he believes to be the desired outcome).
4. Create options (brainstorm about possible solutions).
5. Evaluate options and decide on solution.
6. Write an agreement and close.

When to Use

Due to the proactive nature of mediation, it has proven best used in child-centered schools and those with a humanistic philosophy. The time reserved for involving students in such activities usually comes from academic instructional time. The question then becomes, "How do we use our time in school, and how will educators balance these time demands?" This translates into the need to get community support if peer-mediation implementation is to be effective. The strategy is essentially a preventive one in the guise of an interventionist approach. This approach works quite well with other group-guidance approaches such as judicious discipline.

Strengths

The model's strength is that it is a proactive process for teaching positive techniques to resolve social conflict, with clear directions for administering and monitoring the program.

Weaknesses

The program's weakness is that it requires a great deal of time and commitment from staff, administration, and children. Teachers must be on the lookout for students who use the mediator role poorly, so an intervention can be made.

PRACTICE EXERCISE:

Do Mini Case Study number three at the end of this chapter. Be sure to use the IOSIE method to analyze the situation and explain how you would resolve the problem using a judicious discipline model, or a skillstreaming approach, or peer mediation. Be sure to justify your approach. Could all three approaches be used? How?

POSITIVE ACTION

Carol Gerber Allred (1996) developed a model to measure the success of a school and classroom objectively. Included in her measurement is a demonstrated improvement in social skills and emotional skills as well as increased parental and community involvement. These three factors are related to what Gerber calls "positive actions." The model is based on a philosophy that maintains that individuals feel good about themselves when they perform positive actions. This is consistent with the traditional understanding that the building of good character leads to classes and schools that are well disciplined. When students demonstrate self-discipline, and display evidence of good character, effective classroom management is assured. The positive action model addresses philosophy, concepts, curriculum, and community involvement (see Figure 6.3). Each of these components are interrelated and intended to be applied in a systematic fashion; the expected outcome is a school or classroom that functions at the level that both parents and teachers desire.

The program is essentially a philosophy that unites all program components into a comprehensive school reform model that achieves well-managed classrooms and schools. It is structured and contains twelve hundred lessons that are scripted for all curriculum areas from kindergarten to grade twelve. This makes it easy for teachers to use. It also has a curriculum for parents that corresponds to the school curriculum and involves parents in home teaching, mentoring, role modeling, and decision making.

FIGURE 6.3   Positive Action Model

1. *Philosophy.* We feel good about ourselves when we undertake to perform positive actions. Allred claims that our thoughts lead to actions, and those actions lead to feelings about ourselves, which lead to both positive and negative thoughts. An example would be viewing learning to read as a positive action in the same category as learning to be responsible and respectful. She believes that through instruction, good character can be advanced in society. When academics are considered as positive actions and the school and community reinforces this, they encourage both educational excellence and responsible citizenship.

2. *Unit concepts or guiding principles.* The model provides a prepackaged program that claims to develop good character sequentially step by step. In order to feel good about ourselves the strategy claims that we must identify and implement positive actions. In this program positive actions are focused on the body, mind, and emotions, which are presented by teachers in seven scripted units entitled:

   Unit 1. *Self-Concept:* What it is, how it's formed, and why it's important (philosophy taught) (mind)

   Unit 2. *Positive Actions for Your Body and Mind* (nutrition, cleanliness, critical thinking) (body)

   Unit 3. *Managing Yourself Responsibly* (positive actions, feelings) (emotions)

   Unit 4. *Treating Others the Way You Like to Be Treated* (kindness, fairness, respect, cooperation) (emotions)

   Unit 5. *Telling Yourself the Truth* (refusing to blame others, keeping your word) (emotions)

   Unit 6. *Improving Yourself Continually* (setting goals, persistence, problem solving) (mind)

   Unit 7. Review

3. *Classroom Curriculum:* The lesson program contains a variety of methodologies that address all learning styles and recognize multiple intelligences.

4. *School Climate:* This strategy ties together the activities and coordinates the curriculum lessons into a schoolwide program by creating opportunities for practice of lessons learned in class.

5. *Parent and Community Involvement:* The program encourages collaboration among school, home, businesses, and institutions.

What is unique about this strategy is that it includes a focus on increased academic achievement, attendance, and positive behaviors that evidence a strong moral character. Other behavior approaches focus only secondarily on academic success; in Allred's model it is inclusive and the results are measurable, as seen in a decrease in violence, disciplinary referrals, suspensions, and drug and alcohol use. This she claims can be achieved concurrently with the inclusion of the positive action curriculum, which includes approximately 140 child-centered daily lessons for grades K–6. Each teacher gets a kit that includes a manual and age-appropriate lessons. Parents are also provided with a Positive Action Family Kit, which helps families identify and practice commonly accepted positive behaviors.

The principal's role is to provide the primary leadership and guidance for the program at the school level. The principal can delegate with a high degree of confidence because plans for administration and implementation are thoroughly developed and easy to follow. It is up to the principal to ensure that the model becomes a factor in identifying and reinforcing positive actions.

Allred also explains how a positive action committee consisting of teachers from every grade, a guidance counselor, the principal, the assistant principals, school nurse, aides, custodial staff, and parents can be formed, devoted to developing positive actions. All members have one vote using a school-based management/shared decision making (SBM/SDM) consensus model. Various members take responsibility for appropriate portions of the program. The committee oversees curriculum implementation, is responsible for school-climate activities, resolves issues and concerns, directs the parent community program, and directs how monies are to be spent for the program. The primary role of the committee is to set goals, make plans, implement activities related to curriculum, and evaluate strengths and weaknesses. Positive action committee procedures deal with the following four areas:

1. *Assessment.* Measurable goals that address expectations are developed.
2. *Planning.* Action plan based on assessment is formulated.
3. *Implementation.* Tasks are set, and progress is reported to committee.
4. *Evaluation.* Empirical measurement and information obtained from student, teacher, and parent surveys determine how well program accomplished the goals that were set.

When to Use

Character education programs go hand in hand with effective management programs. Allred's model is a highly formulated program with a schoolwide focus. The model utilizes a preventive approach that also focuses on academic achievement, which separates it from most other character-development programs.

Strengths

Good character education is easily transformed into good management programs. When shared values reflect core beliefs, there is less likely to be disciplinary problems. Allred's positive action materials are abundant and easy to follow.

Weaknesses

Implementation can be difficult since it requires total school support and a high degree of parental involvement. Critics question whether a scripted program devoted to the development of character is necessary; teachers instill values and model good character without such programs. Other critics say that character education has little to do with class management.

PRACTICE EXERCISE:

Do Mini Case Study number four at the end of this chapter. Be sure to use the IOSIE method to analyze the situation and use a positive action strategy to change the direction of the class and resolve the case problem.

KEYS TERMS TO FOCUS ON

efficacy in action

learning zones

cooperative discipline

hands-joined approach

skillstreaming

judicious discipline

peer mediation

positive action

DISCUSSION QUESTIONS

1. How could you use the efficacy in action model to motivate students to improve their behavior and academic efforts?

2. Explain how cooperative discipline can be viewed as both a preventive and interventionist strategy.

3. Show how group-guidance approaches such as judicious discipline and efficacy in action can be used concurrently.

4. Evaluate the statement that the positive action model is a character-education program in the guise of a classroom management program. Is character education necessary for effective classroom management? Explain.

5. Compare the skillstreaming model and peer mediation with regard to their similarities and differences.

MINI CASES FROM THE FIELD

Analyze the following mini case studies using the IOSIE method, from the perspective of group-guidance management models discussed in this chapter. Each study should be analyzed using the specific model suggested as a plausible solution.

1. The students in your seventh-grade social studies class seem lethargic and lacking in positive enthusiasm. No one volunteers, and all are anxious to leave as soon as the bell rings. Children relate to one another in a disrespectful fashion. You have spoken to most of the boys in the class and they profess to not understand what you are talking about. The girls all complain that the boys are pigs and mess up everything they do. The boys appear to have

taken a perverse pride in being called pigs by the girls. They have started to call the girls ugly, and make weird sounds when any girl moves about the room. Your class seems to be going down the drain, both academically and socially. Analyze this mini case study using the IOSIE method and justify the use of the efficacy in action approach to place this class on the right track both scholastically and behaviorally.

2. Millie Wilson, an adorable five-year-old in your kindergarten class, has been disrupting the class by having temper tantrums when she does not get what she wants. She insists on playing in the dollhouse and will not let any other children into the house. If you tell her she must share the space, she looks at you and cries and lays on the floor, blocking the entrance to the dollhouse. You notice that other children are following Millie's lead and also having temper tantrums. Her parents have told you she does the same thing at home. Analyze this brief study using the IOSIE method to decide how you would deal with this situation if you had to use a cooperative discipline strategy.

3. Children in your tenth-grade social studies class are totally out of control with regard to their interpersonal relations. They make disrespectful statements to one another that lack any empathy or concern for the feelings of their classmates. They are constantly pushing each other and allowing their aggressive tendencies to direct their actions. You have observed the boys pushing their smaller classmates out of their way upon entering or leaving the classroom. Abdul Hassan complains to you that his classmates are always calling him names and making disparaging remarks about his religion. The situation comes to a head when you discover that Abdul is planning to fight Tim Elemis after school because he can't take their taunts any longer. You act immediately and notify the principal, who calls the boys to his office to prevent any violence from occurring. You reflect as to the appropriate course of action to take. Analyze this case using the IOSIE method and describe and justify how this situation could be addressed by using a skillstreaming approach, the judicious discipline model, or peer mediation. Which of these models would be the most effective in this case, and why?

4. Your third-grade class is not doing well academically. The students are at a reading level that is one to two years below grade level. You have worked hard trying to improve their performance, but have not achieved results. The class's general deportment has been persistently poor. The students seem to share a value system advocating "might is right" and "do unto others before they do unto you." You have observed children going through their classmate's book bags. Toys brought in for show-and-tell have been found broken or have just disappeared. You are unable to tolerate this situation any longer. Analyze this case using the IOSIE method and explain how you would implement a positive action strategy to change the direction of this class. Why do you feel this strategy has a good chance of succeeding?

REFERENCES

Albert, L. 1996. *Cooperative discipline: How to manage your classroom and promote self-esteem.* Circle Pines, MN: American Guidance Service.

Allred, C. 1996. *Positive actions for living.* Twin Falls, ID: Positive Action Co.

Goldstein, A. P., and E. McGinnis. 1997a. *Skillstreaming the adolescent.* Champaign, IL: Research Press.

Goldstein, A. P., and E. McGinnis. 1997b. *Skillstreaming the elementary school child.* Champaign, IL: Research Press.

Goldstein, A. P., and E. McGinnis. 1988. *How to teach students prosocial skills.* Videotape. Norman Baxley Associates, producers. Champaign, IL: Research Press.

Howard, J. 1998. *Efficacy in action: Working to get smart.* Videotape. Bloomington, IN: Efficacy Institute and Phi Delta Kappa International.

Landau, B., and P. Gathercoal. 2000. Creating peaceful classrooms: Judicious discipline and class meetings. *Phi Delta Kappan* 81, 450–54.

Schrumpf, F., and D. Crawford. 1992a. *Peer mediator conflict resolution program guide and student manual.* Champaign, IL: Research Press.

Schrumpf, F., and D. Crawford. 1992b. *Conflict resolution in schools.* Videotape. Baxley Media Group, producers. Champaign, IL: Research Press.

Vygotsky, L. 1930/1978. *Mind in society.* Cambridge, MA: Harvard University Press.

CHAPTER SEVEN

INDIVIDUAL-GUIDANCE MANAGEMENT MODELS

FOCUS POINT

1. Individual-guidance models have long-term effectiveness in positively changing students' behavior.

Teachers are in general agreement that the purpose of classroom management is to provide for a positive learning environment and to assist children in developing a sense of personal responsibility. Individual-guidance models utilize limited teacher control; students are understood to be the primary agents of change. This approach can make implementation difficult for teachers, especially with respect to establishing a time frame in which the desired outcome is achieved. Yet many analysts see a limited control model as most effective, over the long term, in positively influencing student behavior.

GINOTT MODEL

The Ginott model, developed by the psychologist Haim Ginott (1976), utilizes interpersonal communication methods that encourage humanitarian classroom environments. Ginott maintained that discipline results from interaction between student and teacher. Disciplinary "victories" occur when intervention is focused on specific incidents of misbehavior rather than a student's character. The model purports to support positive student self-concepts. This is achieved through quality teacher-student interaction. Ginott advocates positive verbal intercepts. He conceives of the teacher as a role model whose behavior is key to classroom discipline. Teachers are seen as modeling the behaviors they wish to see in their students. The role of the teacher is to direct students away from bad behavior and lead them to socially acceptable behavior that is positive and lasting. Ginott's methods are organized around three basic themes: (1) congruent communication; (2) fostering independence and self-respect; and (3) avoiding the perils of praise.

Congruent Communication

Congruent communication involves conveying acceptance rather than rejection, and avoids blaming and shaming. Teachers are instructed to avoid insults and intimidation and instead demonstrate sensitivity to students' needs and desires. The point is to encourage self-esteem while de-escalating potential conflict. (See Figure 7.1.)

Fostering Independence and Self-Respect

Ginott (1993) believed that, because of their basic understandings about power structures, children are more likely to consider teachers as enemies than friends. The reason for this is that children "are dependent on us, and dependency breeds hostility." To lessen dependency and, hence, hostility, teachers should encourage autonomy and facilitate instruction in personal problem solving. Ginott believed that students had to learn to be autonomous and responsible. He further believed that positive communications helped to build student self-respect, which in turn produced better classroom discipline.

Facilitating Responsibility.   Ginott believed that in order for students to develop self-discipline, teachers must:

- *Facilitate student autonomy.* Children need to make choices relating to their behavior; if students become dependent on the teacher to determine appropri-

---

FIGURE 7.1   Essential Precepts of Congruent Communication

1. *Deliver sane messages (messages that are a logical and rational directive that is not influenced by the concept of the punishment).* Examples: If a child forgets his gym clothes, tell him it is impossible for him to participate. If a child fails to turn in homework, remind him to turn it in tomorrow so he can get proper credit. If a child is cheating tell him you need to keep your eyes on your own paper, that way you can always claim to have done your own work (Edwards, 1997).
2. *Express anger appropriately.* Anger must be expressed without insult. Teachers should simply describe what they observe and state how they feel using I-messages (statements that begin with "I"). You can attack the problem rather than the person by directing your anger at the behavior, not the individual. Avoid using labels. Ginott claimed that labeling was really "disabling." Avoid criticizing students. Instead, provide help and advice on how a student can improve. Never use hurtful sarcasm. "Verbal spankings do not improve performance or personality. They only ignite hate" (Ginott, 1985, 62).
3. *Show empathy for students' feelings.* It is better to acknowledge that tests are scary than to argue with a child that she has nothing to fear. False assurances should be avoided. Always validate what a student feels.
4. *Be brief.* Students close their minds to overtalkative teachers.

ate behavior, hostility will inevitably ensue. Start by giving them choices about small things (e.g., going to the bathroom by themselves; the number of problems they are given for homework). Autonomy with respect to day-to-day behavior helps develop in children personal responsibility and autonomy.

- *Guide emotion.* Instead of telling children how they should feel, help them clarify their emotions. This directs them to solve their own problems. Try to withhold your own opinion. Your intervention should focus on acknowledging/respecting student feelings. Act as a sounding board, not a font of wisdom.

Avoiding the Perils of Praise

Ginott believed that teachers have to be very careful in how and when they bestow praise. Praise that promotes dependency trains children to respond to external stimuli rather than their own internal standards. Feelings of self-worth become connected to receiving praise. Appropriate praise tells students what they have accomplished while letting them draw their own conclusions about its value. Teachers should offer interpretations rather than evaluations. Statements should be devoid of value judgments about personalities and only express positive feelings about student work. Ginott also cautions teachers not to be condescending or manipulative. For example, instead of saying, "Good job, Bill," say "I appreciate the way you set up your paper; it makes it easy to read."

Disciplining Students

According to Ginott, the most critical aspect to discipline is finding effective alternatives to punishment. Punishment serves to enrage students and make them uneducable. It leads to more misbehavior, which in turn encourages more-severe punishments. It does not deter misconduct; it simply makes students more cautious. Ginott believed that attempts to instill values in children through punishment proved fruitless; values cannot be forced on students.

In Ginott's conception, discipline problems are prevented through loving, warm, and patient action on the part of the teacher. A child who spills milk should be treated in the same way as an honored guest who spilled a drink. This approach focuses on the problem and not the individual. A teacher's actions and intentions are primary in setting the tone of the classroom. Ginott commented:

> I have come to a frightening conclusion that I am the decisive element in the classroom. It is my personal approach that creates the climate. It is my daily mood that makes the weather. As a teacher, I possess tremendous power to make a child's life miserable or joyous. I can be a tool of torture or an instrument of inspiration. I can humiliate or humor, hurt or heal. In all situations, it is my response that describes whether a crisis will be escalated or de-escalated, and a child humanized or dehumanized. (Ginott, 1993)

When to Use

Ginott's model conveys empathy and acceptance; it resonates with teachers who believe that results are achieved through kindness rather than punishment. The model is based on commonsense ideas about meeting students' emotional needs. Ginott's model works well in setting an overall positive tone between teacher and student. It can readily be combined with other management methods, even those that are on the other end of the spectrum, such as the Kounin model (Chapter 5).

Strengths

The model aims at the development of a positive self-concept that leads to self-respect, which is key to avoiding discipline problems. By fostering independence and autonomy in students, teachers avoid circumstances that promote student rebellion and misconduct. The model encourages positive relationships between teachers and students by advocating sane communications. The approach emphasizes dealing with student feelings, which allows the teacher to assume the role of caring teacher and facilitator.

Weaknesses

Critics take issue with the model's long list of do's and don'ts. Many feel that a comprehensive set of principles would be more helpful for teachers. The model has no specific steps for dealing with discipline problems, and insufficient support for teachers who are used to a more traditional role in dealing with students.

PRACTICE EXERCISE:

Do Mini Case Study number one at the end of this chapter. Be sure to use the IOSIE method to analyze the situation and use the Ginott model as a guidance approach to resolve the situation presented in the mini study.

CHOICE THEORY AND REALITY THERAPY

How can you effectively get students to choose to work and behave appropriately? The psychiatrist William Glasser developed choice theory (1965, 1969, 1986, 1990, 1997, 1998), the basic premise of which revolves around satisfying five basic psychological needs, which Glasser views as genetic: (1) belonging and love, (2) power and achievement, (3) fun and enjoying work, (4) freedom and the ability to make choices, and (5) survival (see Figure 7.2). The assumption is that once these five needs are met, children have no need to misbehave. Disruptive classrooms are defined as environments that interfere with the educational process and infringe

FIGURE 7.2   Basic Genetic Psychological Needs

Love/belonging

- At least one person who cares about me in an unconditional, accepting way
- Groups that accept me as a member
- Self-love, nurturing

Power/competence

- The ability to create and maintain an impact on the world
- Things I do to feel capable
- Influencing others

Freedom

- Freedom from being manipulated
- Freedom to express myself
- Freedom to make my own decisions
- Availability of options

Fun

- Humor, laughing, jokes
- Activities that give me pleasure
- What I do when I don't have to do anything

Physical/survival

- Food, shelter, safety

---

on the rights of others. Disruptive behavior is caused when the inner needs of students are not met and children then choose to misbehave.

Glasser concludes in his work that individuals are knowingly responsible for their own actions as a result of having free choice. He refers to choice theory as the antithesis of traditional stimulus-response theory. In Glasser's view, stimulus-response theory simply does not work. According to Glasser, we choose what to do based on what we believe in, not as a reaction to a specific stimulus.

In refuting stimulus-response theory Glasser revisits the Russian physiologist Ivan Pavlov's (1927) classic experiment related to the physiology of salivation. Pavlov saw that a dog salivated when his lab assistant entered the room with a tray of meat. He followed the same feeding procedure but substituted a flashing light before the dog was fed. The dog was observed salivating at the flashing light even though no meat was present. The light stimulus, Pavlov concluded, created a conditioned response that had caused the dog to salivate. Glasser contends that

Pavlov's conclusions were wrong. Had he used cats instead of dogs, his results would have been different. We answer a ringing phone because we choose to, not because it is a stimulus we are conditioned to respond to.

Glasser claims that our needs are satisfied through a process, which depends on learning pictures contained in our mind's eye, not through stimulus response. These pictures are stored in our minds as long as they satisfy us. A student's picture of learning formed in his quality world is based on his perceptions of what he feels creates quality in his learning and life. His picture of a caring teacher who gives easy tests may not be compatible with the teacher's picture of a diligent, self-motivated student. This scenario will certainly cause management problems if the teacher's role in implementing choice theory is not understood.

A quality classroom is a place where student work fosters a sense of personal responsibility. The conditions needed to establish a quality classroom are a warm, caring, and sharing environment that stresses self-evaluation and relevant interaction. When the teacher creates an atmosphere and activities that satisfy student needs, students will choose to behave appropriately. Glasser marks the distinction between an authoritarian teacher and a teacher leader. An authoritarian teacher uses punishments and rewards, drives students, relies on authority, "knows how," and creates confidence. A teacher leader uses persuasion, leads students, relies on cooperation, "shows how," and creates enthusiasm. It is Glasser's contention that the teacher leader is more apt to create the quality classroom.

The teacher is viewed by Glasser as a facilitator and modern manager, not a lecturer and controller. Students who won't work and have lost their learning picture need to be guided into achieving their quality world. Teachers need to change the structure of teaching by using learning teams and ignoring past failures and focus on present achievements. Glasser's learning-team model is an attempt to demonstrate relevance by empowering students through involvement. It does away with individual competition and memorization by using a team-model concept similar to that found in sports, music, and dramatic productions. The team model moves away from a short-term focus on rote learning and looks to long-term assignments based on depth and involvement.

Teachers are urged to see their students as a team. To establish a functioning learning team you must tailor team assignments that demand cooperation structured so students see the benefit of achieving established objectives. The key to this approach is to give students as much responsibility as they can handle. This can be accomplished using a variety of management strategies. Glasser believes that a wide range of approaches, including traditional ones, can be seen as supporting choice theory. (See Figure 7.3 for a comparison of the learning-team and traditional approaches.) Choice theory blends quite smoothly with a constructivist view of education. Children not only have free will and choice but also can construct their own meanings to create their own quality world.

Choice theory is an explanation of how the brain functions as a control system that selects behaviors. It is an internally motivated psychology, in which all behavior is understood to initiate from within us, and not as a result of an outside stimulus, as is the case with behaviorist theory. It states that all behavior is chosen

FIGURE 7.3   Comparison of Learning-Team Approach and Traditional Approaches

LEARNING-TEAM MODEL	TRADITIONAL APPROACH
1. Students gain a sense of belonging by working in heterogeneous teams.	1. Students work as individuals.
2. Students achieve success from motivation, see that knowledge is power, and want to work harder.	2. No motivation from belonging, no motivation if student doesn't succeed. Don't see knowledge as power.
3. Strong students feel fulfilled by helping weak students and feel power and friendship of high-performing team.	3. Strong and weak students hardly get to interact with and know one another.
4. When a weak student contributes it is helpful and need-fulfilling.	4. Weak students contribute less and are not valued.
5. Students depend on themselves and the team, not just the teacher.	5. Students depend solely on the teacher. No incentive to help one another.
6. Learning teams build a structure for getting past superficial facts to vital knowledge.	6. Students are bored and don't want to work.
7. Teams choose how to prove they have learned the material with encouragement from the teacher.	7. Teacher-designed evaluation encourages little more than studying for a test.
8. Teachers can change team membership. Sometimes all members get the team score, other times individuals score, to create incentive.	8. Students compete as individuals; winners and losers are evident.

except for the odd reflex reactions such as sneezes, itches, or twitches. To make choice theory work, Glasser advocates using a process known as reality therapy.

Reality therapy is a method of educational counseling and human interaction that doesn't infringe on the rights of others and allows individuals to implement personal choice. Glasser believes that when choices are understood, responsibility is developed. Reality therapy is a set of techniques for managing classroom behavior, which leads to meeting a student's basic psychological needs. Reality therapy (also called responsibility training) utilizes four questions intended to lead children toward understanding their actions and taking responsibility for their behavior.

1. What do you want?
2. What are you doing?
3. Is it helping you? (Explanation)
4. What is your plan now?

There is no necessity to ask the questions in any specific order. Never, however, ask why a student is misbehaving, as that only leads to excuses. The most difficult aspect of this approach for some teachers is that there is no punishment incurred for poor behavior. A student's self-control, rather than enforced control from without, is seen as emphasized. The teacher must accept the fact that he doesn't lose power and authority by giving up control. In reality you gain power by giving it up. A good leader (teacher) gains respect, not power.

When to Use

Reality therapy is most effective when used as an intervention technique immediately after an incidence of misbehavior has occurred. Children may have difficulty at first responding to the four questions the model utilizes. They have been indirectly trained throughout their educational experiences to expect a management approach based on stimulus response and behavior modification rather than one that attempts to meet their needs. Since there is no direct punishment involved teachers tend to feel that the student has gotten away with misbehavior. If the intervention has worked the immediate problem has been resolved and the process becomes preventive, since the student has been guided to reflect upon his inappropriate action.

Strengths

Reality therapy, in the context of choice theory, is effective with most students. It is easy to implement, as the questions the model utilizes are succinct and straightforward. Individual-guidance approaches tend to be the most effective, in the long term, with students who have specific behavioral problems.

Weaknesses

Not all teachers feel comfortable in the role of a guidance counselor. In moving from a more traditional management approach, teachers may feel that reality therapy allows students to "get away with" bad behavior. The program also takes time away from standardized class work.

PRACTICE EXERCISE:

Do Mini Case Study number two at the end of this chapter. Be sure to use the IOSIE method to analyze the situation and Glasser's reality therapy as your approach to resolving the situation presented in this mini case study. Explain the difference in how a person using assertive discipline might attempt to resolve the problem.

RESTITUTION MODEL

Diane Chelsom Gossen developed the restitution model (1993) as an outgrowth of her work with William Glasser and his choice theory and reality therapy. She developed an internally motivational model in which students were expected to discipline themselves. The model is proactive in that it creates the means necessary for students to react to their own environment. The restitution model is the opposite of behaviorist psychology, which advocates a stimulus-response approach to discipline. Restitution is defined by Gossen as a systematic and creative approach to self-discipline that enables students to strengthen themselves by repairing their mistakes. It gives students the opportunity to live up to the ideal person they want to be instead of behaving in order to please others or avoid discomfort. Most understand restitution as applying to the victim of an action, as in the case of a monetary judgment awarded for a specific loss. The focus of this model, however, is on self-restitution, where the offender restores himself back to the person he wants to be. The model focuses on developing long-term solutions. Chapter 1 listed Gossen's five types of classroom manager: the punisher, the guilter, the buddy, the monitor, and the manager. The restitution model sees the teacher's style of management as key to the fostering of responsibility in the student. The teacher as manager is the optimal management type to implement the restitution model. In Gossen's conception, managers use noncoercive questioning to help students recognize responsibility. Criticizing and guilting as well as complimenting and reinforcing are avoided. Children are spoken to in a calm, stress-free tone and nonthreatening body language is employed. Your tone of voice reflects what position of control you use. Words are only 10 percent of any message you deliver. How you convey a message is more important than the specific words you use. Your vocal tone carries 35 percent of the message; your body and face carry the other 55 percent. Remember that to discomfort your student is to control him; the use of coercive behaviors and punishments, because they are external controls, does not teach or encourage self-discipline. These methods are used to encourage children to act in ways that reflect agreement with previously established class beliefs. If this procedure is utilized students will understand and be responsible for their actions.

Remember, if self-control is not initially achieved, monitoring student action in order to keep rules and effectuate positive controlling behaviors is recommended. If a child resists restitution, then provide a consequence until the child is ready to practice self-discipline. Never force the issue; a forced restitution is no restitution at all. The focus of restitution must always be on assisting students in strengthening themselves.

Gossen accepts Glasser's rationalization with regard to the genetic needs inherent in all human beings. She views these needs as keys to understanding how to manage situations in which inappropriate behavior occurs.

Gossen is concerned with finding out why people behave. Three reasons are given for good behavior: (1) to avoid pain, (2) to gain a social reward, and (3) to achieve self-respect. Children look to avoid the pain (consequences) associated with misbehavior, so they behave. Children might behave because of peer pressure, to be one with the group, or because they feel they will gain self-respect by doing the right thing. If you can get a child to behave because he understands that self-discipline leads to self-respect you will have achieved a great victory for that child's future. Gossen claims that you can understand what a person believes in by the way he relates to the reasons for good behavior as viewed through his responses to three simple questions: (1) What happens if I don't do it? (2) What do I get if I do it? (3) Who am I if I do this? Gossen also outlines the differences between punishment and discipline. Punishment, she claims, only reinforces failure, and if it works at all it is only for a brief period, since ownership is not taken. Punishment tends to weaken the interchange between teacher and student while subjecting the child to feelings of guilt and loss of self-esteem. Discipline, according to Gossen, is the opposite of punishment. Discipline is self-induced and arrived at as a result of individual choice. Punishment is an extension of the teacher's need or desire to exert individual control over a student's actions.

Establishing the Social Contract

In order to implement the restitution model you must develop a social contract with students and understand Glasser's choice theory. The process by which everyone in the school agrees to classroom and school beliefs is called establishing a social contract. Gossen suggests that the best way to avoid failing in establishing a restitution model is to keep to the rules, which consist of not forcing restitution, monitoring your actions, gaining the acceptance of participants, and limiting the number of restitutions. The problem with implementing a restitution program in many cases is that most of society's assumptions are based on stimulus response theory, which is contrary to choice theory (see Figure 7.4).

FIGURE 7.4   Comparison of Stimulus Response Theory and Choice Theory

STIMULUS RESPONSE THEORY	CHOICE THEORY
■ We are externally motivated.	■ We are internally motivated.
■ We are controlled by others' behaviors.	■ We can only control ourselves.
■ We all share a single reality.	■ Each of us has a separate reality.
■ Positive reinforcement is desirable.	■ Positive reinforcement is coercive.
■ Mistakes are bad and should be avoided.	■ Mistakes help us to learn.
■ Change bad behaviors by guilt and discomfort.	■ Behavior is purposeful and misbehavior is chosen.

When to Use

Restitution can be used as both a preventive and interventionist strategy. If a child has been taught to practice self-control he also has succeeded in practicing restitution. This guidance approach focuses on helping individual students in becoming the person they wish to be.

Strengths

Through the restitution model, successful students achieve self-discipline, which is what every management approach advocates. Teachers can see and evaluate their level of effectiveness by student responses. It creates a child-centered class that encompasses positive values.

Weaknesses

Teachers have difficulty using an approach that is dependent upon a total guidance background. The strategy demands consistency and a great deal of time to implement. Results are not immediate, and the teacher can at times be an easy mark as a result of not punishing a child for admitted misbehavior.

CURWIN AND MENDLER MODEL

Richard Curwin and Allen Mendler's (1988, 1999) major contribution to school discipline has been in developing strategies for improving classroom behavior through maximizing student dignity and hope. They focus on chronically misbehaving students by suggesting methods for motivating students that ensure success and help students learn to behave responsibly. They aim to improve the behavior of chronically misbehaving students, behavior that puts a child in danger of failing, while assisting the child in preserving his personal dignity. The model centers on providing needed help for those who are behaviorally at risk of failure by restoring hope. It is based on the primary tenets that student dignity and hope are essential factors in achieving lasting results. The social contract and the insubordination rule are concrete tools to use. A social contract (class rules formulated with students) is used to enforce consequences for misbehavior. The insubordination rule is only used if a student refuses to accept the consequence for his misbehavior. The student is not allowed to return to class until he accepts responsibility for his actions. Creative responses, active listening, the use of I-messages, highly motivating lessons, and keeping disciplinary discussions private help to de-escalate situations and are all strategies used with this model. Teachers must recognize that schools exist for students, not teachers. The teacher's only reason for existence is to benefit the student by assisting him to learn and behave responsibly.

Discipline plans should be created that address the three dimensions of discipline: prevention, action, and resolution. Curwin and Mendler believe students can be helped to regain hope by making learning more attractive. In their book *Discipline with Dignity* (1988, 32–46) they point out that while interesting activities and success are crucial to restoring hope, equally important is dignity. Chronically misbehaving students usually do not respond to traditional methods of discipline. They have become immune to scolding, lecturing, sarcasm, detention, extra writing assignments, isolation, names on the board, or trips to the principal's office. Curwin and Mendler claim a 25 to 50 percent success rate with chronically misbehaving students by following their "principles of effective discipline." The principles include the acceptance of discipline as necessary for effective teaching to take place and the understanding that short-term solutions are rarely effective. The principles also stress treating students with dignity. Essentially the principles focus on having students understand that they cannot learn without practicing self-discipline. Teachers must assure students that they will always be treated with dignity and respect. This goal can only be achieved through teacher action. Students should also understand that there will be consequences for misbehavior. These consequences have been explained to students and students have agreed to them. Stress the concept that when one takes ownership (responsibility) for one's actions one is on the road to resolution of those problems.

The model's principles of effective discipline are:

- Discipline is the key to effective teaching.
- Students must always be treated with dignity.
- Discipline must not interfere with the motivation to learn.
- Effective solutions usually take time to achieve.
- Responsibility is more important than obedience.

These basic principles focus on long-term behavioral change, not quick fixes. The rules that are agreed upon must make sense and not interfere with the learning process. The prime concern for the teacher is to assist in aiding the student to develop responsibility by modeling appropriate behavior. When these principles become part of a student's being, change is on the way.

Curwin and Mendler, in the article "Zero Tolerance for Zero Tolerance" (1999), demonstrate how their model contradicts the traditional zero-tolerance idea of treating all discipline offenses the same way. They state that one size does not and cannot fit all. Zero-tolerance policies are inherently unfair since they enforce discipline without acknowledging personal dignity and instilling hope. They sum up their model by advocating what they call an "as tough as necessary" policy. Discipline through dignity and hope is an approach that succeeds because it is based on a classic principle of Western civilization: treat others as you want others to treat you. Discipline according to this model requires a two-stage approach: stabilize and teach.

When to Use

This guidance approach can be used in most situations. It allows for intervention and consequences for the short-term and acts as a preventive deterrent in the long run. It is an option to be considered when dealing with children who have special needs. According to Curwin and Mendler (1999), it has a success rate of 50 percent for these children, a rate that can only be improved if implemented in mainstream classrooms.

Strengths

Curwin and Mendler's is the only model that offers an approach other than a behaviorist strategy to work with children who have special needs. They claim the approach has a success rate of 40 percent with students labeled as incorrigible. It is a student-centered model that is concerned with student rights and dignity. An emphasis is placed on better instruction and sincere compassion, which are essential for preventing discipline problems. The model encourages teachers to let the small things go and focus on the underlying problems.

Weaknesses

Some criticize the model as unrealistic, since most teachers are not prepared to utilize a strategy that is based solely on a guidance approach. The model places too much blame on school policies and teacher actions for misbehavior. Too much prominence is placed on creating a student-centered model. Children don't necessarily know what is in their best interests; they need strong leadership and direction on the part of teachers in order to succeed. The model also requires a great deal of planning and forethought, which may be unreasonable to expect from a teacher burdened with large classes.

PRACTICE EXERCISE:

Do Mini Case Study number three at the end of this chapter. Be sure to use the IOSIE method to analyze the situation and describe how you would use the Curwin and Mendler model to salvage a seemingly hopeless situation.

TEACHER EFFECTIVENESS TRAINING: GORDON MODEL

The psychologist Thomas Gordon developed two programs, one that trained parents and one that focused on training teachers in behavior management. In his first two books on parent effectiveness training (PET), published in the 1970s, parents learned the skills necessary for establishing positive relationships with their children. He followed these with a teacher effectiveness training (TET) program (1975). His primary goal with TET was aimed at improving the quality of interactions between teachers and students. Gordon maintained that the only true effective discipline is self-control that occurs internally in each child. Teachers who influence students can assist in the development of student self-control. "You acquire more influence with young people when you give up using your power to control them . . . and the more you use power to try to control people, the less real influence you'll have on their lives" (Gordon, 1975).

Teachers have basically three types of relationship times with students: (1) teaching/learning time, when teacher and students are on task, attentive, and participating; (2) student-owned problem time, when students experience upsets or problems that distract their attention from learning tasks; and (3) teacher-owned problem time, when the teacher must deal with unacceptable student behavior and is distracted from teaching tasks (Gordon, 2005). Teachers who practice this approach use interpersonal communication skills and problem-solving strategies to assist students with their problems and effect changes in student behavior. The specific skills focus on behavioral observation, identifying the problem, demonstrating understanding, being understood, expressing recognition, confrontation, and a form of win/win problem solving.

Effectiveness training makes the following assumptions (Edwards, 1997). It assumes that students can learn to manage their own behavior, because as human beings they can make choices. It further assumes that when teachers are assertive in behavior management, students commonly rebel. It also adheres to the belief that rewards and praise may be detrimental to a student's intrinsic motivation since they support dependency. A major assumption is that students can solve their own problems when teachers practice the essentials found in TET and actively listen to them, give appropriate I-messages, and clarify problem-solving techniques (see Figure 7.5).

FIGURE 7.5 Essentials of Teacher Effectiveness Training

- *Active listening* involves carefully attending to and demonstrating understanding of what another person says.

- *I-messages.* Students will alter their misbehavior when teachers deliver appropriately constructed I-messages. These are statements that focus on how the speaker is feeling about another's behavior. *Example:* I need quiet so that I'm able to pay attention. Confrontive I-messages attempt to influence another to cease unacceptable behavior. *Example:* I can't hear what anyone is saying when you all call out. Preventive I-messages attempt to forestall future actions that may later become a problem. *Example:* I hope we will behave when our guests arrive.

- *Problem solving* is a process in which people clarify a problem and put forth solutions. They select one solution that is acceptable to all, implement it, and evaluate it.

Problem Ownership

Gordon created a visual device called the "behavior window" to help clarify the concept of problem ownership. Contained in the window are skill clusters, which are needed to deal with the three types of behavior problems, those belonging to students, those belonging to the teacher, and those that are really no problem (see Figure 7.6). These skills can be defined as:

1. *Helping skills.* These include listening skills and methods for avoiding communication roadblocks. You help a child in need both academically and socio-emotionally.
2. *Preventive skills.* These include preventive I-messages, collaborative rule setting, and maintaining harmonious relationships within the classroom. *Example:* You move a child's seat because a talkative fellow student is distracting him.
3. *Confrontive skills.* These include modifying the environment, recognizing primary feelings, sending nonconfrontive I-messages, shifting gears, and using a no-lose method of conflict resolution. *Example:* I am afraid that if you do not do your homework you will have difficulty understanding the next day's lesson.

Procedures for Resolving Discipline Problems

Gordon believes that effective discipline cannot be achieved through either coercion or the use of rewards and punishments. He believes that discipline must be developed and nurtured within the character of each individual. Rewards and punishments are considered to be aimed at controlling students and therefore ineffective ways of achieving a positive influence on children. Influencing is viewed by Gordon as qualitatively different from controlling. Influencing requires teachers to forgo using coercive power methods. Basically what Gordon is advocating can be viewed as a four-step procedure to resolving discipline problems.

FIGURE 7.6 The Behavior Window

PROBLEM OWNER	ACCEPTABILITY TO TEACHER	SKILL CLUSTERS
1. Behavior problem only for student (student owns the problem)	Acceptable	Helping skills
2. Student's behavior causes no problems	Acceptable	Preventive skills
3. Student's behavior a problem for teacher	Unacceptable	Confrontive skills

Misbehavior Is Needs-Satisfying. One of the first steps for resolving discipline problems is for teachers to recognize that children are needs-satisfying beings just as teachers are. Teachers have to accept that behavior, both good and bad, is undertaken to satisfy needs. Once this is understood, the objective becomes to create a procedure for developing worthwhile goals such as self-control and self-discipline as part of a preventive approach to resolving discipline problems.

Encourage Problem Ownership. Children have to be encouraged to take ownership of their own problems. Ordering, warning, moralizing, offering solutions, lecturing, name calling, or, worse, putdowns are all methods that utilize punishments and rewards that block effective communications and deter children from taking ownership of their problems. Even the seemingly innocent use of praise and reassurance, aimed at making problems go away, is not a solution but an extension of a rewards approach used to control students. Questioning and sarcastic humor are also ineffective approaches to encourage problem ownership or to resolve student problems.

Establish Good Relations. The third step in resolving discipline problems is to establish good relations with students. This can be accomplished only when teachers learn to speak the language of acceptance and actively listen to their students. Children need an opportunity to think through problems and feelings and choose courses of action without undue interference. Teachers have to listen and decide if they or the student owns the problem. Teachers must seek to understand without judging.

Establish Clear Communications. Teachers can effectively inform children of how they feel about their behavior by well-constructed I-messages. I-messages must specifically inform students about the behavior, which is causing a problem for the teacher. Establish clear communications through the use of sane I-messages. Effective I-messages tell students exactly what their inappropriate behavior is, its tangible effect, and how their teachers feel about their behavior. Gordon suggests that if resistance occurs at this stage you could switch to active listening in order to re-establish good relations.

When to Use

Teacher effectiveness training is essentially a preventive approach that focuses on an individual-guidance strategy. Teachers who have empathy for student needs can use this approach quite successfully. As with most guidance approaches, the key is in the communication between teacher and student.

Strengths

This approach encourages independence and autonomy as well as promoting self-control for students. Teacher-student relations and interactions tend to improve.

Students are encouraged to be introspective and reflect on and deal with their personal problems and feelings. Teachers learn how to express their needs to students. Students learn how their behavior affects others. It provides a framework by which students come to understand that teachers have needs and feelings just like they do.

Weaknesses

It can be difficult for teachers to transition from behaviorist tendencies of telling and controlling to an approach that depends on actively listening to students. Teachers may find it hard to deal with differences in values between themselves and their students. Transmitting I-messages can be difficult for teachers to master, if they are used to making direct commands with respect to student behavior. TET is not a comprehensive preventive discipline model.

TRANSACTIONAL ANALYSIS

The California psychiatrist Eric Berne (1910–1970) developed transactional analysis as a method of dealing with behavioral disorders. He concluded that behavior is an outgrowth of information stored in the subconscious mind that has been learned by interacting with others. He believed that most of our experiences in life are recorded in our subconscious minds in an unaltered fashion. These unaltered experiences are part of each individual's total being and become part of the way we behave. The acceptable and unacceptable behavior exhibited by students is subconsciously designed to get reactions and determine how others feel about us. Wilder Penfield's (1952) work is cited as evidence that all of a human being's experiences are permanently recorded in the brain, which is viewed as an information-storage system. This would be similar to having a prerecorded video that we store and can view at a later date. Thomas Harris, who worked with Berne, wrote *I'm OK—You're OK* (1967), which popularized transactional analysis. Educators who use transactional analysis have an understanding of personality and functioning that reaches across the fields of learning and unifies the educational experience.

The Three Ego States

Berne, in seeking to simplify complex interpersonal transactions, recognized the human personality as made up of three ego states. He considered each of these states an entire system of thought, feeling, and behavior through which individuals interact with one another. He defined these ego states as "consistent patterns of feelings and experiences directly related to corresponding consistent patterns of behavior" (1966). One's ego states are created from life experiences, which are retained in the brain and have both conscious and unconscious expression. Behaviors stemming from these ego states can appear out of the blue, seemingly without conscious thought. But these states, from an individual perspective, are clear, purposeful, and well formulated. The ego states have the accuracy of a video recording that can be turned on or off at will. According to transactional analysis, all people have three ego states, and the interaction between them forms the foundation of transactional analysis theory. These transactions refer to the meaningful communications and exchanges between individuals, which transactional analysts are trained to recognize (Steiner, 2000).

1. *The parent ego state* is a vast collection of experiences from the first five years of life. Children during this stage are understood to record their experiences as they occur, without any "editing." Behaviors employed to control others are instinctive and issue from this state.
2. *The child ego state* is "recorded" at the same time as the parent ego state. This recording includes the responses children make as to what they see and hear. Exuberance and self-centeredness issue from this state. Feelings, both positive and negative, rule.
3. *The adult ego state* monitors both the parent and child ego states and alters the automatic behaviors that would ordinarily occur. When children realize that they are able to successfully manipulate their environment, the adult ego state emerges.

Failure to make the transition to the adult state locks one into a behavior pattern that prohibits personal and social adjustment. Harris (1967) identifies four outgrowths of this transaction process, which he calls the four "life positions": (1) I'm not OK; you're OK; (2) I'm not OK; you're not OK; (3) I'm OK; you're not OK; (4) I'm OK; you're OK. These are probably the best-known expressions of transactional analysis. The last establishes and reinforces the position that recognizes the value and worth of every person. This theory basically regards people as "OK" and thus capable of change, growth, and healthy interactions.

The premise of transactional analysis is that individuals need to feel adequate. By understanding the basic concepts one can use transactional analysis as a method to positively manage classroom behavior. The key is in our understanding that both children's acceptable and unacceptable behavior is designed to ascertain how others feel about them. According to Berne, teachers who use "stroking" techniques (i.e., encouraging cajoling, humoring) for all children will be a positive influence in their lives. People need strokes, the interpersonal recognition that allows them to survive and thrive. Understanding the healthy patterns of stroking is a key to understanding transactional analysis (see Figure 7.7).

Games Students Play

Berne viewed certain socially dysfunctional behavioral patterns as "games." These childish repetitive actions are intended by children to obtain strokes but instead they reinforce negative feelings and self-concepts. To achieve their goals teachers

FIGURE 7.7   **Fundamental Ideas in Transactional Analysis**

1. There are three ego states (child, parent, and adult).
2. Problems can occur if an individual is trapped in the parent or child ego states.
3. There are four "life positions" that describe how individuals feel about themselves and others.
4. Human beings have a basic need to feel capable and accepted ("I'm OK").
5. The best way to treat others is to fulfill in them the basic need for acceptance ("You're OK").
6. Transactions can be analyzed as an outgrowth of information stored in the child's subconscious.
7. To increase the adult ego state and regulate the child and parent ego states is the primary goal of transactional analysis.

need to stay in the adult ego state when they interact with students. Teachers must avoid playing behavioral games and supply necessary stroking in order to prevent problems. They should first determine the purpose of the game the student wants to play and then refuse to play, then provide stroking. The following are some of the classic games children play.

1. *Uproar* is an attempt to provoke the teacher to react in a negative fashion. Students can then claim they are being picked on. Tactics used include tapping, talking out, causing any type of disturbance.
2. *Clown* is to act the fool and distract the teacher from her instructional mission. Students believe they can hide their lack of knowledge by clowning around.
3. *Stupid* is to act dumb so as not to be called upon by the teacher. Students use this game to hide ignorance of content being taught.
4. *Chip on his shoulder* is when a student feels that he can intimidate the teacher by use of inappropriate language or postures so as not to be called upon in class.
5. *Make me* is another attempt to intimidate the teacher. A student would be resistant to providing information, for example, if the teacher requested a parent's phone number.
6. *Late paper game* is the game played when students provide excuses in order to hand in a paper late. (Ernst, 1972)

Once the nature of a student's game playing has been determined, the teacher should be careful not to play it. Make the student understand that you know the game they are playing, and that it is counterproductive. Use positive statements to reinforce the child's self worth. A teacher who practices transactional analysis views children as capable of deciding what they want for their lives, and as capable of making correct decisions.

When to Use

This preventive approach is quite appropriate in any situation in which the teacher wishes to provide individual guidance. The strategy cannot be used as an intervention technique. It could, however, be used in conjunction with another strategy such as reality therapy.

Strengths

This model is supported by a great deal of research on the subconscious mind. It promotes self-analysis and self-correction. It has applications beyond the classroom in students' personal lives. It helps children avoid destructive roles often played in interpersonal relationships. It helps children understand their own messages and those of others. It provides a framework for communication and understanding.

Weaknesses

Overcoming the automatic behaviors coming from the parent and child ego states may be difficult. Transactional analysis cannot be applied as readily to discipline problems other than those involving verbal exchanges. Students may not have the language, cognitive skills, or reasoning necessary to employ this technique. Making distinctions between the ego states is difficult. Teachers need training in process, which is lengthy and time consuming.

PRACTICE EXERCISE:

Do Mini Case Study number four at the end of this chapter. Be sure to use the IOSIE method to analyze the situation and describe which model, the Gordon, restitution, or transactional analysis, you would use in the future. Be sure to support your decision based on your own beliefs.

Then, take the Classroom Management Quiz, which appears in Appendix B, to determine which management style best matches your personal beliefs.

KEY TERMS TO FOCUS ON

Ginott model

sane messages

choice (control) theory

reality therapy

learning-team model

Curwin and Mendler model

restitution model

Teacher Effectiveness Training

behavior window

I-messages

transactional analysis

ego states

DISCUSSION QUESTIONS

1. How would the Ginott model deal with a child who is late with his assignments? Would the model ever use punishments?

2. Glasser believes that all behaviors are chosen. He would argue that a person answers a phone by choice, not by reflex. Why?

3. Defend or critique Curwin and Mendler's beliefs regarding zero tolerance.

4. How does Gossen's definition of "restitution" differ from the traditional definition?

5. Describe why the Gordon model and transactional analysis are often looked at as fringe models for classroom control.

MINI CASES FROM THE FIELD

Analyze the following mini cases using the IOSIE method from the perspective of the individual-guidance management approaches discussed in this chapter. Each study should be analyzed using the specific model suggested as a plausible solution.

1. Bobby Merrow is a fourth grader who seemingly lives to destroy the smooth functioning of your class. He has repeatedly tested your patience with his disruptiveness. His misbehavior takes the form of ignoring your actions toward him and by denying that you gave certain instructions. He talks behind your back and makes remarks and strange sounds when no one is looking. The other children laugh at this attention-seeking behavior. His parents claim he is well behaved at home, except when his birth father sees him on the weekends. His homework is rarely completed on time, especially work that was assigned over the weekend. Analyze this mini case using the IOSIE method and describe how you would use a guidance approach based on the Ginott model to address Bobby's behavior problems.

2. For the better part of the year, you have attempted to guide Henry Wolfinger, a child in your second-grade class, toward appropriate behavior. He constantly makes excuses about both his poor conduct and his unsatisfactory schoolwork. He seems incapable of taking responsibility for his behavior, and his excuses are often untruthful. It seems that he has forgotten the meaning of telling the truth. One day you are in the schoolyard during recess and see Henry and a group of children arguing. The children claim Henry took their ball and will not give it back. Henry claims that the ball is his and they can't play with it. You've gone to a workshop on classroom management, seeking to discover a more effective approach to dealing with behavioral problems. You decide after analyzing the situation using the IOSIE method that you will use Glasser's reality therapy method as an educational counseling tool in this situation. A colleague sees you using the reality therapy question formulation with Henry and asks you to justify your questioning technique as opposed to the punishment he would have inflicted for the child's misbehavior. Explain to your colleague your rationale in taking this approach with Henry.

3. Clark Olney is a learning-disabled child who has been mainstreamed into your tenth-grade English class. He has been frustrated all semester, attempting to keep up with the class. Because of his frustration he has begun to act out and lie about his class work. You have previously attempted to control his misconduct

through the use of traditional behavior modification techniques. Needless to say he has not responded positively. On one particular occasion he became enraged and stormed out of the classroom, slamming the door behind him. You immediately notified security and your supervisor with regard to Clark's leaving your room. A hearing is scheduled with Clark, his parents, the guidance counselor, and the assistant principal. You reflect about what you should say at the hearing, which is to be held in three days. After analyzing the situation using the IOSIE method you decide that you will explain how you will attempt to use the Curwin and Mendler model to salvage a seemingly hopeless situation. Describe in detail why and how you would attempt to use the Curwin and Mendler model in dealing with this case.

4. Your supervisor, Mr. Ravitch, after observing your sixth-grade class, tells you that he is not satisfied with your approach to classroom management. He refers to your constant yelling and ordering the children to behave. He says he has seen you frequently fly off the handle when a child responds to you in a way you feel is inappropriate. He suggests that you should move away from the assertive discipline model you profess to have been using, since it is obviously not working. He suggests you try using a guidance approach to deal with misbehavior. He further offers you a choice between the restitution model, the Gordon model, and transactional analysis. After analyzing this mini study using the IOSIE method, prepare a response to your supervisor in which you select one of the management strategies he suggests and explain your decision.

REFERENCES

Berne, E. 1966. *Principles of group treatment.* New York: Oxford University Press.

Berne, E. 1964. *Games people play.* New York: Ballantine Books.

Curwin, R. L., and A. N. Mendler. 1999. Zero tolerance for zero tolerance. *Kappan* 81 (2), 119–20.

Curwin, R. L., and A. N. Mendler. 1988. *Discipline with dignity.* Alexandria, VA: Association for Supervision and Curriculum Development.

Edwards, H. C. 1997. *Classroom discipline and management.* 2nd ed. Upper Saddle River, NJ: Prentice Hall.

Ernst, K. 1972. *Games students play.* Millbrae, CA: Celestial Arts.

Ginott, H. 1993. *Teacher and child: A book for parents and teachers.* New York: Colliers.

Ginott, H. 1985. *Between teacher and child.* New York: Avon.

Ginott, H. 1976. *Teacher and child.* New York: Avon.

Glasser, W. 1998. *Choice theory: A new psychology of personal freedom.* New York: Harper Collins.

Glasser, W. 1997. A new look at school failure and school success. *Phi Delta Kappan* 78, 596–602.

Glasser, W. 1990. *The quality school.* New York: Harper and Row.

Glasser, W. 1986. *Control therapy in the classroom.* New York: Harper and Row.

Glasser, W. 1969. *Schools without failure.* New York: Harper and Row.

Glasser, W. 1965. *Reality therapy.* New York: Harper and Row.

Gordon, T. 2005. *Our classroom management philosophy.* Gordon Training International. www.gordontraining.com/schools.html.

Gordon, T. 1975. *TET: Teacher effectiveness training.* New York: Peter H. Wyden.

Gossen, D. C. 1993. *Restitution: Restructuring school discipline.* Chapel Hill, NC: New View Publications.

Harris, T. A. 1967. *I'm OK—you're OK.* New York: Avon Books.

Pavlov, I. P. 1927. *Conditional reflexes,* trans. G. V. Anrep. London: Oxford University Press.

Penfield, W. 1952. Memory mechanisms. *AMA Archives of Neurology and Psychiatry* 67, 178–98.

Steiner, C. 2000. *A compilation of core concepts.* Pleasanton, CA: International Transactional Analysis Association. www.itaa-net.org/ta/coreconcepts/coreconcepts.htm.

PART III

CASE STUDIES FOR ANALYSIS

The case studies in Part III will help you develop a discipline strategy to meet the challenges of your classroom. A good strategy must be comprehensive and contain in its design a preventive process and an intervention process. It should be based on your own core values regarding the level of teacher classroom control you desire. Your strategy should be built on a consequence, guidance, or group-guidance approach, and/or a combination of various traditional management models. If the traditional models discussed in Part II are inadequate, think about constructing your own. A good approach will encourage good classroom behavior, prevent discipline problems, and provide a procedure for intervention that can be easily implemented.

In order to expedite the process of developing your own strategies, follow the IOSIE method in analyzing each of the cases studies. Read each case in its entirety following each of the IOSIE method steps:

- *Identify the problem* in all its aspects.
- Prepare a list of short- and long-term *objectives* that would resolve the identified problem.
- Develop a long-term *solution* for the identified problem and explain how the management strategy you choose will help solve the identified problem. (Use one of the management strategies discussed in Part II.)
- Describe the personnel, materials, and resources needed to *implement* your strategy.
- Finally, reflect on the approach and *evaluate* the results.

The process of developing an individual strategy is essentially based on a common sense approach rooted in management theory and practice. The objective of these case studies is to provide you with an opportunity to analyze behavioral problems from the perspective of the teacher while using multiple strategies. In most cases there is no single right answer; solutions are usually complex and multifaceted. View each case from as many perspectives as possible. The basic idea of this exercise is to translate theory into practice

Put yourself in the role of the teacher and read straight through each case. React to the episode as if it were occurring to you. What would your primary concern be? Identify the immediate problem and your immediate objectives. Next, write down your reactions and your personal response. Reread the case in order to be clear on the stated and unstated facts. Try to determine a long-term approach for resolution by consulting the various management strategies outlined in this book. If working in groups, actively listen and use brainstorming techniques to share ideas and reflect on various perspectives presented in the case analysis.

Define and identify the behavioral problem. The solution should consist of both long- and short-term alternatives. Decide on your plan and implement it. The final step—crucial to determining success—is to assess achievement of objectives. If your plan has not worked, prepare another plan. At this juncture you may have to look at the problem from different perspectives—those of the parent, principal, and student. Be aware that differing views on appropriate actions may exist. The IOSIE method provides a guideline for analyzing case studies and selecting a course of action to rectify misbehavior.

CHAPTER EIGHT

CASE STUDIES FROM THE FIELD

Now you have an opportunity to practice the skills and employ the classroom-management strategies and models discussed throughout this text. The case studies correspond with the three management model types we have previously discussed in Chapters 5, 6, and 7. The following charts provide an easy-to-use glance at the case studies. The first chart indicates the specific strategy suggested for use in your analysis of each case. In most cases, however, any of the strategies can be used with any of the cases; your own management style is the determining factor. The second chart breaks the cases down by grade level. If you feel comfortable with a particular model or strategy, by all means use it; if it does not work, use a different approach.

Strategies to Use with Case Studies

STRATEGY	CASE NUMBERS
Most Teacher Management Models (Consequences Models)	
Assertive Discipline	2, 7, 19
Jones Model	3, 15, 22
The Kounin Effective Momentum Model	11, 18
Logical Consequences	1, 15, 19
Traditional Model	8, 12, 22
Behavior Modification	1, 9, 10
Relative and Moderate Teacher Management Models (Group-Guidance Models)	
Howard's Efficacy Approach	9, 10, 13
Alpert's Cooperative Discipline	4, 17

STRATEGY	CASE NUMBERS
Judicious Discipline	1, 11, 13
Skillstreaming	2, 16
Positive Action	12, 17
Peer Mediation	2, 16
Least and Limited Teacher Management Models (Individual Guidance Models)	
Ginott Model	5, 14, 20
Reality Therapy	3, 6, 13, 14
Curwin and Mendler Model	4, 17
Restitution Theory	5, 7, 20
Teacher Effectiveness Training	9, 16, 21
Transactional Analysis	6, 8, 21

Case Studies Categorized by Grade Level and Title

CASE NUMBER	TITLE	GRADE LEVEL
1	A Violent Six-Year-Old	Kindergarten
2	Let Me Get to the Wardrobe	Fifth Grade
3	Are You Really a Special Child?	Ninth Grade
4	I Don't Want to Go to Junior High School	Sixth Grade
5	Love in High School Is for Real	High School
6	Is It Child Abuse?	Special Education
7	Destroying School and Personal Property	Senior Jr. High School
8	Always Fighting	High School
9	Tantrums	First Grade
10	They're Picking on Me	Fifth Grade
11	It's Not Fear	Sixth Grade
12	I Am Going to Tell My Mother	Senior Jr. High School
13	There Is Really a Good Reason	Sixth Grade
14	To Report or Not to Report	Seventh Grade
15	Management by Program	Fourth Grade
16	My Child Never Lies	High School
17	Is This a Case of Cultural Diversity or Child Abuse?	Special Education
18	Does Good Teaching Make a Difference?	Fifth Grade

CASE NUMBER	TITLE	GRADE LEVEL
19	The Bomb Threat	High School
20	What's That Smell?	Seventh Grade
21	AIDS Is More Than a Sickness	Third Grade
22	What the F—?	High School
23	But I Do Everything Right!	Fourth Grade
24	First Graders Can Be Difficult	First Grade
25	Why Is He Bored?	Third Grade
26	Is Toileting Appropriate for the Fifth Grade?	Fifth Grade
27	Is Scripted Education the Solution?	Fourth Grade
28	A Differentiated Classroom in High School	High School
29	Homework in High School	High School
30	Advanced Placement and Honesty	High School
31	Reading in High School	High School
32	Dealing with Violent Behavior in Middle School	Middle School

■ ■ ■ ■ ■

CASE STUDY ONE
A VIOLENT SIX-YEAR-OLD

Keys to analyzing this case:

- Outline the case using IOSIE.
- Consider behavior modification, logical consequences, and judicious discipline as plausible options for a long-term solution.

Billy Jones was a handsome six-year-old boy with beautiful blue eyes, curly auburn hair, and a smile that would melt any mature heart. He stood no more than forty-two inches and weighed less than thirty pounds. It was said about Billy that "when he was good he was very good; when he was bad he was a terror." Billy was a natural leader and had a way about him that both fascinated and annoyed the other children in his kindergarten class. He was with foster parents who were older adults and overly authoritarian in their approach to Billy's constant outbursts and misbehaviors.

Ms. Blanco was twenty-two, just out of college, and this was her first teaching assignment since she had successfully completed student teaching. Her first few weeks had gone exceptionally well. Her class of twenty-one children had jelled quickly. The children liked her and she liked the children.

Billy was brought to class by his foster parents, who seemed only too happy to be rid of "the little troublemaker." No sooner had they left, however, a disheveled woman in her late teens came to the classroom with a letter from the court giving her custody of Billy. Billy refused to go to his mother and tried to hide behind a fellow student. Principal Capitan was called, and he coaxed a hysterically crying Billy into the hallway. Mrs. Sknoot, the guidance counselor, helped the principal escort both Billy and his mother to his office.

After that incident, Billy's behavior in the classroom gradually grew worse over the next two months. Billy constantly hit and pushed other children and took their belongings. When he was confronted he would lie and say the objects were his. He would then scream, knock over furniture, and run about the room as if playing tag in the schoolyard. Ms. Blanco attempted to contain Billy by scolding him and complaining to his mother, who had regained custody. Billy's mother agreed to every suggestion Ms. Blanco made; however, Ms. Blanco felt she was not following up on her suggestions, including having Billy stay in his room until all his homework was completed, and not speaking to Billy unless his behavior and work improved.

The final straw occurred the second week in November. The principal had scheduled to formally observe Ms. Blanco teach a language arts lesson. Ms. Blanco had prompted, prepared, and pestered her children to be on their best behavior. She had even pleaded with Billy, who just smiled at her. The class acted appropriately during the opening portion of the lesson. The children had been read a story about a naughty goat that had not listened to its mother when told not to eat or play in farmer Gray's carrot patch. As Ms. Blanco sat in her rocking chair, with the Big Book prominently displayed to her side, Billy began to roll on the floor until he reached the foot of her chair. He then proceeded to clutch her right leg with both arms. Ms. Blanco looked at the principal, quietly sitting in the rear of the room. Ms. Blanco decided she would just ignore Billy and finish her lesson as if he were not present. This approach didn't seem to work; Billy just got bolder and began to sing.

DISCUSSION TOPICS AND QUESTIONS TO PONDER

1. Identify the immediate problem in this case and describe what actions you would take to resolve it.
2. Based on the logical consequences model, identify some of the causes of Ms. Blanco's difficulty with her lesson.
3. Why did the principal remain in the back of the room when Billy acted out?
4. Could the judicious discipline model be used to teach Billy appropriate class behavior? How?
5. What do you think about the teacher's perspective on the problem? Were her suggestions to Billy's mother appropriate?
6. Describe how a behavior modification program would work in this case.
7. What should have been the role of Billy's mother in this situation?
8. Explain how other school personnel could have helped in this situation.
9. What are some of the hidden issues in this case?
10. What would be your short-term plan? How would it differ from your long-term plan?

WHAT WOULD YOU DO IF . . . ?

1. Billy complained that he was afraid his mother would not come to pick him up at dismissal?

2. A group of concerned parents of children in your class expressed their concern that Billy was disrupting the learning process in your class, and further insisted that you either do something about it or get him out of your class?
3. The principal felt Billy would be better off in a different class with a more experienced teacher?
4. Billy was found to be sharing his medication with his classmates?
5. During your whole class lessons, Billy refused to participate?

CASE STUDY TWO
LET ME GET TO THE WARDROBE

Keys to analyzing this case:

- Outline the case using IOSIE.
- Consider assertive discipline, skillstreaming, and peer mediation as options for a long-term solution.

Jane Chavez was a very bright eleven-year-old who appeared to be moving flawlessly into adolescence. Both her parents were professionals who were actively involved in the school's parent-teacher association. Mrs. Chavez was running for president of the PTA with her husband's total support. Both parents were very proud of their daughter, who had never let them down. She was, in their eyes, the perfect child.

Mrs. Thomas, Jane's sixth-grade teacher, did not hold these views. Mrs. Thomas was a ten-year veteran with a sterling reputation as a teacher of the gifted. Her class's yearly rendition of Charles Dickens's *A Christmas Carol* was the highlight of the Darby Elementary School's holiday program. This year, she was concerned about the casting of the coveted role of Tiny Tim. Kylie Aims, a quiet, reserved student, would be ideal for the part; he had that ethereal innocence that the role required. As Mrs. Thomas reflected on who should get the part, Jane or Kylie, she came to a conclusion: She could either do the right thing or give into indirect parental pressure. She decided for Kylie. From that point on, her class was never the same.

During the following months, a series of unexplained incidents took place. Test papers displayed on the sides of the class wardrobe disappeared as soon as they were hung up. Children's pens and pencils were constantly stolen from schoolbags stored in the wardrobe. Kylie's jacket was torn and marred with black ink, and Jane's gym shoes were missing. More seriously, children refused to store their belongings in the wardrobe, and insisted upon carrying their coats everywhere.

Children began to take sides as either Jane or Kylie's friend, but not both. The problem came to a head when two students claimed that Jane was responsible for all the incidents because she wanted to get back at Kylie for stealing her part as Tiny Tim in the holiday presentation.

Mrs. Thomas tried to control her anger and outrage at Jane's behavior. She decided to request that the principal suspend Jane from school. She reasoned that she needed to act assertively and decisively to restore her classroom to the safe and secure learning environment it had always been. Jane could not go unpunished for having committed so many wrong deeds; Mrs. Thomas would teach Jane a lesson she and her parents would never forget. Mrs. Thomas's only concern was what the principal would say about her request, but she was convinced she was acting in the best interests of her students.

DISCUSSION TOPICS AND QUESTIONS TO PONDER

1. Identify the immediate problem in this case and describe what actions you would take to resolve it.
2. Justify and explain Mrs. Thomas's use of what she considered assertive discipline.
3. Describe how the skillstreaming model could have been used to resolve the problem between Jane and Kylie.
4. Explain the type of procedures that should have been developed to monitor the vandalism that occurred in the class wardrobe.
5. Did Mrs. Thomas really act in the best interests of her students?
6. What are some of the hidden issues in this case?
7. How do you think the principal will respond to Mrs. Thomas's request? Why?
8. Describe how peer mediation could have been used to address the issues in this case study.
9. How could the parents help alleviate this situation?
10. What would be your short-term plan? How would it differ from your long-term plan?

WHAT WOULD YOU DO IF . . . ?

1. Jane's parents complained to you that Jane's suspension was based on uncorroborated information and was not only unjust but also discriminatory on your part?
2. Kylie came to you and said Jane's friends were harassing him? If his parents claimed that Jane's actions were causing their son emotional distress?
3. You saw children gathering outside your classroom in order to make faces at Kylie?
4. Jane said she was not responsible for what was going on, that it was Kylie who was behind everything, and that Kylie had told her as much?
5. The principal asked you why you had not consulted him when these incidents got out of control?

CASE STUDY THREE
ARE YOU REALLY A SPECIAL CHILD?

Keys to analyzing this case:

- Outline the case using IOSIE.
- Consider the Jones model or reality therapy as options for a long-term solution.

Kurt Willy was a very quiet boy who displayed little or no emotion. As a fourteen-year-old ninth-grade student at Victory Memorial Junior Senior High School, he had really never fit in to the middle-class, suburban, bedroom community. Kurt's parents were both in the armed services and were constantly posted to different locations every two or three years. Victory, which he had just begun, was the fifth school Kurt had attended since he began going to school.

Kurt had always been a loner until he met Jose Atkins. Jose, at ten, was much younger than Kurt and was just starting the sixth grade at Victory. Jose saw life as a bowl of cherries he could indulge in. After school he loved to go exploring and wandered about the community, getting into trouble. He liked to graffiti storefronts with his tag, "Little Munster." Kurt would escort Jose on his graffiti expeditions; it gave him a feeling of excitement and danger. It didn't take long before Kurt began to develop a taste for his own graffiti. The difference was that Kurt decided to practice his art on Victory's classroom walls.

Mr. Niceman, Kurt's social studies teacher, had a problem. Someone was vandalizing his classroom and the principal was holding him responsible for the room's appearance. Principal Meanly said that classroom management was the responsibility of the classroom teacher, and any teacher who could not control his class did not deserve to receive tenure.

Mr. Niceman spoke to every child in the five classes he taught. No one admitted to knowing anything about the graffiti, or the obscene sayings interspersed with the drawings. One youngster claimed there was a new boy in school who bragged about being a graffiti artist. Mr. Niceman wondered what he should do; he doubted it would be any child from outside his own classes, but who knew?

The graffiti was not present during the day, but always appeared the next morning. It was assumed that the vandalism occurred after three. Most of the graffiti had been done with a black waterproof marker, which happened to be found in the corner of the room where Kurt sat. Mr. Niceman thought that Kurt was a little strange because he was so quiet. He would never have thought that Kurt could be the cause of all his problems—or could he? Mr. Niceman decided to set a trap. He would stay in his class, hidden in the closet after the children were dismissed, and wait to see what would happen. Sure enough, at about ten minutes after three Kurt returned to the room and walked to his desk. He produced a large black magic marker and promptly began to graffiti the rear wall with an obscene picture. Mr. Niceman exited the wardrobe and shouted in as loud a voice as he could, "What is the matter with you? Are you a special education child?"

DISCUSSION TOPICS AND QUESTIONS TO PONDER

1. Identify the immediate problem and describe what actions you would take to resolve it.
2. How could the Jones model have been used when Mr. Niceman confronted Kurt?
3. Describe your impression of the principal's actions with regard to his view of the teacher's role in relation to classroom management.
4. How could Mr. Niceman have used reality therapy during his confrontation with Kurt?
5. Evaluate Mr. Niceman's method of finding the culprit and suggest an alternative solution.
6. Design a guidance-focused approach to resolve this problem. Explain why it would be necessary.
7. Explain how other resource personnel could have been used to solve the immediate and long-range problems.
8. Identify and analyze hidden issues of this case.
9. Compare and contrast the immediate problem and the long-term problem.
10. Upon reflection, what do you really think of the way Mr. Niceman handled the problem?

WHAT WOULD YOU DO IF . . . ?

1. The principal asked you to organize a school cleanup campaign to eliminate the problem of graffiti?
2. Kurt's parents came to school, confronted you, and claimed that Kurt had said you had hit him?
3. Kurt's parents said they would discipline their son by giving him a beating he would never forget; when you told them that was not allowed, they told you to mind your own business?
4. A group of irate community members write you a letter explaining that they have seen one of your students defacing both their property and school property?
5. The PTA president visits your class and asks you what you are doing to clean up the graffiti that has been plaguing your classroom?

CASE STUDY FOUR
I DON'T WANT TO GO TO JUNIOR HIGH SCHOOL

Keys to analyzing this case:

- Outline the case using IOSIE.
- Consider cooperative discipline and the Curwin Mendler model as options for a long-term solution.

Kathy Philips was a ten-year-old African American student in the sixth grade at Twain Elementary School. Upon completion of the sixth grade, Kathy was scheduled to go to Pierce Junior High School. Throughout her school career, Kathy had been labeled as a child with a chronic behavior problem. She was a girl who liked to eat and showed limited self-control when it came to food or to behavior in general. Kathy weighed close to two hundred pounds and was just shy of five feet six inches tall. Both her parents were severely overweight, despite the fact that they constantly denied any weight problem. Kathy was the apple of their eye and could do no wrong; both parents felt that because of Kathy's quick wit, she would be a success in life. The faculty of Twain Elementary did not share their views.

Kathy also was fearful of being considered a failure. It was not beneath her to bully her classmates. She intimidated many because of her size and aggressiveness, which accounted for her limited academic success. For example, she coerced a shy girl named Jane into doing her language arts and social studies homework, and bullied Connie, an introverted girl, to do her mathematics and science homework. All in all, Kathy had a very comfortable elementary school experience; she had parents who felt she could do no wrong and a network of students who did her work. From a ten-year-old's perspective, life was good.

This all changed when Mrs. Rightway took over the class in January. Mrs. Laissy, her former teacher, was on maternity leave and would not return until the following September. Mrs. Rightway was a mature woman who had become a teacher later in life after a successful career in the business world. She was a structured person who had always lived by a set of strict rules. The last thing in the world she expected to deal with when she became a teacher was to have a child like Kathy. It didn't take Mrs. Rightway too long to figure out that Kathy had a host of problems—physical, family, social, and academic.

The question was, how to handle Kathy? What did Kathy hope to achieve by her misbehavior? Mrs. Rightway decided to speak to Kathy privately. Her first question to Kathy was, "Why do you behave the way you do?"

Kathy responded, "Because I am who I am; what did I do to you, anyway?"

Mrs. Rightway had never been spoken to in that fashion. She didn't like it and would not tolerate it. She gave Kathy a note for her parents and told her to write a composition: "How to properly show respect to your teacher." Kathy's parents were to sign the essay. Mrs. Rightway also threatened to have Kathy held back from going to Pierce Junior High School if her disruptive behavior continued.

Kathy began to cry and cursed Mrs. Rightway under her breath. She ran out of the room and screamed, "You suck! I don't want to go to Junior High School anyway!"

On her way home that afternoon, Kathy looked at the note and thought about what Mrs. Rightway had said. She laughed and tore the note to pieces.

DISCUSSION TOPICS AND QUESTIONS TO PONDER

1. Identify the immediate problem and describe what actions you would take to resolve it.
2. Describe and analyze Kathy's actions and motives with regard to the cooperative disciple model.
3. Describe your feelings about Mrs. Rightway's way of dealing with Kathy.

4. Compare and contrast Mrs. Rightway's handling of the situation. What did she do correctly? Where did she fail?
5. How could the theories of Curwin and Mendler have been used in this case study?
6. Design a program focused on Kathy's problems related to her family, social outlook, academic failure, and physical problems.
7. How could other personnel assist Kathy with her problems?
8. How would you involve Kathy's parents to help with the many problems facing their daughter?
9. What would be your short-term plan? How would it differ or reinforce your long-term plan?
10. Reflect on the path that Kathy has taken. How would you gain her respect?

WHAT WOULD YOU DO IF . . . ?

1. Kathy's parents complained that you had threatened their daughter with non-promotion, and they claimed that her behavior had nothing to do with academics?
2. You observed Kathy assigning her classmates, who are obviously frightened of her, various tasks as if they were her servants?
3. The principal told you that Jane and Connie's parents had complained that Kathy was intimidating their daughters?
4. Mrs. Laissy called you and told you not to believe everything the students tell you, and that she wanted you to leave well enough alone and not cause trouble by disturbing Kathy?
5. The children in your class voted Kathy the class president?

CASE STUDY FIVE
LOVE IN HIGH SCHOOL IS FOR REAL

Keys to analyzing this case:

- Outline the case using IOSIE.
- Consider Gossen's restitution theory and Ginott's model as options for a long-term solution.
- Review strategies for working with and understanding gangs (see Appendix A).

Velez Cortez was a shy, petite, raven-haired Hispanic girl who was sixteen. She had a face like an angel painted by Botticelli and the body of a mature Venus. Her physical attributes were negatively balanced by her emotional immaturity. The adolescent boys at Harrison High had voted her as the girl they would most like to be stranded on a desert island with. Velez, for her part was unaware of the reaction she created in the opposite sex. She knew she was pretty, but coming from a very strict

Hispanic family she led a restricted social life; she rarely was allowed to go out with boys unless they were approved by her father and somehow related by blood to the family. Velez, in the eyes of her family, was a sincere sweet child who should be protected from the evils and hardships of the world. According to her parents, Velez led an idyllic life for a teenager.

Velez did not see her life that way. She envied the other girls, whose parents would let them go out on dates and stay out on weekends as late as one o'clock. The girls even told her they were allowed to kiss boys if the boys were really nice. Velez longed to share her peers' social life and not have her parents' rules and regulations.

Velez's life changed when Tommy Harding entered Harrison High and her third period social studies class. Tommy had a reputation as the leader of a group known as the "Undesirable Ones." His so-called gang was new to Harrison High. In fact, Principal Russo was convinced there were no gangs in his school—just teenagers who hung out together. Tommy was the forbidden fruit that Velez had longed for. She felt that he was so cute and really smart, despite what some teachers said about him. For his part, Tommy thought Velez was the most desirable girl in school. So began their relationship. Tommy gave Velez his club jacket; she became his girl and, as Tommy said, his property. As time and their relationship progressed, Velez's life slowly deteriorated.

Mr. Karnes, Velez's social studies and homeroom teacher, saw the change in Velez. She was no longer the happy, innocent girl she had been at the start of the school year. Velez had never been his best student, but now she was not only failing social studies but all her other classes. He thought, "What should I do?" When he spoke briefly to Velez about Tommy, she nearly bit his head off, saying that her love for Tommy was real and no one would be allowed to come between them. If they tried, she would kill herself. Mr. Karnes knew he had to act but was unsure about what was expected of him.

DISCUSSION TOPICS AND QUESTIONS TO PONDER

1. Identify the immediate problem and describe what actions you would take to resolve it.
2. How should Mr. Karnes have responded to Velez's suicide threat?
3. Could Mr. Russo have done anything to possibly prevent this situation from arising? What are some effective antigang strategies that could have been used?
4. How could support personnel have helped to resolve a potentially disastrous situation?
5. Explain how Gossen's restitution theory could be used in this case.
6. Compare Gossen's approach with what Ginott would have advocated in analyzing this case.
7. How could Velez's parents have been involved in resolving some of the peripheral problems related to this case?
8. Elaborate in detail the specific steps Mr. Karnes should take.
9. How could Mr. Karnes have helped to build Velez's self-image? How could congruent communication have been used?
10. What would be your short-term plan? How would it differ from your long-term plan?

WHAT WOULD YOU DO IF ... ?

1. Velez's parents came to school and blamed you, as her teacher, for not having told them of the terrible company she was keeping? What if they wanted to also see the principal to report your misconduct?
2. Tommy confronted you in the hallway between periods and shouted out that you should mind your own business if you know what's good for you?
3. Mr. Russo expressed his disbelief that you could have been so insensitive to Velez's feelings, and asked you to apologize to her?
4. Graffiti appeared everywhere denouncing you as a creep and a goody wimp?
5. Velez was absent from your class for more than a week?

CASE STUDY SIX
IS IT CHILD ABUSE?

Keys to analyzing this case:

- Outline the case using IOSIE.
- Consider reality therapy or transactional analysis as options for a long-term solution.
- Review the physical and behavioral indicators for child abuse and child maltreatment (see Appendix A).

Ms. Kalahari dismissed her class, stood in the school doorway, and reflected about the Brandizzi family. The family always went home together after school, with mama and papa leading the way. Mr. and Mrs. Brandizzi were well overweight, more than five hundred and fifty pounds combined. They had two children, fraternal ten-year-old twins who were the center of Mr. and Mrs. Brandizzi's lives.

The age of the twins was where their similarity ended. Gina was thin and frail and lagged in physical development when compared to her peers. She weighed all of fifty pounds at four feet ten inches, while her brother, Gerard, was taller than Gina and weighed one hundred and fifty pounds more than she did. Gina was shy and timid with a speech disorder, and rarely looked anyone in the eye. She was easily forgettable; she usually stood with her head lowered and her eyes focused on the ground. Her brother, in contrast, was loud and crass and too large to be ignored. Because of his booming voice and deafening laugh, he was a child who consistently made his presence felt.

As Ms. Kalahari looked down the block after the family, she couldn't help thinking that they had a comical aura about them. The children came late to school every day, were unkempt and dirty, and had rotten teeth. Gerard always demanded his breakfast regardless of the time he arrived at school. His sister, Gina, would lower her head and go directly to her classroom where she would beg or steal food from her classmates. The other children constantly complained that both brother and sister smelled. Most refused to sit any where near them or to be their friends.

Ms. Kalahari was Gina's teacher, and Mrs. Borden was Gerard's teacher. Both teachers had spoken many times about the best way to deal with these children and their obese, argumentative parents, who claimed that their special children were perfectly normal. The parents insisted on Gina and Gerard's brilliance, despite their having been recently evaluated with IQs of 64 and 66, respectively. Mr. and Mrs. Brandizzi further claimed that they had been tricked into allowing their children to be placed into special education classes.

Principal Stone had spoken with the family on many occasions with regard to problems ranging from tardiness to family hygiene. Her last discussion with the parents had centered around placing the entire family on a diet except for Gina. She had also threatened to take further action if the parents did not comply with her wishes.

Ms. Kalahari and Mrs. Borden were both aware of Principal Stone's ongoing dialogue with the family. They also were concerned with Mr. Brandizzi's temper when confronted with any suggestion of fault on his part with regard to his children. They were worried that they and Mrs. Stone might be in jeopardy if the father were confronted. Adding to the existing problems, the nurse had just verified that both children had lice again and had to be sent home until they were cured.

Ms. Kalahari and Mrs. Borden asked each other what they could do; should they be quiet or should they start something that they did not know how to finish?

DISCUSSION TOPICS AND QUESTIONS TO PONDER

1. Identify the immediate problem and describe what actions you would take to resolve it.
2. Describe the physical and behavioral indicators that point toward the possibility of child maltreatment. What further information would you need before you registered a complaint?
3. Describe your feelings about the actions or inactions of Mrs. Kalahari and Mrs. Borden.
4. Compare the teachers' actions with those of the principal. Is there evidence of congruence?
5. Explain the legal obligations at play in this case study. Were the teachers' concerns justified?
6. How should the children have been interviewed, and by whom?
7. Evaluate the possible effectiveness of reality therapy as a long-term solution.
8. How could transactional analysis have been used in this case study?
9. Which counseling technique, reality therapy or transactional analysis, would have a better chance of success in this situation?
10. Upon reflection, what should be done for this family—parents and children?

WHAT WOULD YOU DO IF . . . ?

1. You were served with a subpoena to appear at a custody hearing? Mrs. Brandizzi is divorcing her husband and wants you to testify as to her fitness as a parent.

2. Mr. Brandizzi came to school and threatened to report you to the board of education if you didn't apologize for reporting him to child welfare and accusing him of child abuse?

3. The principal reprimanded you for filing a complaint to child welfare without first informing her?

4. You observed Gina crying and sobbing to herself in a corner of the schoolyard during her lunch period?

5. Gerard came to you and claimed that his father is always picking on him and that he punishes both him and his sister by depriving them of food?

■ ■ ■ ■ ■

CASE STUDY SEVEN
DESTROYING SCHOOL AND PERSONAL PROPERTY

Keys to analyzing this case:

- Outline the case using IOSIE.
- Consider restitution theory or assertive discipline as options for a long-term solution.

The wind blew cold on Mr. Harris's face. The chill was as deep as his regrets for acting inappropriately. How could he have been so stupid to believe the tale of woe that Chad Plotkin had handed him? He knew eleven-year-old Chad was a child who wanted attention and found it by making up stories. When Chad had first come to him, Mr. Harris should have realized there was something wrong with Chad's story. How could he have known that Tania Jones was behind all the vandalism that had so recently plagued his seventh-grade classroom and Marcus Junior Senior High School? The incidents had started right after the unsuccessful Martin Luther King Friendship Dance in mid-January.

Tania was an articulate African American child with piercing black eyes who said exactly what she felt. Tania led many causes, all focusing on bettering the lives of her fellow students. With her domineering personality, however, she made as many enemies as she made friends. Her prime adversaries were the local neighborhood kids, who resented any outsiders, especially those who were bussed to school from the other part of town.

At first, the court-ordered integration plan seemed easy for the upper-middle class, liberal, suburban community to handle. The leaders of the community welcomed the opportunity to be a part of the American experience and foster the civic respect and responsibility that they had voted for. What had not been considered was the reaction of those in the minority, who opposed any type of change. The first sign of trouble was at the Friendship Dance; stink bombs had been set off and the gymnasium walls had been painted with racist slogans. Principal Caulfield apologized for the scurrilous behavior of a few, and insisted that the dance should continue. This decision proved to be misguided, as it resulted in arguments and taunts for the rest of the evening.

The following weeks saw a gradual lessening of positive relations among students, faculty, and community. It seemed that all attempts to bring people together only exacerbated the situation. This was so until Mr. Harris, at the request of Principal Caulfield, called a meeting for all the student leaders to discuss how to put student and community relations back on track. He had already done the same thing in his class, and the results had been wonderful. His class was the only one in school that showed positive intergroup student relations. He had achieved this by being assertive and conciliatory in his actions. The children trusted him, and he would lead them.

Things continued to be positive until Chad named Tania as the primary instigator of the racial problems, destruction of school property, and theft of personal property. Mr. Harris had gotten very angry and had confronted Tania in front of the students. He said that he believed that she was the cause of all the problems confronting the school. Tania just looked at Mr. Harris with disbelief and said, "You teachers are all alike. You wouldn't know the truth if it hit you in the face."

DISCUSSION TOPICS AND QUESTIONS TO PONDER

1. Identify the immediate problem and describe what actions you would take to resolve it.
2. Why was Mr. Harris stricken with his own behavior? Was his reaction appropriate for his actions?
3. How should Mr. Harris have behaved? How did his actions differ from those of Principal Caulfield? What could the principal have done to alleviate the situation?
4. Were Tania's reactions out of order? In what respect?
5. Evaluate the effectiveness of using assertive discipline as a long-term or short-term solution.
6. How effective would restitution theory have been if it were the basis for a long-term or short-term solution?
7. How could community resources be used to resolve the problems facing the school?
8. Compare the positive and negative actions taken by Mr. Harris. What could Mr. Harris do to correct his mistakes?
9. Identify and analyze hidden issues in this case.
10. Upon reflection, compare the immediate and long-term problems presented in this study.

WHAT WOULD YOU DO IF . . . ?

1. Tania's parents approached you after school and accused you of causing them and their daughter a great deal of grief with your false accusation?
2. Chad told you that Tania's friends threatened him with violence if he did not rescind his story?
3. Mr. Caulfield asked you come up with a new plan to put the school back on track regarding racial relations?

4. Concerned business leaders visited you and suggested that you leave well enough alone and concentrate on teaching your classes rather than interfering in things you know nothing about?
5. The president of the student government asked for your support in her reelection campaign?

CASE STUDY EIGHT
ALWAYS FIGHTING

Keys to analyzing this case:

- Outline the case using IOSIE.
- Consider the traditional model and transactional analysis as plausible options for a long-term solution.
- Review effective strategies for the prevention of bullying (see Appendix A).

Carl Waller would have been a four-letter man at Jefferson High School if they gave out awards for misbehaving freshmen who had been kept back twice. Carl was frustrated with school, and ignorant with regard to what he was supposed to be learning. He felt justified breaking any school rule imaginable. He was a poster child for inappropriate behavior. His problems at school usually stemmed from inappropriate behavior, including bullying and harassing fellow students.

After reading the last paragraph in Carl's confidential record, Mrs. Jonas, his newly assigned ninth-grade history teacher, was ready to scream. What was she to do with Carl? How could she prepare for a child who was sure to bring a wave of conflict to her third-period freshman class? She decided that she needed a specific plan that would prevent problems with Carl and would protect the younger students in her class.

After a great deal of reflection and discussion with her colleagues, Mrs. Jonas decided that the best way to avoid problems were to keep them as far from you as you could. She decided that Carl would sit as far from her and the other students as physically possible. He would not be allowed to leave the room until every other student had. She would place rules and regulations in the form of posters about the room that exclaimed, "No Fighting, No Talking, and Just Learning!" Doing this, she felt, would establish her as a no-nonsense disciplinarian.

The first day Carl attended class was miraculously problem-free. Carl behaved in a respectful fashion and appeared to mind his own business. It didn't last too long; when one student placed a tack on Carl's seat, Carl reacted true to form by grabbing tiny Jim Blaine who sat beside him. He began to choke Jim, exclaiming, "Who put the tack on my seat?" The dean, Mr. Sanchez, resolved the incident by speaking to both youngsters, threatening to suspend anyone involved in placing a tack on any student's seat. He also said that Carl did not have the right to take the law into his own hands. Both boys were sent back to class.

This incident sparked a series of fights that took place after school. In addition, the class's tone changed drastically from one of academic curiosity to one in which students were sullen and nonparticipatory. Mrs. Jonas knew her plan had not worked. No child would come forward to say they were being bullied. What could she do?

DISCUSSION TOPICS AND QUESTIONS TO PONDER

1. Identify the immediate problem and describe what actions you would take to resolve it.
2. How do you feel about Mrs. Jonas's plan to contain Carl? How could it have been made to succeed?
3. Evaluate the support Mr. Sanchez gave Mrs. Jonas. Were his actions appropriate? What else could he have done?
4. Was Mrs. Jonas's implementation of a traditional management model appropriate in this case?
5. How could support personnel help to resolve this potentially disastrous situation?
6. How could transactional analysis have been used?
7. Does Carl fit the profile of a bully? How could Mrs. Jonas have discouraged his harassing behavior?
8. Reflect on the path Carl has chosen. How would you gain his respect?
9. How could Carl's parents be involved in dealing with these misbehavior problems?
10. What would be your short-term plan? How would it differ from your long-term plan?

WHAT WOULD YOU DO IF . . . ?

1. Carl came to you after class and said you never gave him a chance, and that he wanted to turn a new leaf but was not allowed to?
2. Carl's parents asked to have Carl transferred out of your class, and the assistant principal, Mr. Blake, said you must meet with the parents and convince them to keep Carl in your class?
3. The guidance counselor, Mrs. Creed, asked you to prepare a plan to help Carl?
4. Another student blamed you for starting the malicious rumor that he put the tack on Carl's chair, just because he liked to fool around?
5. Your class wanted to discuss Carl and his behavior?

CASE STUDY NINE
TANTRUMS

Keys to analyzing this case:

- Outline the case using IOSIE.
- Consider behavior modification, teacher effectiveness training, and/or the efficacy approach as options for a long-term solution.

- Review the environmental model in order to provide an ecological analysis of the student's behavior (see Chapter 1).

Catherine Weiner was a seven-year-old second grader who had recently transferred to Elmont Elementary. She appeared to be a shy little girl with a desire to learn and to be helpful. Her mother told the principal that appearances can be misleading, and warned that Catherine had an aggressive streak if she did not get her way. She also said that Catherine did not respond well to criticism; it usually made matters worse. Her previous school had allowed her to play with her small fire truck, which she always had in her possession. This seemed to thwart her raucous behavior.

Ms. Bumble, a recent graduate from Teacher's College, was assigned Catherine and told of the intake interview. She felt confident that she could handle Catherine since she had been an exemplary disciplinarian as a student teacher. She was offered the position at Elmont because both her sponsor teacher and administration felt she knew how to control a class. At times she could be quite stern; she wanted her classes to be the best behaved in the school.

Unfortunately Ms. Bumble's management style was one that Catherine could not abide by. Every afternoon after lunch, Catherine would look out the window and raise her hand for permission to go to the toilet. Ms. Bumble denied her permission, because Catherine had been toileted at lunch. Catherine would insist and start playing with her fire truck. At this point, Ms. Bumble would threaten to take her toy if it were not put away; Catherine would then begin to cry and sob. When Ms. Bumble did take the fire engine, Catherine's sobbing would turn to loud, hysterical, uncontrollable crying and striking out. Catherine had to be removed from the class and sent to Mr. Aptekar, the guidance counselor.

The next day, Mr. Aptekar asked to meet with Ms. Bumble to discuss Catherine. When Ms. Bumble entered his office, he offered her a seat and said, "What do you think about Catherine?" Ms. Bumble responded that in the few weeks Catherine had been in her class, she constantly misbehaved and had tantrums.

Mr. Aptekar asked if she were aware of all the confidential information on Catherine Weiner. Ms. Bumble said, "Some, but not all."

Mr. Aptekar continued, "There is no official record that Catherine ever had a problem with tantrums, only the mother's statement upon having her registered. The tantrums began when she entered your class. In her other school they let her play with her toy fire engine. Her records indicate that she has always been a highly motivated child with good grades. Catherine's mother believes that the problem is the way you relate to her. I asked the mother if her recent separation from her husband, who worked for the fire department, had caused any noticeable distress for Catherine. She responded that her husband's girlfriend looked very much like you, but aside from that, she hadn't observed any outward stress on her daughter's part. Her father still saw her every week and seemingly had a good relationship with his daughter."

Mr. Aptekar concluded the meeting by asking Ms. Bumble to prepare a management plan to deal with Catherine's tantrums. He also suggested that she consider allowing her to play with the fire engine to see if that would help. He told her to look at the situation as if it were an action research project, where the problem was to discover the cause of Catherine's tantrums and the data collected would lead to a solution.

After the meeting, Ms. Bumble reflected on how she could help Catherine and accommodate Mr. Aptekar's requests. She also wanted to let Catherine's mother know that she really cared about her daughter. But those tantrums would have to go!

DISCUSSION TOPICS AND QUESTIONS TO PONDER

1. Identify the immediate problem and describe what actions you would take to resolve it.
2. After analyzing this case study with the environmental model, answer the following questions:
   - What is the problem behavior?
   - Where does it occur?
   - How often does it occur?
   - Under what conditions does it occur?
   - How could the environment be changed to resolve the problem?
3. How do you feel Ms. Bumble is handling the tantrums?
4. Which approach should be used? Why?
5. Was Mr. Aptekar correct to share the confidential information with Ms. Bumble? Why?
6. Outline a behavior modification strategy that a behaviorist might recommend.
7. Compare and contrast the approaches taken between a teacher effectiveness strategy and behavior modification.
8. Assess the positive actions, as opposed to the negative actions, taken by Ms. Bumble. What could Ms. Bumble do to correct her mistakes?
9. What is Ms. Bumble likely to discover as a result of her action research project?
10. Compare the immediate and long-term problems.

WHAT WOULD YOU DO IF . . . ?

1. Mrs. Wiener came to school requesting her daughter be taken out of your class because you had not met her needs, and claimed you failed to provide a sound and secure emotional environment for her daughter?
2. Mr. Aptekar invited you to meet with both parents and explain your take on what has been happening to Catherine?
3. The principal asked you why you appear to be unable to control Catherine when she becomes upset?
4. The principal asked you to prepare a plan that is acceptable to Catherine's parents that will assist in maintaining her in your class?
5. The guidance counselor asked you for a list of people who might help keep Catherine on the proper course?

CASE STUDY TEN
THEY'RE PICKING ON ME

Keys to analyzing this case:

- Outline the case using IOSIE.
- Consider the efficacy approach and behavior modification as plausible options for a long-term solution.
- Review the conflict resolution skills discussed in the Appendix section on Bullying, "Effective Strategies for the Prevention of Bullying."

Mr. Doddered sat alone in his fifth-grade classroom contemplating his next move. He was at a loss; he had tried everything to protect ten-year-old Brian Condotti from the bullies at Peterson Elementary School. He visualized Brian, a very sweet child with a pleasant disposition, who had absolutely no self-esteem. Even when Brian was academically successful, he acted as if he had failed a final examination.

Mr. Doddered thought about the numerous meetings he had had with Brian's parents to speak about their son's lack of self-esteem. They were nice people who really cared for their only son. Mrs. Condotti, a petite woman who was very religious, told Mr. Doddered that they had always sheltered Brian and were afraid God would take him as He had taken their first child, who died as the result of a hit-and-run accident. She felt her protectiveness justified, even if it caused Brian to become dependent. Mr. Condotti, a big burly man, sat quietly in his seat until asked for his opinion, and then said in a booming voice, "She treats him like a little girl rather than a healthy young boy." He was afraid to go near his own son because his wife said he treated him too roughly.

As a result of that meeting, Brian was placed in every physical activity that the school offered. He was forced to join the softball team, the volleyball team, and his class's basketball team. In each case, Brian failed miserably. He was not athletically inclined and found great difficulty relating to his more aggressive teammates. Mr. Doddered had also attempted to coach Brian at lunchtime, without much success. Brian just did not know how to deal with criticism, and cried whenever he was teased.

Mr. Doddered was at his wit's end as to how he would build Brian's self-esteem. He finally decided to take assertive action and punish all the boys in the class for being so nasty to Brian. If that didn't work, he was prepared to call and speak to every parent in the class. He also made up his mind to make Brian the class monitor. He expected that Brian would gain self-esteem with his newfound authority. He could now officially report any misconduct that occurred in the class. Mr. Doddered felt he was finally on the right path to helping Brian be the person he wanted to be. Unfortunately, Brian's self-esteem not only declined, but became nonexistent. The next day at lunchtime, Mr. Doddered saw Brian cowering in the corner of the playground, crying, surrounded by a group of boys. When Brian was asked what happened he said, "They're picking on me."

DISCUSSION TOPICS AND QUESTIONS TO PONDER

1. Identify the immediate problem and describe the steps you would take to resolve it.
2. Was Mr. Doddered acting appropriately by meeting with the parents? Who else should have been involved in these conferences? Why?
3. Evaluate Mr. Doddered's plan with regard to its ability to deal with Brian's lack of self-esteem.
4. How could an efficacy approach been used to help build Brian's self-concept?
5. If you were to implement a behavior modification strategy, what type of reinforcers would be appropriate for Brian? Make a list of in-class and out-of-class reinforcers.
6. Develop a behavior management intervention plan and address the following points:
   - What is the target behavior?
   - What type of baseline data is necessary for you to proceed? How will you obtain the data?
   - Describe your reason for intervening. Reflect on what you would do if Brian's parents didn't see the problem.
   - What intervention methods would you select? What reinforcers?
7. How could you use conflict resolution skills to deal with Brian being bullied and harassed by his classmates?
8. What would you do if the students could not resolve their conflict with Brian?
9. Why would asking them to agree to disagree be a plausible last step?
10. Upon reflection, compare and contrast the immediate and long-term problems and analyze how they should be resolved.

WHAT WOULD YOU DO IF . . . ?

1. Mr. Condotti came to you to complain that you were as bad as Brian's mother who also overprotected him from the real world?
2. Mrs. Condotti thanked you for helping Brian adjust and protecting him from the bullies in his class?
3. The guidance counselor asked you to leave Brian alone and to let him find his own way to achieve self-esteem? He further explained that he has been working privately with Brian.
4. The principal told you he has received anonymous phone calls claiming that you were seen talking in a closed room with a young boy?
5. The principal asked you if you would like to have Brian removed from your class?

■ ■ ■ ■ ■ ▬▬

CASE STUDY ELEVEN
IT'S NOT FEAR

Keys to analyzing this case:

- Outline the case using IOSIE.
- Consider judicious discipline and effective momentum as plausible options for a long-term solution.
- Review the psychodynamic model and the counseling techniques necessary to make individual guidance approaches successful.

Mr. Coder could not understand what had happened to his new sixth-grade class. In his five years of teaching he had never experienced anything like this. The entire class was not settling down. There were many instances of arguments, pushing, tattling, and bouts of abusive name-calling. This had never happened before. He had never had a class that showed so little concern for one another. There were very few positive interactions among the children, resulting in a total lack of class cohesiveness. Mr. Coder knew he had to develop a plan to improve the social climate in the class in order to promote a more positive class atmosphere.

As if that weren't bad enough, the principal, Mrs. Strengths, had just told him that she thought his class would be perfect for a new student transferring from another school. Mrs. Strengths handed Mr. Coder eleven-year-old Clyde Wiggins' confidential folder. Mr. Coder read that Clyde had been transferred from Power Elementary School to Calmer Elementary School due to what his school record claimed was an unrealistic fear of loud noises. The anecdotal record never said he was school phobic but it was noted that he had a possible fear of school. There was no evidence of any testing. Could it be because of Clyde's father? His father was a member of the local school board and was very domineering. Dr. Wiggins, a pediatrician, had won his seat on the board by his campaign slogan, "Caring Education Leads to a Caring Child."

The class took an immediate dislike to Clyde, inappropriately commenting on his haggard, frail appearance and unconventional dress. Mr. Coder overheard some of these remarks as he introduced Clyde to his new class but did nothing about them. Clyde, for his part, looked frightened and scared standing in his green-checkered trousers. He had a naturally pale complexion that bordered on gray when he was frightened. He had no self-esteem. In his first meeting with the class he had been met with disrespect, and was practically laughed out of the room as tears swelled his eyes.

As time went by, Mr. Coder finally decided to both work on building Clyde's self-esteem and improving the social climate in his class. The first action he undertook was to reprimand the class and ask them individually to apologize for their poor manners. The children came up one by one to Clyde in a grudging way and said they were sorry for the way they had carried on.

The following day all seemed to be going well until just before dismissal when Clyde asked to speak to Mr. Coder privately. Clyde said he appreciated Mr. Coder's attempt to protect him but it really wasn't necessary. He could handle his own problems, and besides, he exclaimed in a loud voice, "it's not fear that's going to get the class to like me."

DISCUSSION TOPICS AND QUESTIONS TO PONDER

1. Identify the immediate problems and describe the steps you would take to resolve them.
2. How could Mrs. Strengths have supported Mr. Coder?
3. Do you agree or disagree with Mr. Coder regarding his belief that Clyde's problem was a lack of self-esteem? Why?
4. Outline a judicious discipline strategy that might be effectively used with this class.
5. Explain how Clyde's treatment by his classmates would be handled using a judicious discipline approach.
6. How could the psychodynamic model be implemented to aide Mr. Coder in dealing with Clyde?
7. Describe how the effective momentum strategy would be used to develop class cohesiveness.
8. What should be the roll of Clyde's parents?
9. How could other personnel have been used to resolve the classroom problems and Clyde's problem?
10. What would be your short-term plan? How would it differ from your long-term plan?

WHAT WOULD YOU DO IF . . . ?

1. Clyde's father came to visit and complained that you were interfering in the process by which Clyde would gain self-esteem?
2. The principal asked you to let her see your assignments before you gave them to the children?
3. The assistant principal asked you for a list of students who are not behaving in your class? Upon receiving the list, she asks you to explain what you have done for each child?
4. You saw Clyde physically beating a classmate in the schoolyard?
5. Students in your class claimed Clyde is a bully and only plays at being shy?

■ ■ ■ ■ ■

CASE STUDY TWELVE
I AM GOING TO TELL MY MOTHER

Keys to analyzing this case:

- Outline the case using IOSIE.
- Consider the positive action model and the traditional model as plausible options for a long-term solution.
- Analyze the problem using the performance problem checklist.

Carol Goodman was a strong-willed young lady of thirteen, who in a brief period of time had become a dominant presence at Brady Junior Senior High School. She had an exceedingly high opinion of herself, combined with the nerve, disposition, and belief that there was very little she could not do. Her self-esteem and self-assurance were off the chart. She was aggressive, continually setting goals and achieving her objectives with ease. An overwhelming majority had elected her the president of the freshman class within three months of her being admitted to the school. Her philosophy could be summed up as "the ends justify the means."

Mrs. Gizzard had been teaching for more than twenty years at Brady. During that time she had never met a girl like Carol who exerted such control over her classmates. Carol had good qualities that made her a leader among her peers; however, she had the potential to be a tyrant. You were either for her, or against her.

Mrs. Gizzard had seen how Carol had treated Mary Blaine, a girl who was overweight with a dreadful case of acne. When Mary told Carol in a class discussion that believing feminism was the wave of the future was passé, a major confrontation occurred, resulting in Mary being ostracized from her friends and classmates.

Mary went hysterically to Mrs. Gizzard and asked her to help her stop Carol from being so mean and spiteful. Mrs. Gizzard calmed Mary and told her she would look into the matter. After a brief investigation, Mrs. Gizzard found that most of the students who interacted with Carol were traumatized by her and were fearful of her vengeance and wrath.

Mrs. Gizzard decided that she would consult with the guidance counselor to see if there was a confidential record about Carol. She discovered that Carol had a history of tormenting students who did not agree with her. Mrs. Gizzard decided that she would meet with Carol and call for a meeting with her parents.

When Carol met with Mrs. Gizzard she was in a hostile, contentious mood. Carol told Mrs. Gizzard to mind her own business and leave her alone. She said she would tell her mother and complain to the principal that Mrs. Gizzard was picking on her for no apparent reason. She didn't understand how Mrs. Gizzard could believe Mary Blaine's story; everyone knew she was a liar.

Mrs. Gizzard was sorry that she had ever gotten involved. What was she going to do now? Carol had turned the tables on her. She had to do something to correct the situation.

DISCUSSION TOPICS AND QUESTIONS TO PONDER

1. Identify the immediate problem and describe the actions you would take to resolve it.
2. Analyze the problem using the performance problem checklist:

Describe the problem.
- What is the performance discrepancy that exists between Carol and Mrs. Gizzard?
- Is this discrepancy worth pursuing by Mrs. Gizzard?

Enhance competence.
- Is a social skill deficiency evident?
- Does Carol have the ability to overcome this deficiency?
- Is the social skill crucial to Carol's well being?

■ Can teaching this skill be simplified?
■ Does Mrs. Gizzard have what it takes to teach this skill?

Develop a solution.
■ Which solution is best?
3. Analyze the problem using the IOSIE model.
4. Compare and describe the differences between the performance checklist and the IOSIE model for analyzing episodes such as this case study.
5. How would this case have been handled using the traditional model?
6. How would this case have been handled using the positive action model?
7. Compare and describe the differences between the traditional and positive action model.
8. If you were Mrs. Gizzard, how would you have attempted to resolve the issues involved in this case?
9. Identify and analyze the hidden issues in this case.
10. Upon reflection, compare and contrast the immediate and long-term problems presented.

WHAT WOULD YOU DO IF . . . ?

1. Carol's parents came to school and requested that the principal transfer Carol out of your class?
2. Carol's father requested that the principal reprimand you for acting improperly toward his daughter? If he implied that your tenure be revoked?
3. The guidance counselor asked you to meet with Carol's parents to discuss their concerns?
4. Mary Blaine's parents complained to the principal that you never consulted them about the trouble their daughter was having with Carol?
5. The Blaines and Goodmans want to go to the school board to have your license revoked?

CASE STUDY THIRTEEN
THERE IS REALLY A GOOD REASON

Keys to analyzing this case:

■ Outline the case using IOSIE.
■ Consider judicious discipline, reality therapy, and the efficacy approach as plausible options for a long-term solution.

Mr. Martini could not believe the view he saw from the window of his fourth floor classroom in Brooklyn Heights. The picture that formed in his mind was one of a voyeuristic fantasy world devoid of reality, covered in dust. The children in his sixth-grade class returning from lunch interrupted his thoughts. They were acting in an unruly fashion, yelling, pushing, and crying out for no apparent reason. Yet there was a reason, and Mr. Martini knew exactly what it was. An act of unmitigated violence had occurred in New York City that had affected the lives of all Americans directly and indirectly. The effects on his sixth-grade class, one month after the attack on the World Trade Center on September 11, reflected that of adult society. Reactions had grown from disbelief to fear to an assortment of positive and negative reactions, beginning with prayer and patriotism and concluding, for some, with prejudice, discrimination, bigotry, and hate.

Mr. Martini had worked at the Heights Elementary School for the past three years. He had been an excellent student in college and was well on the road to being one of the most effective teachers in the Heights School. During the attack, Mr. Martini had comforted his children. At the direction of the principal, Mrs. Sanchez, he contacted parents to come to school to pick up their children. His heart almost burst every time there was no response to his phone calls. In the aftermath, Mr. Martini discovered that his class had been directly affected; both Claire Simms' father and Ricardo Fontana's older brother had died as a result of the attack.

His only Arabic student, Abdul Sama, had been kept out of school by his parents after the attack for six days. When Mr. Martini finally contacted them it took a lengthy conversation to convince them to send Abdul back to school. Mr. Martini had promised that no harm would come to Abdul because of his religion and place of birth. He had made similar promises to other children who had come from Islamic countries.

That was before the hate mail and graffiti. Some unknown assailants in Mr. Martini's class were targeting Arabic children. Mrs. Sanchez directed Mr. Martini to find out who was responsible for this outbreak of bigotry. She asked him to reflect and prepare a plan of action for resolving this untenable situation. She also suggested that he give some thought to the possible consequences that could be meted out to the perpetrators.

While walking down the hall to Mrs. Sanchez's office, Mr. Martini wondered if his plan would work. He had decided to appeal to reason. The children were acting out of anger, and besides there was a good reason for their actions, even though they were misguided.

DISCUSSION TOPICS AND QUESTIONS TO PONDER

1. Identify the immediate problem and describe the actions you would take to resolve it.
2. Was Mr. Martini's reasoning flawed? Explain your position.
3. How could judicious discipline have been used to help resolve this situation?
4. Elaborate in detail how reality therapy could have been used to assist those students affected directly by the actions of September 11.
5. How could the efficacy approach have been used to draw out positive patriotic feelings, rather than those that led to negative undemocratic actions?
6. Were Mrs. Sanchez's actions appropriate? What other actions could she have taken?
7. Upon reflection, what should be done for the children and parents in this school?
8. Explain the legal obligations at play in this case study.

9. Compare the teacher's reactions with those of the principal. Did either one act in the best interests of the children? Explain.
10. How would your short-term plan differ from your long-term plan?

WHAT WOULD YOU DO IF . . . ?

1. Abdul's parents accused you of allowing bigotry to fester in your classroom?
2. A coalition of Arabic leaders visited with the principal and demanded your removal from the school?
3. The Simms and Fontana families claimed you are un-American because you spend so much time worrying about the Arabic families and pay little attention to those families that were directly affected by September 11?
4. You attempted to use a judicious discipline approach and the children insisted on condemning children of Arabic ancestry?
5. The principal demanded that you stop using the efficacy approach since it is viewed as flag-waving and "putting oil on the fire"?

CASE STUDY FOURTEEN
TO REPORT OR NOT TO REPORT

Keys to analyzing this case:

- Outline the case using IOSIE.
- How could an individual guidance approach, such as the Ginott model or reality therapy, be used as an option for a long-term solution?
- Review the physical and behavioral indicators for child abuse.
- What rules govern reporters of child abuse?
- Consider the procedures to follow when responding to a child abuse disclosure.

Mr. Woodward had been a middle school teacher for all of six months. In that brief period of time he felt he had experienced young adolescents in all their dimensions, from innocent child to bullying predator. He found that a great deal of interaction occurred during the homeroom period he monitored every day. He used this twenty-minute time period to take care of daily routines and to get to know his students as individuals. Mr. Woodward felt that a social-emotional approach to his students was the way to go. He believed he could do more for his students by caring than just being the strict authoritarian that his more veteran fellow teachers advised.

Lucinda Brown was a bright happy student who got along well with her classmates and most of her teachers. She liked Mr. Woodward because he reminded her of the father she had never known. Her mother's new friend was OK, but he really didn't care about her. He only tolerated her because he liked her mother. She wished Mr. Woodward would care for her mother.

Mr. Woodward often noticed Lucinda staring at him intently. She had always been well groomed for an eleven-year-old seventh grader, but lately she seemed withdrawn, and her personal appearance was disheveled. When he looked at her, he noticed that she was hesitant to make eye contact. Something was wrong.

Mr. Woodward decided to give Lucinda a pass to meet with him after her lunch period. When Lucinda finally arrived she appeared nervous, was fidgeting with her hand, and still refused to make eye contact. Mr. Woodward asked her how she felt and she responded that she was fine. Mr. Woodward pressed the conversation and suggested that she seemed to be different and preoccupied lately. She finally made eye contact and just shrugged. Mr. Woodward pressed on and directly asked her if anything was bothering her, she shook her head. Mr. Woodward decided to tell Lucinda that he was available if she ever wanted to talk.

As Lucinda was leaving the room, Mr. Woodward noticed bruises on her arm and shoulder. He blurted out, "What happened to your arm?"

Lucinda responded that she had fallen yesterday while riding her bike after school. Mr. Woodward replied, "Lucinda, that's just not true. Those bruises didn't happen yesterday. Did someone hurt you?"

Lucinda blurted out, "I will tell you only if you promise not to tell anyone."

Without thinking, Mr. Woodward agreed to Lucinda's terms. She then proceeded to relate a tearful story about how her mother's boyfriend, who had been unemployed for months, became violent when he drank.

"I am so sorry," Mr. Woodward said.

As Lucinda left, she reminded Mr. Woodward of his promise not to tell anyone about her bruises.

DISCUSSION TOPICS AND QUESTIONS TO PONDER

1. Identify the physical or behavioral indicators that point toward a possibility of child abuse.
2. Based on what Lucinda said, would you need more information before you registered a complaint?
3. Who would you register your complaint with? Why?
4. Are there legal obligations at play in this case? Explain.
5. What actions should Mr. Woodward have taken?
6. What long-term approach should Mr. Woodward push for?
7. How should Lucinda's mother be involved in this case?
8. Should the police be called? Why?
9. Should the principal be notified? Why?
10. What role, if any, should the school guidance counselor and/or psychologist play in this study?

WHAT WOULD YOU DO IF . . . ?

1. The principal told you that Lucinda is a compulsive liar and is always making up stories?
2. The guidance counselor claimed to know the mother's boyfriend as a loving man and potential parent?
3. The mother's boyfriend came to school and says he is going to marry Lucinda's mother. He claims Lucinda is just making up stories and that the bruises were

caused by Lucinda trying to learn to ride her dirt bike, which he bought for her. He also claims that he is employed?

4. Lucinda returned to your class and says she was lying because she does not like her mother's boyfriend?

5. Mr. Woodward keeps his promise and tells no one of the information he is privileged to?

CASE STUDY FIFTEEN
MANAGEMENT BY PROGRAM

Keys to analyzing this case:

- Outline the case using IOSIE.
- Consider logical consequences or the Jones model as plausible options for a long-term solution.
- Think in terms of compromise.

Collins Elementary School was an inner-city school that had consistently failed to get more than 30 percent of its fourth-grade students to read on grade level. Parents were at a loss when it came to their children's inability to read and pass the state tests. After a great deal of consultation and angry endless meetings, the administration and parents agreed on a skills-based literacy program to be implemented the coming year. Every child in the school would have instruction in the reading skills necessary to pass the state standardized tests for three periods daily, with the option of more periods if necessary. The faculty was divided as to whether they should change their programs and institute this new skills-based approach. Many felt that such a stress on skills and rote exercises was not what reading was all about. However, they decided to go along, feeling that was all they could do.

One teacher had very serious reservations about the new skills-based program.

Ms. Manes had just completed her first year as a fourth-grade teacher at Collins Elementary School when the new policy regarding reading instruction was decreed. Ms. Manes didn't feel she needed a new approach; she was especially proud of the success of her present reading program, which was based on great books and assorted classic children's literature. She feared her children would lose the joy for reading that she had tried so hard to instill.

The new literacy program began that following September amid appropriate fanfare. Prizes, including money, were offered to children who improved and bonuses were offered to teachers whose classes achieved grade level in reading. Teachers were not given a choice regarding the merit bonuses; they were all expected to participate, and they did. All went well in Ms. Manes's class for the first month and a half of the new term. Then the complaints and acts of misbehavior began during the skills sessions. At first it appeared that the children hated to work in their skills books. They claimed it was boring and dull. Ms. Manes told the children they had no choice; they had to do the required work. She also threatened to punish those who did not work diligently. These actions only increased the class's frustration and the misbehavior. Ms. Manes had to do something to regain control of the class.

Ms. Manes decided to abandon the skills based program and return to her own literacy program based on reading good books. This seemed to work well; the children were happy and the work ethic of the class was restored. Ms. Manes informed her students' parents of her decision. Mrs. Alter, the assistant principal in charge of reading, visited the class and claimed to be shocked at Ms. Manes' inappropriate action in unilaterally disbanding the school's reading initiative in her class. She said she had received parent complaints about Ms. Manes' mismanagement of her class's reading program. As she left the room, she looked at Ms. Manes and directed her to get with the program.

DISCUSSION TOPICS AND QUESTIONS TO PONDER

1. Describe the management problem that is at the core of Ms. Manes' problems.
2. Evaluate the way Ms. Manes resolved the question of how to teach reading in her class.
3. How could a logical consequences approach have been used to resolve discipline problems in the class?
4. How could the Jones model have been used to solve the problem of misbehavior in Ms. Manes class?
5. Were Ms. Manes' actions appropriate? What other approach could she have taken?
6. Was Mrs. Alter's reaction reasonable considering the situation? Explain.
7. Compare the teacher's reactions with those of the assistant principal. Did either person act in the best interests of the children? Explain.
8. How could the parents and the principal have been used to resolve the problem?
9. What would you do if you were expected to teach a program that you found to be the cause of classroom disruption?
10. What type of compromise could resolve the problem between Ms. Manes and Mrs. Alter regarding the reading initiative?

WHAT WOULD YOU DO IF . . . ?

1. Only a few parents complained that the skills program frustrated their children?
2. You attempted to use the Jones model and the class was still unruly?
3. The principal requested that you speak at a parent-teacher meeting regarding your reasons for not following the schools skills-based reading program?
4. Half the parents wanted the skills-based program and half wanted your good books approach?
5. The assistant principal threatened to bring you up on charges of insubordination?

■ ■ ■ ■ ■

CASE STUDY SIXTEEN
MY CHILD NEVER LIES

Keys to analyzing this case:

■ Outline the case using IOSIE.
■ Consider teacher effectiveness, skillstreaming, or peer mediation as plausible options for a long-term solution.

Mrs. Wong had never been so angry and upset in her entire life. How dare Mr. and Mrs. Karbul not take her word with regard to Cindy's behavior? This whole incident would never have occurred if children and parents showed respect for teachers. When she was a child, she was sure her parents would have sided with her teacher in any dispute she might have been involved in. She reflected on what her parents' reaction would have been if one of her teachers had told them that she never accepted responsibility for her actions. She was sure they would have sided with her teacher. What ever happened to society and its perception of teachers?

Cindy Karbul was delighted to see Mrs. Wong's distress. Cindy felt Mrs. Wong deserved worse than that; she was the most boring teacher Cindy had ever had. She had tried to get her tenth-grade English class changed to Mr. Henson's class. He was a man she would love to learn from. She fantasized that she might even be able to teach him something. Besides, school was such a bore; you had to make things happen if you were ever going to have fun. Good thing her parents believed everything she ever told them. Why should she do all the homework Mrs. Wong assigned? Homework only got in the way of her social life.

She had told Mrs. Wong that she would do her work when she had the time. That wasn't a reason for Mrs. Wong to yell at her and call her irresponsible. Teachers never listened!

Mrs. Wong tried to calm down and review the steps that had led to her predicament. Cindy was a self-consumed adolescent who was at a stage in her life where she felt she knew it all. When she had demanded that Cindy hand in her work on time or fail, Cindy went wild. She claimed that Mrs. Wong never explained anything and when she asked her to explain, she never listened. This was totally untrue. All Mrs. Wong's other students were able to hand in their assignments on time. Cindy was just a manipulating liar.

The call she had made to Cindy's parents had been most courteous. She had asked to meet with both parents so that they could straighten out Cindy. Unfortunately that was not what had happened. Mr. and Mrs. Karbul had gone directly to the principal to complain about Mrs. Wong. They claimed that she was persecuting their daughter by assuming that their daughter had a problem. Both parents believed that Mrs. Wong had a problem. They said she did not relate to children and was living in another century. If that wasn't bad enough, Mr. Bluff, the principal, had sided with the parents. He asked to meet with her the following day, and at that meeting he said that Mrs. Wong had better lighten up and review her classroom management procedures. He then asked her to prepare a plan to rectify this situation.

Now was the time for her to decide what she intended to do about Cindy. Mrs. Wong decided that she had been too easy. In the future she would be more persistent in stating her expectations and her feelings. She would speak in a firm voice while maintaining eye contact. She would place demands on all her students and make sure they were enforced. That's what she was going to tell Principal Bluff. She would be more assertive in confrontations and clearly define the consequences so that no student could ever say she never explained anything.

DISCUSSION TOPICS AND QUESTIONS TO PONDER

1. Identify the immediate problem in this case and describe the actions you would take to resolve it.
2. Who owns this problem?
3. How would you describe Mrs. Wong's decision to be more assertive in her dealing with Cindy and the rest of her students?
4. How could Mrs. Wong have used a skillstreaming model to assist in managing the class and Cindy the way she felt they should be managed?
5. Effective skillstreaming deals with feelings and how one can positively express their views. How does this statement apply to Mrs. Wong's problem and to Cindy's?
6. How could Mrs. Wong have involved other students in handling this case?
7. Would peer mediation have worked in resolving the problems you have identified in this case study?
8. Review the steps Mrs. Wong proposes to take to resolve her problems. Evaluate her decisions.
9. What would you have suggested Mrs. Wong do to assist her in resolving a potentially disastrous situation?
10. What would your short-term plan be? How would it differ from your long-term plan?

WHAT WOULD YOU DO IF . . . ?

1. Mr. Bluff said that Mrs. Wong had to change her management practices and insisted that her authoritarian approach could never work with a child like Cindy?
2. Cindy said that Mrs. Wong was lying when she said that all the other children do their work in her class?
3. Mr. and Mrs. Kabul had a change of heart and asked for your help with Cindy?
4. Mrs. Wong claimed she knew that the Gordon model is the best way to handle this situation but she didn't have the personality to change her behaviorist tendencies to actively listen to students?
5. Cindy asked you for help with her problems?

■ ■ ■ ■ ■

CASE STUDY SEVENTEEN
IS THIS A CASE OF CULTURAL DIVERSITY OR CHILD ABUSE?

Keys to analyzing this case:

- Outline the case using IOSIE.
- Consider the Curwin Mendler model, cooperative discipline, or positive action as possible options for a long-term solution.
- Review the definitions of child abuse and child maltreatment.
- Review behaviorist methodology to understand a traditional approach to this case.

Mr. Tangelos had been teaching in the Mayberry School for twenty years. Midway through his tenure he had decided to become a special education teacher. He felt a need to help children who, through no fault of their own, were at a disadvantage. Children, whom he believed, needed a caring, understanding teacher who would always be there for them. It was said that Mr. Tangelos was a wonderful person and a fine teacher with a warm and kind disposition.

Then one day Mohammad Ashawi, a second-grade student in special education, came to school and refused to change for gym class. Mr. Tangelos asked him what was the matter and received no response except, "I am not going to gym." Mohammad was a handsome, articulate, seven-year-old who usually would be more than anxious to be involved in any athletic event, especially gym class. His behavior seemed strange to Mr. Tangelos. Mohammad was finally coaxed to go to gym with the promise that he did not have to change his clothes or participate in any activities since he had finally claimed he did not feel well.

Mr. Quinlan, the principal, saw Mohammad limping while on the way to gym class. He asked Mr. Tangelos what the problem was. Mr. Tangelos relayed what Mohammad had told him.

Mr. Quinlan said, "He's limping; did you examine his feet?"

Mr. Tangelos said he had not. Mr. Quinlan decided to investigate further, and brought Mohammad back to his office. Upon the removal of Mohammad's sneakers and socks, unexplained marks were noted on the souls of his feet. When confronted with this, Mohammad claimed he was bad and his father had punished him. He said he was sorry and would be good in the future. He also begged Mr. Quinlan and Mr. Tangelos not to tell his father he had told on him. Mr. Quinlan called for Mrs. Green, the guidance counselor, to bring a camera to take pictures of the marks on the soles of Mohammad's feet. He phoned his superintendent to inform her of the situation; he was told to make sure of his facts before taking any other actions.

A call was then made to Mohammad's home, over his protests, asking both parents to come to school. An hour later Mr. Ashawi and his brother arrived at Mr. Quinlan's office, outraged and upset over the way they had been spoken to on the phone. Mr. Quinlan asked Mr. Ashawi to calm down and listen to what he had to say. When he was confronted with the marks on little Mohammad's feet, and Mohammad's accusation, Mr. Ashawi quietly stood up and said, "Yes, I did that. As his father I have every right to discipline my son when he is disobedient."

Mr. Quinlan said, "You admit beating him on the soles of his feet?"

"In my country when a child misbehaves he must be punished," Mr. Ashawi replied.

At this point, Mr. Quinlan exclaimed that under no circumstances was beating a child on the soles of his feet permissible. Mr. Ashawi became enraged and grabbed his son by the arm and left Mr. Quinlan's office. Mr. Tangelos followed and called to the security officer to get the police—Mohammad was being kidnapped. Mr. Quinlan stepped forward and directed Mr. Tangelos to be quiet and let the police handle this situation.

The police arrived two hours later with Mr. Ashawi and Mohammad. They explained that a complaint had been filed at the police station against Mr. Tangelos for child abuse and against Mr. Quinlan for discrimination and harassment. Mr. Tangelos looked at Mr. Quinlan and asked, "What next?"

DISCUSSION TOPICS AND QUESTIONS TO PONDER

1. Identify the immediate problems in this case and describe what actions you would take to resolve them.
2. In your opinion, what should happen next?
3. Was this incident precipitated by any lack of knowledge regarding Mohammad's culture? Explain your view.
4. Could using a management program, such as positive action or the Curwin and Mendler method, have avoided misunderstandings?
5. Could Mr. Tangelos have handled this situation more effectively? How?
6. Was the guidance counselor used appropriately? What should have been Mrs. Green's role? The role of the superintendent?
7. Could Mr. Quinlan have dealt with Mr. Ashawi more efficiently? How?
8. What are the legal implications of Mr. Ashawi's complaints?
9. How could a long-term solution be implemented in this case?
10. Is this a case of cultural diversity or child abuse? Explain your answer.

WHAT WOULD YOU DO IF . . . ?

1. Mohammad denied that he had said his father had beaten him?
2. Mr. Ashawi said he was sorry and asked you to give him a second chance?
3. Mr. Ashawi claimed his wife was psychotic and she was the one who had really beaten Mohammad?
4. Mrs. Green said you were not listening and you did not recognize a case of cultural diversity when faced with one?
5. Mr. Quinlan said there is nothing wrong with a person from Mr. Ashawi's country beating a child on his feet?

■ ■ ■ ■ ■

CASE STUDY EIGHTEEN
DOES GOOD TEACHING MAKE A DIFFERENCE?

Keys to analyzing this case:

- Outline the case using IOSIE.
- Consider the Kounin effective momentum model as a solution to the problems presented in this study.

Ms. Sands tried every possible way to control her unruly fifth-grade class at Arlington Middle School. She had tried every consequence method known to mankind, from behavior modification to assertive discipline. Nothing seemed to work with these children. Now her assistant principal, Mr. Cohen, wanted to see her to review a classroom observation he had made.

Ms. Sands reflected on what had led up to Mr. Cohen's request. First was the fight between Billy and John. The boys claimed that they were bored and something about being a duffer head? It was just silly nonsense. Ms. Sands reprimanded them and had them write a thousand times, "I will not fight in class." This had worked until Betty screamed out that Juan was throwing spitballs at the girls. Ms. Sands warned Juan that he should never throw anything at anyone, and followed with a lecture on how terrible it would be if the paper had gone into someone's eye; they could become blind. The whole class thought that funny and laughed. Ms. Sands lost control of the class and behavior deteriorated. Ms. Sands decided immediately to punish the class by not allowing them to go to gym class or play at lunchtime. She also prepared a list of punishment homework to add to the regularly assigned homework. This pattern of generally disorderly behavior had been established as the norm.

As a result of Ms. Sands' disciplinary measures, a group of parents had requested that their children be removed from her class. The assistant principal suggested that the two of them meet with the parents as a group in order to explain the class situation before any transfers were approved. Mr. Cohen then proposed to visit her class so that he could have enough information to speak knowledgeably at the meeting.

During Mr. Cohen's visit to the classroom, he saw children not paying attention. Ms. Sands had her back turned to the class while she was writing notes on the chalkboard. Mr. Cohen walked about and asked the children what they were learning. He received answers such as "I don't know" and "She's so boring I could cry." Mr. Cohen asked the children what was wrong with the class; they overwhelmingly responded, "Ms. Sands!" Before leaving the class, Mr. Cohen told Ms. Sands that she should prepare a plan to improve her performance before their meeting with the parents.

The meeting proceeded fairly well until Mary's mother accused Ms. Sands of terrifying her daughter so badly that she wet the bed and had nightmares about school. Ms. Sands laughed and said that really couldn't have happened. Other parents also spoke out, saying that it was obvious that Ms. Sands was insensitive and never really listened to their children. One parent added, "She is not listening to us now!"

Betty's father, Mr. Jenkins, made a conciliatory gesture and said, "Maybe we can come to a compromise where Ms. Sands stops punishing innocent children." Ms. Sands responded that she had no way of knowing who was innocent; the children blamed each other for any misbehavior.

Ms. Sands guessed the meeting hadn't gone to well; it was even worse than Mr. Cohen's visit.

DISCUSSION TOPICS AND QUESTIONS TO PONDER

1. Identify the immediate problems and describe the actions you would take to address them.
2. How could Mr. Cohen have supported Ms. Sands?
3. Were Ms. Sands' actions appropriate with regard to her students' parents? Explain.
4. How should Ms. Sands have responded to the parents?
5. Was Mr. Cohen using good judgment in asking the children to describe their feelings with regard to Ms. Sands? Explain your answer.
6. Reflect on the actions Ms. Sands has already taken. How could they be improved?
7. How could the key behaviors found in the Kounin model have been used to alleviate many of the problems described in this study?
8. Describe how the teacher negatively influenced the children through the use of the ripple effect? How could this be turned about?
9. Why do you think the children disliked Ms. Sands?
10. Prepare a plan that you would present to Mr. Cohen if you were Ms. Sands.

WHAT WOULD YOU DO IF . . . ?

1. The parents stopped sending their children to your class?
2. Mr. Cohen moved every child who wanted out of your class?
3. The parents agreed that the children should be punished and that you were too lenient?
4. Mr. Cohen switched your class?
5. The children said they were forced to misbehave by the class bully?

CASE STUDY NINETEEN
THE BOMB THREAT

Keys to analyzing this case:

- Outline the case using IOSIE.
- Consider logical consequences and/or assertive discipline as plausible options for a long-term solution.
- Review the risk factors for violence and the reports on the prevention of violence in schools.

Mr. Hamilton felt he would never know if he had acted appropriately in dealing with Jessie Brown and the gang called the Precinct Breakers. Jessie seemed a stereotypical fifteen-year-old inner-city kid until you dug a little harder. Early on he evidenced a pattern of isolation from his peers. They considered him different, or as some claimed, weird. His cumulative records showed that Jessie had always had difficulty with social relationships. When Jessie had first entered his eleventh-grade social studies class, he told Mr. Hamilton that he had little interest in school, but did enjoy history. What he really liked was to read about wars and foreign conquests. His father, a retired policeman, paid no attention to his youngest son, aside from taking him to the rifle range once a month.

Mr. Hamilton had a fine record at Harding High School, at least with the students. The word was that he was one teacher you could depend on and trust with anything. This reputation made Mr. Hamilton feel good; he had always wanted to be the best-liked teacher in school.

His friendliness and tolerant manner had gotten him into difficulties with the school administration in the past, when he had not reported the student writing graffiti on the principal's office door. Unfortunately for Mr. Hamilton, the assistant principal had also seen the student writing the graffiti. As a result of not reporting the student, Mr. Hamilton had an uncomplimentary letter placed in his personnel file.

One day, Jessie confided in Mr. Hamilton and told him that there was a secret club in the school called the Precinct Breakers; they were always picking on kids they didn't like. Recently, they had taken to picking on Jessie because they thought he was a geek. They had, however, given him a choice: If he gave them his lunch money for a week they wouldn't bother him any more. Jessie had thought that it was a fair deal until he realized that the extortion was not going to stop. Mr. Hamilton told Jessie that he would go with him to the police.

"No, please," Jessie said, "you promised that you would never tell anyone anything I told you." Jessie insisted that he had ways to take care of the Precinct Breakers. When Mr. Hamilton asked him what those ways might be, Jessie simply responded, "I'll blow them away."

Mr. Hamilton thought little about Jessie's words until the bomb threats and false fire alarms began. Mr. Hamilton spoke to Jessie about the threats and alarms. Jessie retorted, "What do you think?"

Mr. Hamilton wondered if he had done the right thing in keeping his word to Jessie. Should he go to the principal and let him know about his suspicions?

DISCUSSION TOPICS AND QUESTIONS TO PONDER

1. What are the immediate problems described in this case study?
2. Compare and contrast Mr. Hamilton's problems with Jessie's.
3. Identify and compare the personality problems that both Mr. Hamilton and Jessie have evidenced.
4. Could assertive discipline have been used by Mr. Hamilton to resolve the problems he faces? How?
5. Could the logical consequences model have been employed by Mr. Hamilton to aid him in making decisions? How?
6. Is there anything inappropriate with Mr. Hamilton's desire to be well-liked? Explain.

7. What should Mr. Hamilton have said when Jessie asked him to promise not to say anything?
8. What are the steps that Mr. Hamilton should have taken?
9. Would it have been wise to deal with the Precinct Breakers separately from Jessie?
10. What should Mr. Hamilton do so that problems such as those described in the study do not occur again?

WHAT WOULD YOU DO IF . . . ?

1. The principal found out about the threats from another source and suspended Jessie?
2. You reported your suspicions only to discover later that Jessie was only an innocent victim?
3. The Precinct Breakers beat up Jessie?
4. The guidance counselor said you are derelict in your duties in not reporting what you knew?
5. A bomb was actually found in the school?

CASE STUDY TWENTY
WHAT'S THAT SMELL?

Keys to analyzing this case:

- Outline the case using IOSIE.
- Consider the Ginott model and/or restitution theory as plausible options for a long-term solution.

Mr. Liebowitz was a mature man with an undistinguished career in the garment industry. He hated the twenty years he had spent purchasing and selling wholesale lots of cloth. Finally, he saw an opportunity to change careers and do what he had always wanted to do: become a mathematics teacher. Mathematics was his passion and true love. Teaching and guiding children were just the icing on the cake. Mr. Liebowitz had been able to get into an alternative certification program, which would allow him to be paid by the city while he was trained by the university to become a teacher. He would also receive a free Master's Degree in Education. Life was finally getting good for Mr. Liebowitz.

    Things began to change for Mr. Liebowitz upon the completion of his scheduled two months of university training, when he was assigned to a downtrodden inner-city school as a seventh-grade mathematics teacher. During his first two weeks he adjusted to his new environment and to his assignment to teach five classes daily. His colleagues at the Ross School told him he should enjoy the honeymoon period as long as it lasted, which would not be more than two weeks. His university advisor, Dr. Atwell, warned him not to listen to any negative advice.

Nevertheless, things were going well until the children started to complain about a terrible smell in his classroom. (Mr. Liebowitz suffered from a sinus condition, which made him incapable of judging how bad the smell was.) The children claimed the odor permeated their clothes and caused them to get upset stomachs. Mr. Liebowitz told the children that they should calm down and that the smell would go away. This strategy did not last too long; the only thing that seemed to last was the smell. Class after class now complained of the same awful smell.

Not long after this olfactory disaster, the children in his first period class came to him and complained that the smell came from Rhoda Stanko, a sweet twelve-year-old who had recently immigrated to America. She tried her best, but due to her language deficiency she was having a great deal of difficulty in her studies. She appeared to understand very little of what was said in class. Her parents were lovely people who did not speak a word of English and possibly had hygiene problems.

At first Mr. Liebowitz thought he would have a talk with Rhoda, but he decided it might be taken the wrong way and he might damage her self-esteem. He couldn't speak with her parents, as they didn't speak English. His last choice was to go to the principal, but he couldn't do that either, because the principal would think he couldn't handle his own problems.

Mr. Liebowitz finally decided that the best way to handle the problem was to ignore it, hoping that it might go away. This strategy resulted in his classes becoming unruly. Children who had welcomed Mr. Liebowitz warmly only a few weeks before became unmanageable. Children disrupted the class, constantly requested to leave the room, and finally cut his class. Parents started writing notes asking that some action be taken regarding the smell that permeated their children's classroom. One parent requested that the Environmental Protection Agency be called in. Mr. Liebowitz responded in writing to each parent that he was taking care of the smell. Upon reflection, he realized that it wasn't getting better. He was going to have to take some kind of specific action. Maybe he could have Rhoda transferred to another class.

Mr. Liebowitz received a note from Mrs. Santiago, the assistant principal, asking him to explain all these complaints that she was getting from parents regarding the rotten smell emanating from his room. She asked if he had consulted the custodian.

Just as Mr. Liebowitz finished reading the note, Mrs. Santiago came into his room and took a deep breath and exclaimed, "What in heaven's name is that smell?"

DISCUSSION TOPICS AND QUESTIONS TO PONDER

1. Identify the immediate problem and explain the actions you would take to resolve it.
2. Was Mr. Liebowitz correct to worry about the development of Rhoda's self-concept?
3. How could Mr. Liebowitz have used the Ginott model and stressed a common-sense approach to this situation?
4. Explain how the restitution model would have helped to understand why the students were misbehaving in order to avoid pain.
5. How could the restitution model have been used to resolve this problem?

6. Could Mr. Liebowitz have taken any actions that would have resolved the problems of misbehavior he was facing from his classes?
7. Were their any consequences he could have employed to lessen the misconduct of the offending students?
8. Evaluate the attempts Mr. Liebowitz made to resolve the problem.
9. Should Rhoda's parents have been informed? Should Rhoda have been informed?
10. What would you have done in this situation?

WHAT WOULD YOU DO IF . . . ?

1. The children refused to sit next to Rhoda?
2. Rhoda's parents said there was no hygiene problem with their daughter?
3. Rhoda's parents claimed you and the class are prejudiced against people from their country?
4. After you spoke to Rhoda, she began to cry and claimed that her parents punish her by not allowing her to bathe?
5. Mrs. Santiago asked if you want Rhoda removed from your class?

■ ■ ■ ■ ■

CASE STUDY TWENTY-ONE

AIDS IS MORE THAN A SICKNESS

Keys to analyzing this case:

■ Outline the case using IOSIE.
■ Consider transactional analysis or Gordon's teacher effectiveness training as plausible options for a long-term solution to the problems presented in this case.

David Saverese was an exceptionally handsome youngster. With his jet-black hair and piercing blue eyes he could have passed for an eight-year-old Rob Lowe or a Tyrone Powers from another era. He carried himself with the poise of a future athlete, quite unusual for any third grader. David was a bright child who had been born to the wrong parents. His mother, Louise, had died from a drug overdose when David was six years old. His father, Tony, was a recovering alcoholic and from all appearances was not a healthy man. Despite his physical condition, Tony was attempting to provide a nurturing environment for David, the light of his life.

Mrs. Cole finished reading David's confidential record with a sense that something was missing. David had always been well behaved in her class until recently. After reading of the tragedy that had surrounded his young life, she could understand some of his recent behaviors, even though lately they seemed quite bizarre. Over the past two weeks, David had changed from a quiet, well-behaved child into a raging demon who would not sit still for more than a few seconds at a time and would constantly walk about the room disturbing other children. If she scolded David, he would begin to cry and attempt to run out of the room or fall to the floor. His emotional outbursts seemed to last about five minutes but were increasing in length.

Mrs. Cole was a veteran teacher who had been quite successful in managing her classes in the past. The last straw was when she found David sitting in the men's urinal crying hysterically. He refused to leave, and Mr. Ibarra, the principal of the Sadly Elementary School, had to be called. Mr. Ibarra physically picked David up and carried him out of the bathroom. When things had quieted down, he asked Mrs. Cole why she had not told him about David's bizarre behavior before this incident. Mrs. Cole responded that she thought she could handle it by herself. Mr. Ibarra then asked Mrs. Cole to contact David's father at dismissal and escort him to the office so that they could discuss David's unusual behavior.

At 3:10 that day, Mr. Saverese entered Mr. Ibarra's office escorted by Mrs. Cole. Mr. Saverese kept looking down at his shoes while blowing his nose. Mr. Ibarra got right to the point and asked, "Are you aware of your son's untoward behavior?" Mr. Saverese said that he had been totally informed about David's strange behavior, and he apologized for any damage or harm it might have created. He also explained that he really did not know where to turn. When Mrs. Cole said that she would work with David to control his temper, Mr. Saverese responded, "That's not the problem. The problem is that I have AIDS and David knows I only have a few more months to live."

After the meeting had ended and David had gone home with his father, Mrs. Cole cried. What could she do to help this child survive? What was going to happen to him? What was going to happen to her class if he was allowed to continue to wreak havoc as an outlet for his unfortunate situation?

DISCUSSION TOPICS AND QUESTIONS TO PONDER

1. Identify the immediate problem in this case and justify the actions you would take to rectify the situation.
2. Based on Gordon's teacher effectiveness training model, describe specific actions that Mrs. Cole can take to assist David.
3. Why did the principal, Mr. Ibarra, immediately ask to meet with Mr. Saverese?
4. How would you explain the legal issues that might arise as the result of inappropriate actions on the part of Mrs. Cole and Mr. Ibarra?
5. How can Gordon's behavior window be used to determine problem ownership in this study?
6. Based on your understanding of transactional analysis, what steps could Mrs. Cole take to assist David?
7. Is there anyway to help David feel adequate?
8. How could other personnel have been used to remedy this situation?
9. What are some of the hidden issues in this case?
10. Compare your immediate actions with your long-term goals in this case.

WHAT WOULD YOU DO IF . . . ?

1. David would not come to school for fear of losing his father?
2. Concerned parents discovered that David was HIV-positive and wanted David removed from their children's class?
3. David bit someone after he was diagnosed as HIV-positive?

4. Mr. Ibarra decided to move David to a different class because of the parental requests?

5. The guidance counselor and school psychologist wanted David removed from his father's custody?

■ ■ ■ ■ ■

CASE STUDY TWENTY-TWO
WHAT THE F—?

Keys to analyzing this case:

- Outline the case using IOSIE.
- Consider the traditional model or the Jones model as plausible options for a long-term solution.
- Review preventative and antigang strategies in schools.

Chloe Knight was a typical teenage girl who was interested in boys, clothes, music, and being considered popular with her social peers. She also had the intellectual attributes necessary for eventual success in life, with the exception that at times she spoke without thinking and used profanity when provoked. Unfortunately, it took very little to provoke Chloe. Mr. Hassan, Chloe's new eleventh-grade science teacher, had seen Chloe in action. He had broken up a potential confrontation between Chloe and her archrival, Sara. The argument had begun with Sara contradicting Chloe with regard to a popular local rock group. That was all it had taken for Chloe to lash out at Sara, calling her an f—ing idiot. The boys in the lunchroom had encouraged Chloe to fight with Sara. Mr. Hassan had told both girls to cut it out and go back to eating their lunch. They looked back at him as they left the cafeteria, mumbling to themselves.

That incident had occurred at the start of the school year, and the emotions died down as quickly as they had been ignited. Mr. Hassan was thinking about that incident when he received a transfer slip placing Chloe into his third-period class with Sara. What should he do? He resolved to wait and see, a strategy that proved to be ineffective.

As soon as Chloe entered the classroom, she made a distasteful face when she saw Sara. Sara said, "Just what are you looking at, Chloe?" Mr. Hassan looked at both girls and warned them that fighting was not allowed, and if they didn't like it they should get out before he threw them out. From that point on the girls became the best of friends and conspired and plotted to get back at Mr. Hassan for embarrassing them.

Little disruptions began to interrupt the momentum of Mr. Hassan's class. Chloe and Sara kept up a steady stream of conversation every time Mr. Hassan turned his back to write on the chalkboard. When he faced them and told them to stop talking, they laughed and said he was hearing things and that they weren't talking. They both started to put makeup on during Mr. Hassan's lessons. Mr. Hassan countered by having them write apologies to the class for interfering with their science lesson. The incidents didn't stop; the more repressive Mr. Hassan became the more the level of classroom disruption increased. Classroom noises, gum on seats, and students coming late to class indicated a general decline of the level of respect in Mr. Hassan's class. It wasn't long before Mr. Leisure, the assistant principal, asked to speak with Mr. Hassan.

At the meeting, Mr. Leisure asked for a detailed explanation regarding the misbehavior that was occurring in Mr. Hassan's class. Mr. Hassan asked Mr. Leisure how he knew about the problems in his class. Mr. Leisure responded that everyone knew; it was written all over the handball courts in the schoolyard.

DISCUSSION TOPICS AND QUESTIONS TO PONDER

1. Identify the immediate problem presented in this case study.
2. What actions would you take to resolve the immediate problem presented?
3. Describe Mr. Hassan's actions with regard to Chloe.
4. How would you deal with Chloe? Who might you consult to assist you? Why?
5. Are their any indications of gang intervention in this study? Explain.
6. What traditional approaches has Mr. Hassan failed to initiate?
7. How could the Jones model have been used to resolve the immediate problems facing Mr. Hassan?
8. Would a guidance approach have been more effective in dealing with a student such as Chloe? Why?
9. How would you have involved Chloe and Sara's parents to assist in dealing with these misbehavior problems?
10. Compare your short-term solution and your long-term strategy for the resolution of these problems.

WHAT WOULD YOU DO IF . . . ?

1. Sara came to you and told you about Chloe's plan to disrupt your class?
2. Chloe said that Sara is the leader of a gang and provokes her because she had refused to join Sara's gang?
3. Mr. Leisure suggested you meet with both girls, the guidance counselor, and their parents?
4. Chloe continued to misbehave despite all your efforts to alleviate the situation?
5. Parents of other children complained that you spend too much time disciplining Chloe and not teaching your class?

■ ■ ■ ■ ■ ▬▬▬▬▬▬▬▬▬▬▬▬▬▬▬▬▬▬▬▬▬▬▬▬▬▬▬▬▬▬

CASE STUDY TWENTY-THREE
BUT I DO EVERYTHING RIGHT!

Keys to analyzing this case:

- Outline the case using IOSIE.
- Consider the best generic approach to take: consequence, group guidance, or guidance.

Mr. Sutter had never experienced feelings of depression or lack of self-worth in all his years of teaching. Everyone liked him, and he liked people. He often referred to himself as a people person, and his students were his people. His principal, Mrs. Frantz, always expressed her high regard for his classroom work and the way he controlled his classes. Children obeyed him, were always respectful, and never spoke until spoken to. Mr. Sutter got along with his colleagues and had a wonderful family life.

This term, however, Mr. Sutter's life had become completely unhinged. Juan Cortez had come into his life and completely disrupted both Mr. Sutter and his fourth-grade class at Elmont Primary School. After almost twenty years of teaching, Mr. Sutter was stumped as to how to handle young Juan. He tried everything that had always worked in the past. He had warned Juan, raised his voice, and finally sent Juan to the principal.

Juan Cortez was a handsome ten-year-old Mexican American boy who had piercing brown eyes with a propensity for anger and disruption. Incidents occurred seemingly without provocation; he would randomly throw things about the room, stand up and shout out obscenities, or yell, "Mr. Sutter hates me." Mr. Sutter usually laughed and told Juan to cut it out and act like a man. After these incidents, Juan would refuse to do any class work. Mr. Sutter scolded Juan when he misbehaved; he would point out that no one likes a child who acts the way he does. When Mr. Sutter's patience finally wore thin, he would send Juan to the principal's office. Mr. Sutter could not allow Juan to constantly disrupt his class.

At Elmont Primary School, the principal, working with a school support team known as the Pupil Personnel Team/Intervention Team, assumed responsibility for supporting learning in the classroom. The principal was specifically responsible for coordinating efforts to identify students in need of additional help. The team was a proactive group charged with analyzing the whole child and providing teachers with the tools they needed to maintain order and buttress learning. The team consisted of an intervention team leader and core members selected by the principal. Team composition could change depending on the student being discussed, but core members remained the same. Core members were a three-day-a-week guidance counselor, a two-day-a-week psychologist, and two full-time literacy and math coaches.

The team decided to use a consequence approach to control Juan's poor behavior and improve his learning. The team case manager explained the plan to Mr. Sutter by calling it a behavior contract that Juan was obliged to follow. The contract used an anecdotal record format, which was to be developed from daily reports that Mr. Sutter completed and sent to Juan's parents. The parents were expected to come to school on a weekly basis to discuss Juan's progress with Mr. Sutter. The team's rationale for the contract was to match Juan's behavior with appropriate targeted interventions that would resolve his learning and management problems.

Mr. Sutter believed the plan could never really work; it was unworkable. Juan needed to be punished to learn respect and proper behavior. Mr. Sutter didn't have time to keep records and teach classes and constantly meet with parents. It would have been much easier to remove Juan from his class or threaten his parents with parental neglect. Mr. Sutter felt he was not responsible for Juan; it was the team's problem. Juan should be controlled by his parents at home, and in school the principal should take the place of the parents. Mr. Sutter decided to force the team and the principal to do their jobs and control disruptive children. Every time Juan acted up he would have him leave the room to go to the principal's office for an intervention.

That afternoon Mr. Sutter received a letter from the principal. When Mr. Sutter opened the letter, he could not believe that he was being summoned to a meeting with the principal and PPT/Intervention team. What could it possibly be about? He had always done everything right.

DISCUSSION TOPICS AND QUESTIONS TO PONDER

1. Identify the immediate problem in this case. What would be your long-term objectives?
2. Whose plan could have met the objectives of improving learning and behavior, Mr. Sutter's punishment or the Intervention Team's consequence approach? Explain why.
3. Are there any possible alternatives or additional interventions that could or should be attempted? Describe them.
4. Were improving Juan's learning and classroom behavior the only problems?
5. Could Mr. Sutter be considered part of the problem? Why?
6. Describe your feelings with regard to Mr. Sutter's punishment plan. Was it appropriate for this situation? Is punishment ever appropriate?
7. Why would the team want to meet with Mr. Sutter?
8. Was Sutter's philosophy of controlling students through appropriate punishment realistic? Explain.
9. How were the parents to be used to help solve Juan's behavior problem? Were expectations realistic? Explain.
10. Would a guidance, group-guidance, or combination approach been more effective in helping Juan?

WHAT WOULD YOU DO IF . . . ?

1. Juan's parents said that he was afraid of you because he felt you hated him?
2. The principal asked you to write up the steps you were going to implement to help Juan?
3. The principal threatened you with disciplinary action for unprofessional conduct?
4. Juan told you that no one in the school likes him because they don't like Mexican Americans?
5. Juan's grades suddenly improved?

■ ■ ■ ■ ■

CASE STUDY TWENTY-FOUR
FIRST GRADERS CAN BE DIFFICULT

Keys to analyzing this case:

- Outline the case using IOSIE.
- Consider using a guidance approach, such as reality therapy, for both a long-term and immediate resolution to the problems presented in this case.

Tina Twoburn was a beautiful six-year-old child who combined the best features of her American Indian and African American heritages. She could be the sweetest child when she chose to behave, which was not often. She had a fully developed independent streak that tended to encourage her spontaneous reactions to any external attempt to control her behavior. Her parents were quite pleased with Tina's academic performance in Ms. Rodgers' first-grade class. Tina was in the top reading group and appeared to be on the road to academic success despite behavioral lapses. Ms. Rodgers had in a brief two months created a caring learning community where the majority of her class thrived.

This rosy picture changed the day Ms. Rodgers left the school on an extended medical leave and was replaced by Ms. Collins, a new teacher recently graduated from a prestigious university. Ms. Collins had worked as an executive in a bank for ten years before she decided to change her career and become an early childhood teacher. She loved children, and was eager to take over Ms. Rogers' class when offered the opportunity.

One of Ms. Collins' strengths in her previous career was her organizational skill, which she intended to employ in reorganizing Ms. Rodgers' class. For example, children would no longer be allowed to volunteer for reading groups or project committees; they would be assigned as in the real world. Ms. Collins felt it was never too soon to prepare for life. She desperately wanted her new class to succeed and perform much better than they had under Ms. Rodgers. She realized that Tina Twoburn was a force to be reckoned with the first time she acted out.

The first thing Ms. Collins did was to assign Tina to a slower reading group. Ms. Collins felt Tina was struggling with the assignments and that easier work would lessen her hostility. When Tina objected, Ms. Collins said, "Tina, it is for your own good; the work will be easier for you to handle." With that, Tina cursed Ms. Collins and refused to do any work at all. Ms. Collins calmly explained to Tina in front of the class that "nice children do not use toilet words." Tina responded by putting up her middle finger and saying, "I hate you, you're a stupid teacher."

At this juncture Ms. Collins felt she best ignore Tina's outrageous behavior and go on with her lesson. Tina then got up on the table in the rear of the room and proceeded to dance, while kicking and throwing class projects to the floor. Ms. Collins attempted to cajole Tina to come down off the table. She again told the class to ignore Tina's inappropriate "childish" behavior. At this point, Tina threatened to throw a desk at Ms. Collins. Ms. Collins moved to sit on the desk and told the class to leave the room until help arrived.

The next morning two angry parents arrived in school demanding to know what had happened to make their daughter so upset yesterday. Their child claimed that her new teacher Ms. Collins had made fun of her, called her stupid, and would not let her do her work. Ms. Collins was doing everything wrong, and changing everything Ms. Rodgers had done. Mr. and Mrs. Twoburn were upset and demanded an explanation. Ms. Collins called the principal for help.

DISCUSSION TOPICS AND QUESTIONS TO PONDER

1. Identify the immediate problem in this case. What actions would you take to rectify the situation?
2. How could consequence, group-guidance, and guidance approaches be used in this case?
3. Evaluate each of Ms. Collins' actions and discuss their effectiveness.
4. Explain other actions that could have been taken that might have been better suited to this situation.
5. Were Tina's parents justified to be upset? Why?
6. How should Ms. Collins handle this confrontation?
7. Is calling for the principal an appropriate action to take? Why?
8. How could reality therapy have been used to deal with the problems presented in this case?
9. How could assertive discipline have been used to deal with the problems presented in this case?
10. How could judicious discipline have been used to remedy this situation in the long run?

WHAT WOULD YOU DO IF . . . ?

1. The parents took your side and began to beat Tina for not obeying you?
2. The principal sided with the parents and said you used poor judgment in dealing with this case?
3. Tina apologized and asked you not to tell her parents?
4. The school intervention team criticized you for not calling on them before the situation got out of hand?
5. As a result of your efforts, Tina followed your direction but was failing in her academic work?

CASE STUDY TWENTY-FIVE
WHY IS HE BORED?

Keys to analyzing this case:

- Outline the case using IOSIE.
- Consider a guidance approach combined with good instruction, such as the effective momentum model.
- Think about short-term and long-term objectives.

Mrs. Ramos was truly upset. She had worked at Mondale Elementary School for ten years and in all those years had never seen such a nonviolent disruptive youngster. Carl Forrest had been in her third-grade class since the third week of September. He came from an intact and apparently loving family. His father was in the army and had just been assigned to the local military installation in Mondale City. Mrs. Forrest was a nervous woman who had difficulty making decisions. Most of the time she had her hands filled caring for her family, five children ranging in age from six months to nine-year-old Carl. Carl at first seemed to be a child lost in space and time. He constantly stared out the window with a dejected expression on his face. About a month after his arrival his behavior took on a character of its own.

During class lessons he would call out things that were not relevant to the lesson, such as, "Look at the fire engines!" "I've got pencils for sale!" "No one can leave!" Mrs. Ramos continually scolded Carl telling him to refrain from outbursts because they interrupted her lessons. Her efforts only delayed the frequency of misbehavior incidents and never seemed to resolve them. After a period of time, Carl would incur another infraction or shout out again.

One time Carl left his seat without permission to retrieve discarded paper and remnants from the wastebasket. He proceeded to create objects made out of the refuse and placed them in a tissue box for sale to his classmates. Mrs. Ramos attempted to regain control by telling Carl to stop what he was doing and to pay attention to her lesson. Precious instructional time was lost. On another occasion he crawled under the tables and desks in the classroom, then abruptly stood up and told Mrs. Ramos that he had found the things that had been missing from the class activity center.

These incidents of shouting out, disrupting the class, and general misconduct were transcribed in an anecdotal report for the intervention team prepared by Mrs. Ramos in preparation for her meeting with the team and Carl's case manager. She finished her report by stating that Carl constantly interfered with her lessons, seemed very bored, was easily distracted, and was in need of attention. She also said that previous suggestions by the team to institute a program of positive reinforcement had initially worked at the beginning of the year, but as of this date the positive effects had worn off. She further stated in her report that she had never met Carl's father since he had been recently stationed to Iraq, and his mother, who was distraught, "talked the talk but had no control over Carl."

The meeting with the team began by Ms. Abrams, Carl's case manager, asking why the positive reinforcement approach wasn't working. Mrs. Ramos responded, "He just doesn't care. He is bored with everything we do in class. All he wants to do is make those silly little projects out of discarded refuse and crawl under the desks. How could I praise him for disrupting the class?"

"Could you give us an example of a positive reinforcement you used?" Ms. Abrams replied.

"Well, one time I told him that the nice pants he was wearing would become soiled if he continued to crawl on the floor. He just laughed and continued being disruptive until I sent him out of the room."

"Mrs. Ramos, you say he is bored; can you give us a reason?"

DISCUSSION TOPICS AND QUESTIONS TO PONDER

1. Identify the immediate problem and describe what actions you would take to resolve it.

2. Describe the long-range problems Mrs. Ramos faces.
3. Do you feel Mrs. Ramos understands the positive reinforcement approach? Explain.
4. Would a consequence approach be effective in this situation?
5. Were Mrs. Ramos's actions appropriate for the situations she described?
6. How could a guidance approach, such as reality therapy, be used in this situation?
7. Did Mrs. Ramos make effective use of Carl's family?
8. Has Mrs. Ramos been effective in allowing Carl to develop his kinesthetic and creative instincts? How has she done this?
9. What indicates that Mrs. Ramos does not realize that Carl needs to be challenged to achieve?
10. Why is Carl bored?

WHAT WOULD YOU DO IF . . . ?

1. Carl's parents claim that all you do is try to ignore Carl?
2. Carl's father returned from Iraq and visited your class?
3. Ms. Abrams, the case manager, said, "Look at your actions. How have they helped Carl?"
4. The children in your class complained that you were picking on Carl?
5. Carl said you were a boring teacher?

CASE STUDY TWENTY-SIX
IS TOILETING APPROPRIATE FOR THE FIFTH GRADE?

Keys to analyzing this case:

- Outline the case using IOSIE.
- Consider a guidance approach or good instruction, such as the Kounin effective momentum model, as a solution to the problems presented in this case.

Mrs. Castro was the science cluster teacher at Carville Elementary School. She had gotten the position, she felt, because she had a background in science, as the principal had pointed out, and no one else wanted it. She had studied to be a biologist before becoming a teacher and had briefly worked in a pharmaceutical laboratory. This was her third year at Carville, an inner-city school that had high expectations for its students. A major focus of Mrs. Cato, the principal, was to create a learning community. She believed all teachers and children were in the same boat, and all should pull together to improve the school's academic performance. Mrs. Cato, many believed, was fixated on stressing teamwork and professional cooperation. She was fond of saying that each teacher should begin were the other left off. She wanted her staff to become an educational family.

Mrs. Castro wanted to live up to her principal's expectations. The cluster position afforded her ample opportunity to work with other staff members. Her day consisted of teaching five classes, a lunch, a preparation period, and an administrative duty. She viewed her administrative role as an opportunity to meet with parents and teachers and to establish a volunteer ecology club, a personal goal of hers. She felt she was truly supporting the school's goal of creating a learning community. As a cluster teacher, she always made it a point to follow the classroom teachers' suggestions with regard to classroom management. She aimed at being cooperative and professional in all her interactions with her colleagues.

Ms. O'Neill, the lead fifth-grade teacher, had instructed Mrs. Castro to never allow Anne Jeffrey, a precocious ten-year-old, out of her room or out of her sight. Ms. O'Neill explained that when Anne was out of the room, she tended to wander the building and disappear for extended periods of time. On her first meeting with Anne, Mrs. Castro explained to her, "even if you raise your hand to go to the bathroom, I will not let you out of the room." She further told Anne that Ms. O'Neill had directed her not to let her leave the room. Anne mumbled, "Is this a prison or a school? It's just not fair." Anne then proceeded to call out every five minutes, "Can I go to the bathroom?" This continued for the entire period, allowing for little instructional time. Finally, in frustration, Mrs. Castro told Anne in front of the class that if she were good she would consider allowing her go to the bathroom at the end of the period. Anne responded, "I am good."

This scenario was played out week after week, with the same result: Mrs. Castro became annoyed and upset. She had tried everything she could think of to manage Anne, but nothing seemed to work. She had spoken to Anne's father to ascertain if there was a medical problem with regard to toileting. Her father said she was healthy and had never had a problem with toileting. He also said his daughter complained that she was treated like a prisoner, and that her science teacher was boring. Mrs. Castro responded that Anne might not think she was boring if she paid attention in class and didn't constantly try to leave the room.

When she asked Ms. O'Neill for advice, she was told to stick to her guns. She was to demand that Anne obey her as she obeyed Ms. O'Neill. In desperation, Mrs. Castro called Anne aside and told her that if she brought a note from home she would let her go to the bathroom the next time she asked.

DISCUSSION TOPICS AND QUESTIONS TO PONDER

1. Identify the immediate problems and describe the actions you would take to resolve them.
2. Prioritize the problems presented and offer a solution not attempted in the case for each problem.
3. How could a group-guidance approach have been used to rectify the situation?
4. How could consequences been used to have Anne stop her campaign to disrupt and leave the class?
5. How would you describe Mrs. Castro's attempt at a guidance approach?
6. How would your approach differ from Mrs. Castro's guidance approach? Explain.
7. Describe possible ways to motivate Anne during a science lesson.
8. How do you feel about Ms. O'Neill's advice? Was it appropriate for this situation? Why?

9. Who could have assisted Mrs. Castro in resolving the problem of toileting? How could an aid have been employed?
10. What are appropriate procedures for toileting fifth-grade students?

WHAT WOULD YOU DO IF . . . ?

1. Anne's father complained to the principal that you had no right to deny his child use of the toilet?
2. Anne's grades improved despite her annoying behavior in your class?
3. Ms. O'Neill complained to the principal that every time she returned to her class after you had taught them they were essentially unmanageable?
4. One of the interventions recommended by the intervention team was to have Anne join your ecology club?
5. A group of parents went to the principal to complain that you did not allow their children use of the facilities?

CASE STUDY TWENTY-SEVEN

IS SCRIPTED EDUCATION THE SOLUTION?

Keys to analyzing this case:

- Outline the case using IOSIE.
- Reflect on scripted education and its relationship to interactive learning.
- Think about short- and long-term actions necessary to diffuse situations.

Ms. Rienzi had always prided herself on being a team player. She would always side with the majority. In college she had been known for her strict adherence to the rules. The same values regarding faithfulness had always put her in good standing with her professors. Now, in her first position since graduating, she had set out to demonstrate her loyalty to the people who had hired her. The policy of her school and district was that all lessons were to be scripted and follow the newly devised workshop model. It was a rigid policy, but it was one that Ms. Rienzi was sure she could comply with.

The workshop model had been developed to encourage interactive learning, and it required that each lesson be divided into three parts: a ten minute minilesson of whole group instruction; twenty minutes of small group instruction; and a final ten minutes of groups sharing the results of their work. Many had complained when the model was introduced; the principal, Mr. Lucy, said the workshop model was a central office directive and all were required to comply. He expected each classroom at Portage Elementary School to have prominently displayed on their classroom doors a "flow of the day" chart, which was to be a daily preview of the activities taking place that day. And although it was not publicly acknowledged, the chart could also be used by the administration to check if a teacher was on schedule with daily instruction. Mr. Lucy explained to the staff that standards had to be met in every class. He said that the model was really not rigid, but it was to be used as a guideline; teachers would adopt the model to address the specific needs of their children. He concluded his remarks by stating that "one size would fit all if used intelligently by teachers."

Ms. Rienzi set out in September to implement the new school policies in her new fourth grade class. Unfortunately, the children constantly misbehaved, causing delays in the "flow of the day" and the time devoted to the steps in the workshop model. After three months, Ms. Rienzi decided to make a list of all the actions that had caused her to fall behind her schedule. She felt she better be prepared when asked why her class was so far behind the mandated curriculum.

She recounted how Jane and Adam continually got into shouting matches after lunch that would continue for the entire period, slowing the pace of Ms. Rienzi's lesson. To resolve the problem, she told them to let it go, to apologize to each other, to ignore each other, or to just be quiet! She said they wasted time that could not be made up, and if they continued she would contact their parents. This scenario, in one form or another, was played out month after month, with Ms. Rienzi's class falling further and further behind the other fourth-grade classes.

On another occasion, Adam hit another student on the back causing him to yell out, "Get your stinking hands off me!" Ms. Rienzi asked Adam to stop it and to sit down immediately, there were only ten minutes until dismissal. Adam then cursed her and ran out of the room, saying, "I'm going home, I'm not afraid of you." The next day when Adam returned to school, he began to break crayons and throw them at his classmates, who responded by throwing crayons back at Adam. Ms. Rienzi firmly told Adam and others who were throwing crayons that if they did it again she would call the principal.

DISCUSSION TOPICS AND QUESTIONS TO PONDER

1. Identify the immediate problems presented and describe the actions you would take to resolve them.
2. Did the principal explain the new policies clearly? How did his explanation differ from Ms. Rienzi's interpretation?
3. Describe your feelings with regard to the possibility that this so-called workshop model could be used to maintain order in the classroom.
4. Where should Ms. Rienzi's attention have been focused: instruction or classroom management? Why?
5. Are threats effective in encouraging learning? Explain.
6. Explain how a consequence model, such as the assertive discipline approach, could have been used to resolve this case.
7. Explain how a guidance model, such as reality therapy, could have been used to resolve Adam's misconduct.
8. Explain how a group-guidance model, such as judicial discipline, could have been used to resolve this case.
9. What was really at the heart of Ms. Rienzi's problems?
10. Compare your short-term plan to your long-term plan and explain the differences.

WHAT WOULD YOU DO IF ... ?

1. The principal told you were doing a poor job because you were not following the workshop model?
2. The children complained to their parents that you could not manage the class?

3. Adam went to the principal and said you were picking on him?
4. The principal asked you what you thought had to be done to improve learning in your class?
5. The principal said you were the cause of your own problems because you never taught your class proper procedures?

CASE STUDY TWENTY-EIGHT
A DIFFERENTIATED CLASSROOM IN HIGH SCHOOL

Keys to analyzing this case:

- Outline the case using IOSIE.
- Consider your philosophy of education and what you believe is the way children learn.
- What actions have to be taken to make a program effective?

Ms. Cherapond had taught U.S. History at Elwood High School for eighteen years. During that period of time she had come to think of herself as the best lecturer in the school. Her students were always eager to part take in classroom discussions and did well on statewide examinations. This rosy picture of academic success had come to an abrupt end about five years ago with the arrival of students whose first language was not English. In fact, the diversity of languages spoken in the halls and about the building was astonishing; Spanish, Russian, Urdu, and Chinese were but a few. Under a citywide magnet plan, the school had been designated as a special school for international affairs. The school drew students from all over the metropolitan area. To Ms. Cherapond's thinking, the diversity of languages brought a diminution of academic scholarship. She found herself failing more and more students. Nearly 40 percent of her classes could not meet the standards set down in the state guidelines, no matter how hard she worked.

Ms. Cherapond's department chairperson, Mr. Joseph, had encouraged her to implement a different approach to the format she traditionally had used to teach her classes. He wanted her to look at her teaching through a different prism; she could no longer consider herself the font of all wisdom. She should accept the premise that learners are different in many respects and that "one key does not open all doors." The idea was to personalize instruction by meeting the individual needs of a diverse population. Mr. Joseph described this approach as developing a differentiated classroom, one in which students would be held to standards. Teaching should be flexible and shaped to meet the needs of all. Ms. Cherapond had to differentiate her instruction to address this new multicultural student body.

To Ms. Cherapond's ears, this was impractical. She was not going to dumb down the curriculum and create some fuzzy wishy-washy instructional program. It wasn't her fault that her students were not prepared to meet the challenges that she put before them. To her way of thinking, they would just have to fail until the message got across that learning was not going to be a party in her class. Learning was the accumulation of facts, and the one who gathered the most facts would acquire the most knowledge.

The results from the next marking session brought a note from Mr. Joseph to meet in one week. He wished to discuss the appropriate procedures and practices necessary to implement a differentiated classroom. He expected her to be prepared to discuss methods she was going to use to reach her new student population. He was interested in finding out how she grouped for instruction, and if she did not, why? He asked her to prepare a list of the text materials she used in class, such as trade books, videos, transparencies, and electronic materials. He requested she familiarize herself with Gardner's theory of multiple intelligences and prepare a plan for incorporating it into her lesson preparation. He suggested she prepare transparencies to assist visual learners and think about activities for kinesthetic learners. He concluded his note by asking Ms. Cherapond to keep in mind that differentiated instruction was simply a way of thinking about meeting student needs. He was sure that by differentiating her lessons she could improve her classes' performance.

When Ms. Cherapond received the note she could not believe her eyes. How could she gather so much material in one week? What would be the purpose anyway? She would just bring her lecture notes; they had always been good in the past.

DISCUSSION TOPICS AND QUESTIONS TO PONDER

1. Identify the immediate problem and describe the actions you would take to resolve it.
2. Why was Ms. Cherapond failing to meet the needs of her students?
3. Compare Ms. Cherapond's and Mr. Joseph's ideas and educational beliefs.
4. Who should do most of the work in the class, the students or the teacher? What is happening if the teacher is carrying the burden of doing most of the work?
5. Do students learn better when you teach to them or talk with them? Why?
6. Why do children learn more from a hands-on, meaning-based approach than from a rote lecture approach?
7. Would it have made a difference if Ms. Cherapond had offered her students choices in assignments rather than one assignment for the entire class? Why?
8. What was Mr. Joseph attempting to accomplish in the meeting he was going to have with Ms. Cherapond?
9. Did Ms. Cherapond really understand her strengths and weaknesses? Explain.
10. Upon reflection, how would you handle this situation?

WHAT WOULD YOU DO IF . . . ?

1. Students complained that you were culturally insensitive to their needs?
2. The principal said he had spoken to Mr. Joseph and expected you to stop using a lecture method to instruct your class?
3. You were sent for staff development in order to learn how to use the workshop model as a starting point to differentiate your approach to instruction?
4. Your colleagues said that no one had the right to tell you how to teach and you should just ignore Mr. Joseph's directions?
5. You had a conversation with your students in which they told you they wanted a more active class, one with no lecture?

■ ■ ■ ■ ■

CASE STUDY TWENTY-NINE
HOMEWORK IN HIGH SCHOOL

Keys to analyzing this case:

■ Outline the case using IOSIE.
■ Consider a group-guidance approach, such as judicial discipline, as a possible solution to the situation presented in this case study.
■ Reflect on the purposes of homework.
■ Think in terms of long- and short-term objectives.

Mr. Siegel was nearing retirement age. He had taught at Stevenson High School for thirty years. During his tenure he had experienced many things, least of which was the obvious generational shift in the students he taught. There was a time when all he had to do was say it and it was done. Regrettably those days were gone. Students today were more independent and self-directed. To make contact you had to be one step ahead or you would fall two steps behind.

The problem he was facing wasn't the worst that could befall a teacher, it just had never occurred before to the degree in which it was now happening. At least 30 to 40 percent of his students were not doing homework. They were really never prepared. He had attempted to use consequences such as grade reductions and letters home to parents as a means of coercing students to comply with his homework policy, but the percentages remained the same. At lunch one day in the faculty lounge he spoke to a friend of his, Mr. Buel, who claimed he had a similar problem and that he had resolved it to his satisfaction. Mr. Siegel immediately asked Mr. Buel to explain what he did. He said it was simple enough: "I only do self-contained lessons where the assignments are done in class under my supervision. Assignments to be done at home are not mandatory and are only for extra credit." Mr. Siegel flared up and said, "That's ridiculous, homework is the quintessential job of adolescence! A students' responsibility for homework is essentially parallel to an employee's responsibilities to a job. Viewing homework as a job creates a good work ethic that will follow a student into the work world. Homework should be used to reinforce a lesson, or to prepare for a future lesson at home, as the name implies. It is in fact similar to a job: It's not something you want to do, it's something you have to do."

"That sounds great," Mr. Buel replied, "but from what you told me your kids aren't doing homework, so why spin your wheels? With my system you can still reinforce and prepare for the next lesson while encouraging the work ethic of those who do the extra credit choice assignments."

As a result of his discussion with Mr. Buel, Mr. Siegel felt more confused then ever. Should he forget and give up everything he had held for all these years as a history teacher? He reflected on his beliefs; they were clear and concise. Homework furthers learning ability and requires students to discipline themselves as well as learn time management and organizational skills. Long-term group projects help students to learn to collaborate as they would with coworkers. He had to come up with a plan to enhance his assignments as well as encourage his students to do their homework assignments.

The solution he stumbled upon contained three basic components: He would only assign homework that was meaningful and interesting to the students; his assignments would contain hands-on applications that were productive, such as exploring the concept of chronology by creating a family time line; and finally he would ask students how they viewed the importance of homework.

DISCUSSION TOPICS AND QUESTIONS TO PONDER

1. Identify the immediate problems and describe the actions you would take to resolve them.
2. How do you feel about Mr. Buel's solution to the lack of student homework? Does it have a chance for success? Explain.
3. Compare Mr. Siegel's response to Mr. Buel's suggestions. Who made the stronger argument? Why?
4. Consider a compromise between both positions. Describe it.
5. How could a consequence approach have been used successfully in this situation?
6. How could an individual guidance approach have been used?
7. Does Mr. Siegel's plan have a chance for success? Why?
8. How could Mr. Siegel use a group-guidance approach, such as judicial discipline, to resolve this situation?
9. Was Mr. Siegel's final plan realistic? Explain your answer.
10. Upon reflection, what would you do if confronted with this situation?

WHAT WOULD YOU DO IF ... ?

1. Mr. Buel said you are a fool to try to spit into the wind and to just change your homework policy?
2. Other teachers said the same thing Mr. Buel proposed you do?
3. You found that preparing creative homework assignments was time consuming and difficult work?
4. Students didn't like your homework policy and the percentage of students completing homework was worse than before you implemented the new policy?
5. As a result of your group discussion the students decided that no homework should ever be assigned?

■ ■ ■ ■ ■ ■

CASE STUDY THIRTY
ADVANCED PLACEMENT AND HONESTY

Keys to analyzing this case:

- Outline the case using IOSIE.
- Consider a guidance approach or reality therapy as possible solution to the problems presented in this case.
- Think in terms of long-term goals.

Mr. Perrone was an affable man who had spent most of his life in government service. He had been a meat inspector before he decided to change his career and go into teaching. He was an honest man who lived life under a code of strict moral values. He prided himself on being principled, upright, and honorable. As a high school history teacher, he felt he could uphold and pass on these admirable values to future generations. Mr. Perrone was an eclectic scholar, who at an advanced age had reinvented himself. He went back to college, attended a local university career change program, and became a teacher. He learned, through his studies, that appropriate pedagogical procedures and mastery of content were necessary to teach adolescents.

Upon receiving his Masters in Secondary Social Studies, Mr. Perrone was offered a position at Newtown High School, a dream come true. His program consisted of teaching an Advanced Placement American History class, which needed a qualified teacher, and Mr. Perrone had taken courses in college specifically geared to teaching AP classes. Mr. Adler, the social studies chairman, told him that advanced placement classes provide students with the opportunity to experience college-level studies while still in secondary school. The course he was to teach had to be challenging and thought-provoking, while requiring more work and greater depth than a regular course. The course was to be taught as a college-level course. He further explained that eligible juniors or seniors could enroll and receive both high school and college credit. Mr. Perrone told Mr. Adler he was anxious to get started. Mr. Adler said that the previous teacher, Mrs. Robinson, was on maternity leave and did not expect to return to school until next semester. She had left her lesson plans, assignments, and class tests for his use. Mr. Adler said her plans had been refined over the years, and he was sure that Mr. Perrone would have no problem following them.

The students in Mr. Perrone's AP class, consisting of seventeen males and seventeen females, were a delightful group of young people. However, they made it immediately clear to Mr. Perrone that they needed to pass his course and the College Board of New York's test in order to be given appropriate college credit. Mr. Perrone told his students not to worry; they would work together and he was sure they would all do well. He explained that the test was made up of usually eighty multiple-choice questions and some general essay questions based on historical documents. He would prepare them to interpret these documents by using critical thinking assignments. He explained that the test was scored using a rubric, with five as the highest score and one the lowest, with three being the score needed to get college credit. With his introduction completed, Mr. Perrone's classes began at a rapid pace.

Mr. Perrone's best student was Connie Decatur, who stood out because her data-based assignments were flawless. She had all the right answers and was able to synthesize her written responses with real-life situations. This, however, could not be said for the rest of the class. They were struggling, but didn't complain. Mr. Perrone wondered why they were struggling; assignments were handed in on time in impeccable form. Something was wrong. Every time Mr. Perrone questioned students on their answers, he received convoluted responses, it was as if they did not understand what they had written on their papers. Mr. Perrone was convinced that the class was cheating and that Connie was sharing her work with classmates. He spoke to Connie and she said she had done nothing wrong. What was he to do? Fail them all? Report them to the principal and have them

suspended from school? Work on getting Connie to admit her guilt? Mr. Perrone
needed a plan of action.

DISCUSSION TOPICS AND QUESTIONS TO PONDER

1. Identify the immediate problem and describe the actions you would take to re-
    solve it.
2. Whose problem is it really? Why?
3. What should be Mr. Perrone's long-term goal for this class?
4. Describe the actions he can take to achieve that goal.
5. How can he deal with the moral issues presented and still achieve his long-term
    objectives?
6. How could Mr. Perrone use a consequence approach to resolve this situation?
7. How could Mr. Perrone use a group-guidance approach in this case?
8. How would a guidance approach, such as reality therapy, be used in this case?
9. How could each of these approaches be integrated into a solution?
10. Upon reflection, how would you resolve this case?

WHAT WOULD YOU DO IF . . . ?

1. The students denied that they were cheating?
2. Connie said she was innocent and someone else must be cheating?
3. A student came to you privately and said that Connie had a copy of all of Mrs.
    Robinson's assignments from last year and was selling them?
4. You attempted to resolve the issue using a group-guidance approach and the
    students said that everyone cheats?
5. Connie's parents report you to the principal for harassing their daughter and
    calling her a liar?

CASE STUDY THIRTY-ONE
READING IN HIGH SCHOOL

Keys to analyzing this case:

-   Outline the case using IOSIE.
-   Consider the appropriate approach—guidance, group-guidance, or conse-
    quence—that you would use to resolve this situation.
-   Reflect on your role as a subject teacher and content area reading specialist.

Ms. Habeeb had recently graduated from college with a Bachelor of Science in Secondary English Education. She had excelled in literature, especially Victorian authors. Her first weeks at Dickerson High School were a pure delight; she bubbled
over with joy at how her classes were responding to her. Her instructional approach

was to have classes read chapters from their assigned text and come prepared to discuss what they had read the next day. One day she asked them to focus on the elements that go into good fiction. The following day she was shocked to discover that not one of her students had understood her assignment. Carl Georgiadis asked, "What do you mean by elements, is it the same word we use in science? Like when we learned about earth, air, fire, and water?" Ms. Habeeb responded by telling Carl not to be a wise guy and make silly excuses for not reading the assignment. Carl stood up and shouted out, "All you teachers are nuts, all you know is how to make fun of students." He then stormed out of the room and roamed the building. Ms. Habeeb called security and explained that Carl was wandering the halls.

The next day Ms. Habeeb was summoned by her department chairperson, Mrs. Kuncken, to discuss the incident. Mrs. Kuncken asked Ms. Habeeb to explain what had occurred. When Ms. Habeeb finished, Mrs. Kuncken asked her if she knew anything about Carl's background. Ms. Habeeb said she had not had an opportunity to read his cumulative folder or consult with any of his former teachers, and she didn't think it was her job to look into the personal life of a student. Mrs. Kuncken told Ms. Habeeb that she should always attempt to know her students and if she did she might avoid problems such as students running out of classrooms. Carl, Mrs. Kuncken said, was to receive detention and his parents had been called to school for a presuspension hearing.

"Well that is what he deserves," Ms. Habeeb said, "to be punished."

Mrs. Kuncken replied, "No, Ms. Habeeb, I have no desire to punish Carl. He is just suffering the consequences for his actions, which would never have occurred if you had been aware of Carl's story."

"What story are you talking about?"

"Carl was an abused child," Mrs. Kuncken continued, "and comes from a foster home, where he has been making great strides in getting his life on the right track. Carl has severe reading problems and is delayed at least two years. He is finally catching on, but he still has a long way to go."

Ms. Habeeb said, "You mean Carl can't read? Then he doesn't belong in my class. I am not a reading teacher."

"I beg to differ," Mrs. Kuncken responded. "Every teacher is a reading teacher. You have to stop assigning content reading and begin to teach content reading."

"Please, Mrs. Kuncken," Ms. Habeeb said, "Reading is easy."

"Yes, Ms. Habeeb, it is easy, if you already know how to do it."

After the meeting, Ms. Habeeb reflected on what had been said. She could accept the part that she needed to develop more empathy for her students, but was it really her fault that Carl ran out of the room? Shouldn't a sixteen-year-old be responsible for his actions?

Mrs. Kuncken gave Ms. Habeeb guidelines to follow when teaching a direct reading lesson:

- Before giving the assignment, students have to be ready for it.
- Students need to understand the background of, vocabulary in, and purpose of the assignment.
- Students should read the assignment silently.
- Lastly, students should discuss, reread, and follow up the assignment.

Ms. Habeeb thought to herself, "Maybe Mrs. Kuncken is right." She would now be more understanding and teach reading.

DISCUSSION TOPICS AND QUESTIONS TO PONDER

1. Identify the immediate problem and describe what actions you would take to resolve it.
2. Describe your feelings with regard to Ms. Habeeb's views on her role as a teacher.
3. Compare Ms. Habeeb's views with those of Mrs. Kuncken's.
4. Whose argument is stronger? Explain.
5. Design a guidance-focused approach that Ms. Habeeb could use to resolve her problem with Carl.
6. Explain how other resource personnel could be used to assist in solving the immediate and long-range problems presented in this case.
7. Was it fair to impose consequences on Carl? Explain.
8. Explain and analyze any hidden issues in this case.
9. If you were Ms. Habeeb, how would you help Carl to overcome his reading problem? Would you follow Mrs. Kuncken's suggestions?
10. Upon reflection, do you think Ms. Habeeb could change her ways? Why?

WHAT WOULD YOU DO IF . . . ?

1. Carl's foster parents came to school to complain that you had made fun of Carl?
2. Carl said he really liked you and asked you for a date?
3. Mrs. Kuncken observed your classes and said you were not responsive to the needs of your students?
4. Students in the class said you were giving them too much work?
5. Carl asked to transfer out of your class?

■ ■ ■ ■ ■ ▬▬▬▬▬▬▬▬▬▬▬▬▬▬▬▬▬▬

CASE STUDY THIRTY-TWO

DEALING WITH VIOLENT BEHAVIOR IN MIDDLE SCHOOL

Keys to analyzing this case:

- Outline the case using IOSIE.
- Review the risk factors and predictors of youth violence.
- Consider a guidance approach, such as reality therapy, as plausible options for long-term solutions.
- Reflect on the importance of good school relations.

Mr. Pennington was a teacher with a problem. He felt he had made the biggest mistake of his life transferring to the Midlevel Middle School. He had thought that by being closer to his new home in the inner city, life would be easier. In his former school in the outer boroughs of the city, there had been academic problems, and as a result that school was relegated to the lowest rung in the statewide rankings. At Midlevel there were also academic problems, but the real dilemma was the potential for schoolwide violence. Mr. Pennington had experienced children fighting in class over what he believed were gang issues, which seemed to focus on prejudice between the old-time residents and the newcomers. He himself was a newcomer to the area; having recently purchased a beautiful turn of the century mansion, which he was busily renovating. When he brought his concerns to the assistant principal, Mrs. Schiller, who was in charge of discipline, she told Mr. Pennington that he was just responding to rumors and that there had been no threats of violence in the school. In a stern voice Mrs. Schiller said, "There are no gangs at Midlevel and we intend to keep it that way."

The school was located in a neighborhood experiencing gentrification due to the availability of homes, which cost thousands more in other areas. There was a middle-class economic revival through out the Midlevel community. The traditional poverty, community disorganization, and availability of drugs was being forced out of the area by this revitalized spirit and the concern of residents. Mr. Pennington still believed that violence was eminent. He noticed drawings in student notebooks depicting acts of violence. When he questioned the students about their drawings, they would say they were just pictures of action figures on TV.

Isolated graffiti began appearing on some of the buildings surrounding the school, proclaiming "Newbies go to your own home and leave us alone." Mr. Pennington again reported this to Mrs. Schiller, who said the community watch had already reported the graffiti to the police. Mrs. Schiller told Mr. Pennington that the school was safe, secure, and orderly. These conditions, she said, made for a good school environment and were a precondition for learning. She further suggested that it might be a good thing for Mr. Pennington to turn his concern into good classroom lessons that would engage the children and limit any negative ideas that might be circulating.

Mr. Pennington reflected on Mrs. Schiller's remarks and thought that she was putting her head in the sand and didn't want to recognize the signs of potential violence. At that moment Bob Dwyer, a student in Mr. Pennington's fourth-period mathematics class, came running down the hall. He told Mr. Pennington that he was being threatened by the "Bad Street Boys" and was afraid to leave the building. Mr. Pennington knew that Bob was a gossip and had a history of crying wolf. He was a frail, thin boy with a hawklike proboscis that had earned him the nickname of the Nose. His classmates made fun of him, causing him to withdraw from the few social activities he had participated in. Since his parents had broken up, his situation had worsened. Nevertheless, Mr. Pennington felt this was proof that gangs were rampant and he marched with Bob to Mrs. Schiller's office. Mrs. Schiller took Mr. Pennington aside and said she would look into Bob's accusations and act upon them immediately. She also reminded Mr. Pennington that he was not a one-man police force and shouldn't go looking for trouble, because it had been her experience that people will usually find what they are looking for.

DISCUSSION TOPICS AND QUESTIONS TO PONDER

1. Identify the immediate problem and describe the actions you would take to resolve it.

2. Describe the possible at-risk areas for violence that are evidenced in this case.
3. Compare Mr. Pennington's and Mrs. Schiller's attitude toward potential violence.
4. Explain the legal obligations at play in this case study. Were Mr. Pennington's concerns justified?
5. How would you evaluate Mrs. Schiller's handling of the incident with Bob Dwyer?
6. What other supports could have been used to rectify the situation?
7. Why was it a mistake for Mr. Pennington to place all his faith on what Bob said before all the facts were known?
8. How could reality therapy have been employed in this case?
9. How could the adversarial relationship between Mr. Pennington and Mrs. Schiller have been ameliorated?
10. Upon reflection, how could parents and community support be instrumental to a solution?

WHAT WOULD YOU DO IF . . . ?

1. Mrs. Schiller claims you are an unsatisfactory teacher since you are meddling in issues that should not be your concern?
2. Bob is telling the truth and he is sent home alone?
3. Bob's parents accuse you and Mrs. Schiller of not protecting their son and allowing him to be beaten?
4. The police have been summoned to investigate your motives in allowing Bob to go home alone and not calling his parents or the authorities?
5. Mrs. Schiller apologizes and says she should have listened to you?

MAJOR CAUSES OF VIOLENCE

The purpose of this Appendix is to present some of the major causes of violence in our society. Causes of school violence, from bullying to gangs, suicide, sexual harassment, and child abuse are explored from a teacher's perspective. The potential violent problems children bring to school must be dealt with before they ignite into violence, as with Columbine High School and Red Lake High School in Minnesota (Hurst, 2005).

WHAT SOME KIDS BRING TO THE SCHOOL

Children come to school with a myriad of problems. They come from dysfunctional families, where hope and success are just words that appear in newspaper columns. They come to school lacking social skills and the self-discipline necessary for good behavior. Teachers, on the other hand, tend to favor docility, which at times is mistaken for good character. Many want to seed their classes with children who do what they are told. What these teachers appear to value is what children say they dislike: blind obedience. Mager and Pipe (1997)* list these reasons why children don't perform:

- They don't know what's expected.
- They don't have the tools, space, or authority.
- They don't get feedback about performance quality.
- They're punished when they do it right.
- They're rewarded when they do wrong.
- They're ignored whether they do it right or wrong.
- They don't know how to do it.

*© 1997, CEP Press, 1100 Johnson Ferry Road, Suite 150, Atlanta, GA 30342. *www.ceppress.com* 800-558-4237. Adapted from *Analyzing Performance Problems* by Robert F. Mager and Peter Pipe. All rights reserved. No portion of these materials may be reproduced in any manner without the express written consent from The Center for Effective Performance Inc.

Teachers should be concerned with what children bring to school and why they don't perform. If we are alert and act in a caring fashion we can meet student needs and avoid the pitfalls of mismanaged classrooms where violent acts can occur.

YOUTH VIOLENCE

Studies Report Declining Rate of School Violence

There have been many tragedies involving student violence that have caused great concern. This concern has given credence to the general impression that school crime and violence are out of control. This is not so. Crime in the United States has declined over the past decade in nearly every category, including school crime (Spitzer, 1999). Unfortunately, while juvenile crime rates have dropped, youth homicide rates have more than doubled and suicide rates were up (Dohrn, 1997).

Since 1992, crime against students, including theft, rape, sexual assault, robbery, aggravated assault, and simple assault has decreased by nearly a third. There were 101 incidents per 1,000 students in 1998, compared to 144 crimes per 1,000 in 1989 (U.S. Department of Education, 2001).

The U.S. Departments of Education and Justice maintain that schools remain among the safest places for children. In the year 2000, 90 percent of the nation's schools reported no serious violent crime, and 43 percent said they experienced no crime at all. A companion document, *Indicators of School Crime and Safety 2000* (National Center for Educational Statistics, 2004), revealed a significant decline in the number of high school students reported for carrying weapons to school. Weapons reported brought to school declined from 12 percent in 1993 to 7 percent in 1999.

The U.S. Department of Education reported in 2002 that school violence significantly declined since 1993. The numbers of violent acts, instances of students bring firearms to school, and students' tendencies to join school-related gangs have all decreased. Students are at greater risk of suffering from violence outside schools than from within schools (Twemlow, Fonagy, Sacco, O'Toole, and Vernberg, 2002).

Causes of Youth Violence

There are many explanations, none of which address all of the possible causes. Some see *societal factors,* such as poverty, lack of parental supervision, child abuse, domestic violence, and family breakups, as well as *biological factors,* from alcohol to drugs, as primary causes. Others see the *exposure to violence* in the media and on the Internet as factors in desensitizing children to violence. Some even implicate schools as contributors to school violence. Critics even blame teachers as enabling violence by denying and minimizing, excusing, blaming others, and avoiding or ignoring its existence (Remboldt, 1998).

Violent behavior in whatever form it occurs is essentially symptomatic of *psychiatric disorders*. Conduct Disorder, a state of constant disregard for social conventions eventually leading to criminal and antisocial behavior is one of the most frequently diagnosed causes cited in understanding the cause for violence among youth. Substance abuse and dependence also contribute to violent acts. Drugs reduce inhibitions and are dealt within an environment that nurtures violence. A diagnosis of any specific condition does not constitute a prediction of violent behavior. In fact, psychiatric prediction of violence in any setting is difficult. Assumptions should not be made about any student without conducting a careful and thorough evaluation (Schlozman, 2002).

School factors that influence the level of crime are overcrowding, high student-to-teacher ratios, irrelevant curriculums, little academic achievement, apathy, poor facilities, and limited parental support (Rossman and Morley, 1996). Strong indicators of potential violent behavior are evidenced in a school environment that has a poor organization, and in a student's poor academic performance. Schools that tolerate physical and social aggression are going to see outbreaks of violent acts (Schlozman, 2002).

Predictors of Youth Violence

Dwyer, Osher, and Warger (1998) identified a number of still-common risk factors through a clinical interview process. These risk factors warrant immediate attention, even if the student is perceived as nonviolent. Remember, risk factors cannot be used to profile violent individuals; they do not mean a person is violent, only at risk.

HIGH-RISK FACTORS FOR VIOLENCE

- **Violent drawings or writing** indicate that the individual is in need of counseling to assess the root cause of these expressions of written violence.
- **Threats of violence** to others should be immediately assessed and appropriate intervention actions taken. Under no circumstances should threats be ignored.
- **An aggressive history of past violent behavior** indicates that these students are at greater risk for future violent behaviors.
- There is a high correlation between the **torture of animals** and violent behaviors.
- **A relationship breakup** such as a jilted boyfriend or girlfriend often leads to violent behavior directed at themselves or others.
- **Isolation** has been strongly correlated with violent behaviors toward school peers. Students reporting feelings of being isolated from others should be considered at greater risk.
- **Reports of being harassed or picked on** indicate that the student's complaints should be assessed to determine whether or not he or she intends to harm or fantasizes about harming others.

- **Withdrawal** from peers and familial supports can indicate the student is experiencing any of a number of concerns, from depression to helplessness, which warrant evaluation and intervention.
- Students with **inappropriate use or access to firearms,** as demonstrated by shooting at people, homes, or vehicles, or have improper, unsupervised firearm access have a clear potential to harm others and act violently.
- **Substance abuse** does not necessarily predict violent behavior, but students who use psychoactive substances often fail to think logically and experience increased impulsivity. Thus, there exists a strong correlation between substance abuse and violent behaviors.
- **Familial stressors** or family problems can engender feelings of frustration, anger, and hopelessness among students as well as adults.
- **Called different** by peers as weird, strange, or geeky indicate that the individual has an increased risk for violent behavior.
- **Low school interest** indicates a failure to perform in school, which could lead to frustration and, in combination with other factors, violence.

Students who have many of these identified high-risk factors may be experiencing significant emotional problems. These students are at risk of being violent and are unlikely to function adequately without counseling. These thirteen risk factors will not identify every violent student; they are only meant to act as aids in evaluating students at risk of violence.

Can we really determine the causes for youth violence? We can clearly see that there are high risk factors, but can these factors be translated into causes? Identifying and addressing the predictors at appropriate points in development is important if we are to prevent violence. Unfortunately there have been few high quality longitudinal studies of the predictors of youth violence. The Office of Juvenile Justice and Delinquency Prevention (Egley and Arjunan, 2002) conducted a longitudinal study for two years in which they collected data as to the risk factors that preceded violence. The predictors were arranged in five domains: individual, family, school, peer-related, and community and neighborhood factors.

1. **The individual factors** were associated with personality deficits such as hyperactivity, concentration problems, restlessness, and risk taking. Involvement in other forms of violent behavior due to aggressiveness and early initiation to violent behavior were correlated to beliefs and attitudes favorable to deviant or antisocial behavior.
2. **Family factors** were related to parental criminality, child maltreatment, and poor family management practices in general. The low levels of parental involvement led to poor family bonding and conflict as well as poor parental attitudes regarding substance abuse, violence, and parent child separation.
3. **School factors** such as academic failure, low bonding to school, truancy and dropping out of school, and frequent school transitions were seen as predictors of violence.

4. **Peer-related factors** such a delinquent siblings, delinquent peers, and gang memberships were also viewed as predictors of violence.
5. **Community and neighborhood factors** such as poverty, community disorganization, availability of drugs and firearms, combined with neighborhood adults involved in crime with an exposure to violence and racial prejudice were found to be predictors of violence.

Unfortunately, the most that this meta-analysis study could report was that the larger the number of risk factors to which an individual is exposed, the greater the probability that the individual will engage in violent behavior. It further suggested that targeting interventions at groups of risk factors rather than individual components might be more effective in preventing violence (Office of Juvenile Justice and Delinquency Prevention, 2003–2004).

School Intervention

Schools react to crime and violence by relying on policing violence, violence prevention, or a combination of both. The **policing approach** is characterized as a get-tough approach that entails vigilance, tough punishment, and zero tolerance. Techniques include increasing police presence in schools, hiring security guards, installing metal detectors, and allowing school personnel to conduct random, unannounced searches of school lockers. Security cameras, two-way radios, electronic surveillance, and ID cards are but a few of the means used to police students.

A **teaching guidance approach** urges teachers to empower students to control their own actions, and is based on the premise that coercion fails to influence those who are already exposed to violence and abuse on a daily basis. Teachers must face their own prejudices and fears in order to teach students appropriate behavior. The American Psychological Association (ACT Against Violence, 2002) says that violence is a learned behavior and that individuals can be taught nonviolence as well as violence. The key is to begin early and involve the community in teaching nonviolence through violence prevention programs.

The **zero-tolerance approach** grew out of national drug enforcement efforts that aimed at punishing all identified drug transgressions with the same severe punishments, regardless of circumstances. This policy in schools has led to students being suspended or expelled from schools for inconsequential offenses. A sensible application of zero-tolerance policies would hold offenders accountable for their actions and have them accept appropriate consequences. The proper use of zero-tolerance policies can be a useful tool in the effort to prevent school violence (Ewing, 2000).

The literature that advocates zero tolerance in schools stems not only from drug enforcement but also from the Gun-Free Schools Act of 1994. That Act required states that received federal funds to mandate expulsion from school for a minimum of one year for any student bringing a weapon to school. The literature also points out irrational actions taken by schools that have interpreted the Act to mean that any child, regardless of age, should be expelled for bringing a gun to school, the classic case being the first grader who took his father's licensed gun to school for show and tell. Expulsion is particularly destructive since it limits the opportunity for an appropriate education for the offending child. We need adults to talk with students rather than just punish them by limiting their access to education (First, 2000).

The *Interim Report on the Prevention of Targeted Violence in Schools* (Vossekuil et al., 2000) came to the following conclusions.

1. Incidents of targeted violence at school are rarely impulsive. The attacks are typically the end result of an understandable and often discernible process of thinking and behavior.
2. Prior to most incidents, the attacker told someone about his idea and/or plan.
3. There is no accurate or useful profile for the "school shooter."
4. Most attackers had previously used guns and had access to them.
5. Most shooting incidents were not resolved by law enforcement intervention.
6. In many cases, other students were involved in some capacity.
7. In a number of cases, students who were bullied played a key role in the attack.

Violence prevention programs have been implemented in attempts to avoid the conditions that contribute to school violence, such as school cultures and student attitudes. Violence prevention programs aim to teach youngsters how to handle conflict in nonviolent ways and establish school environments that encourage peaceful behavior. *The 1998 Annual Report on School Safety* (U.S. Department of Education, 2001) provides the following list of suggestions to help schools create safe environments:

1. Provide strong administrative support for assessing and enhancing school safety.
2. Redesign the school facility to eliminate dark, secluded, and unsupervised spaces.
3. Devise a system for reporting and analyzing violent and noncriminal incidents.
4. Design an effective school discipline policy.
5. Build a partnership with local law enforcement.
6. Enlist trained school security professionals to design and maintain the school security system.
7. Train school staff, including support staff, in all aspects of violence prevention.
8. Provide all students with access to school psychologists or counselors.
9. Provide crisis response services.
10. Implement schoolwide education and training on avoiding and preventing violence and violent behavior.

11. Use alternate school settings for educating violent and weapon-carrying students.
12. Create a climate of tolerance.
13. Provide appropriate educational services to all students.
14. Reach out to communities and businesses to assist in improving the safety of students.
15. Actively involve students in making decisions about school policies and programs.
16. Prepare and distribute to the public an annual report on school crime and safety.

In situations where violence needs to be deterred, individual teachers can adapt these suggestions by helping develop schoolwide discipline policies and training on how to manage potentially violent situations (National Center for Educational Statistics, 2004). Review your school's code of conduct and create a classroom code of conduct with the students, using their own words. Educate yourself with regard to preventing violence. The key to deterring violence and enhancing safety in classrooms can be boiled down to one word: *care.* When you demonstrate to students that you care, violent acts are highly unlikely to occur.

BULLYING

Effective Strategies for the Prevention of Bullying

Although school shootings of students have gained significant national attention, more routine forms of student violence continue to plague our nation's schools and streets. These less sensational but equally harmful violent behaviors, such as bullying, deserve appropriate response. Bullying is simply defined as when a more powerful person hurts, frightens, or intimidates a weaker person on a continual and deliberate basis. Bullying is also divided into three distinct forms: physical (hitting, shoving, poking, tripping, and slapping), verbal (name calling, insults, putdowns, and racist remarks, teasing), and social (persuading other students to exclude or reject someone) (Ritter, 2002). Bullying is also defined as the exposure of a student repeatedly and over time to negative actions on the part of one or more other students (Olweus, 2003). There are, however, basic concepts that provide insight into understanding bullies and bullying, including:

1. Bullying takes at least two people: bully and victim.
2. Bullies like to feel strong and superior.
3. Bullies enjoy having power over others.
4. Bullies use their power to hurt other people.

Bullying is not a normal, natural part of childhood; it is a deliberate act that hurts young victims both emotionally and physically. It also affects the people around them by distracting, intimidating, and upsetting them. Bullying in the classroom prevents students from learning and teachers from teaching. The role of the teacher in these situations is to teach bullies better social skills, and to teach the victims and others the skills necessary to avoid the actions of bullies. This can be done through a process called *skillstreaming,* through peer mediation, or through conflict resolution skills. Conflict should be viewed by the teacher as normal, and as an opportunity to develop constructive skills to deal with it. Patricia Phillips (1997) describes how her high school attempted to alleviate and resolve conflicts by establishing a "conflict wall" on which was written the classic steps to conflict resolution.

CONFLICT RESOLUTION SKILLS

1. Cool down. Don't try to resolve a conflict when you are angry. Take time out and attempt to resole the conflict when cooler heads prevail.
2. Describe the conflict. Each person should be given the opportunity to explain what happened in his or her own words. (Make no judgments!)
3. Describe what caused the conflict. Be specific and insist upon exact chronological order. (Don't place blame!)
4. Describe the feelings raised by the conflict.
5. Listen carefully and respectfully while the other person is talking.
6. Brainstorm solutions to the conflict.
7. Try your solution.
8. If it doesn't work try another solution.

Briggs (1996) advocates extending social-emotional learning by viewing incidents of conflict as teachable moments for social learning.

If students cannot resolve a conflict, have them agree to disagree; sometimes that is the best that you can do. Violent students often have hypersensitivity toward criticism. They often claim they were being teased, harassed, or being picked on by those they were violent toward. When fifteen-year-old Charles Williams walked into his high school in Santee, California, and sprayed his classmates with bullets from his father's gun, he claimed afterward that he believed nobody liked him because they teased and bullied him every day. Bullying turned out to be a prime factor in two-thirds of thirty-seven school shooting incidents, as reported by Debra Viadero (2003) and the National Center for Educational Statistics (2004). According to Viadero, the shooters all felt they had been persecuted, bullied, threatened, attacked, or injured by others. There appears to be a clear connection between bullying and school violence.

Myths about Bullying Checklist

Many commonly held beliefs about bullying have been recently seen as false, and that childhood assumptions are just that, assumptions.

- Bullying is just teasing.
- Some people deserve to be bullied.
- Only boys are bullies.
- People who complain about bullies are babies.
- Bullying is a normal part of growing up.
- Bullies will go away if you ignore them.
- All bullies have low self-esteem. That's why they pick on others.
- It's tattling to tell an adult when you're being bullied.
- The best way to deal with a bully is by fighting or trying to get even.
- People who are bullied might hurt for a while, but they'll get over it.

(Note the sixth and tenth statements may be true sometimes; all the other statements are false.)

Olweus (2003) disputes several common assumptions about the causes of bullying. He found that many ideas about the causes of bullying receive little or no support when confronted with empirical data. Students who wear glasses, are overweight, or speak differently are not more likely to become victims of bullies. Olweus' research has shown that those who are passive or submissive tend to become victims almost 85 percent of the time. Aggressive victims—those who have a provocative feature to their personality, which makes them a target—account for the rest.

Halting Bullying at School

The National Education Association (NEA) developed programs entitled "Quit It" and "Bullyproof," made up of interactive materials with curricula that highlight discussions and role-playing. The reading and writing activities are aimed at educating children about what kinds of behaviors are hurtful and how to deal with harassment (Froschi, Sprung, and Mullin-Rindler, 2001; Stein and Sjostrom, 2001). While violent incidents are still relatively uncommon, harassment is widespread. A National Institute of Child Health and Human Development (NICHD, 2001) study found that 13 percent of children in grades six through ten had taunted, threatened, or were physically aggressive toward classmates, while 11 percent were the targets of such behavior. Six percent said they bullied others and were bullied themselves. Boys were more likely to be bullies or victims of bullying than girls who were more frequently the targets of malicious rumors, sexual harassment, and jeers.

While the stereotype is that bullies have low self-esteem, they're often self-confident (Posey, 1995). In fact, bullies are often popular and tend to make friends easily. But if bullies feel slighted, they may be tempted to take it out on someone who can't fight back. The reason for these actions is based in familiar coping mechanisms that bullies have learned to function with. Many bullies come from homes where they're harassed themselves, they tend to perform poorly at school, and, by age twenty-four, 60 percent of former bullies have been convicted of a crime.

Victims, on the other hand, generally have poor social skills and few friends. They may be physically smaller than their peers and act and look different. The psychological trauma of recurring harassment puts victims at risk of suffering from depression or low self-esteem as an adult. The younger the child the more likely he is to suffer from bullying. A study done by the National Threat Assessment Center found that of the thirty-seven school shootings since 1974, attackers felt persecuted, bullied, threatened, or attacked. In more than half of the rampages, revenge was the motivation (Vossekuil et al., 2000).

Charles Williams, the fifteen-year-old Santee, California student accused of killing two classmates and wounding thirteen others also was tormented and bullied. Student witnesses said schoolmates burned him with cigarette lighters and accused him of being a faggot. Even when he announced that he planned to "pull a Columbine," two students called him a wimp and dared him to do it (Reaves, 2001). Early intervention might have been able to prevent this tragedy. Training in anger management, impulse control, appreciation of diversity, and mediation and conflict resolution skills can help prevent violence.

The American Medical Association (Ritter, 2002) claims bullying can damage a child as much as child abuse. The AMA has asked doctors to be vigilant for signs that their young patients might be victims of bullying or be bullies themselves. To support their request they claim that half of all children in the United States are bullied at some point in their lives, and one in ten is victimized on a regular basis. In order to identify if a patient is being bullied, the AMA suggests that parents and doctors ask the following questions:

1. Have you ever been teased at school? How long has this been going on?
2. Do you know of other children who have been teased?
3. Have you ever told your teacher about the teasing? What happens?
4. What kinds of things do children tease you about?
5. Do you have nicknames at school?
6. Have you ever been teased because of your illness, handicap, or disability, or for looking different than other kids?
7. At recess, do you usually play with other children or by yourself?

It can be concluded from the AMA report that bullying is just as damaging and insidious as early sexual encounters or drug abuse. The report found that bullies often manifest more violent behavior with age. They tend to suffer from depression, suicidal behavior, and alcoholism as they grow older, while their victims show signs of low self-esteem, have difficulty making or keeping friends, have trouble sleeping, unexplained stomach pains, headaches, and depression (Ritter, 2002).

Dealing with the Bully

There are two things a teacher can do when faced with a bully. First, the teacher must recognize that a student is a victim of a bully; second, the teacher should know how to neutralize a bully. The key indicators for a child at risk follow.

- The child's grades begins to fall;
- a child shows a decrease in interest for school in general;
- a child feigns illness, such as frequent headaches or stomachaches;
- a child chooses ubiquitous routes home, perhaps hiding the fact that he is a victim of a bully;
- a child claims to have lost books, money, or other belongings without a good explanation;
- a child is caught stealing or asking for extra money; or
- a child has unexplained injuries, bruises, or torn clothing.

Bullying may be the cause for any or all of these indicators.

According to Frankel (1996), the way to neutralize a bully is to get as much information as possible and establish consequences if the bullying continues. Frankel also gives recommendations how a major tool of the bully—the victim—can be dealt with. He states that the teacher should get as many details as possible from the bullied student, allowing for expression of feelings in preparation for problem solving. The teacher is also encouraged to show the victim how to make fun of the teasing by using statements such as:

So what?

Can't you think of anything else to say?

I heard that one in kindergarten.

That's so old it's from the Stone Age.

I fell off my dinosaur when I first heard that.

Tell me when you get to the funny part.

And your point is?

The teacher then must follow up by asking the student who used the technique how well it worked. Olweus (2003) has developed four basic principles for adults to assist in the prevention of bullying:

1. Provide warm positive interest and involvement.
2. Provide consistent application of nonpunitive, nonphysical sanctions for unacceptable behavior or violations of rules.
3. Establish firm limits on unacceptable behavior.
4. Act as authorities and role models.

GANGS

The Problem

A great deal of school violence is related to the growth of gangs in various communities. Past research has demonstrated that it is imperative for school administrators, teachers, and concerned parents and community groups to meet with gang leaders. At these meetings, gang leaders should be asked how to make the school a neutral zone for gang members. School leadership should deal with gang leaders in a respectful but firm manner. Under no circumstances are gangs to be permitted to represent their gangs in school by wearing special colors, hats, clothing, or any other symbols. Even though the use of beepers, cell phones, and headphones has become exceedingly difficult to enforce, these items should not be permitted on school grounds. Gang-related graffiti must be removed from all school property. Rules can and should be established by school authorities, and gang leaders consulted as to how they can ensure that the rules are followed. Neighborhood organizations in communities where gangs are prevalent should be called upon to participate. Often their recommendations make the difference between a successful and a failed antiviolence program. By following this process, gang members can be encouraged to redirect their sense of leadership in a positive direction (Curwin, 1997).

Gangs are notorious for getting people to join their organizations by meeting their needs. They provide outlets for marginalized youths to socialize, control territory, and release aggression (Johnson and Muhlhausen, 2005). Gangs are quite apt at using a variety of recruitment tactics, including promising children clothes, shoes, drugs, parties, and money to help pay off their family's bills. They also use sex or the promise of sex to obtain members. The excitement and adventure of gang life, combined with intimidation and threats, make for a fine recruiting campaign. Peer pressure and the requisite status of being a gang member are aided by various symbols (tattoos, uniforms, and so on) to convince youngsters to join gangs. Early discussions with children about the negative consequences of gang membership and providing them with positive ways to get their personal needs met can protect them from gang recruitment efforts. A specially trained school safety coordinator, whose function is to coordinate antiviolence programs and to respond to crisis situations by offering counseling and mediation, is a step in the right direction.

Preventing the Recruitment of Gang Members

Gangs recruit members from youth between the ages of twelve and twenty-five, with the average age for recruitment being seventeen. Many teens join gangs because they are bored, lacking in purpose, or looking for a way to belong (Egley and Arjunan, 2002). But there are other options for young people: sports, recreational, and after-school programs are a great chance to meet new people, explore new interests, develop new talents and skills, and to connect with people who really care about their well-being. Anyone can be targeted for recruitment into a gang, including young people who

- have suffered from drug and alcohol abuse in their families;
- come from broken families;
- are doing poorly in school;
- are truant from school;

- need money;
- live in neighborhoods where gangs exist;
- are weak-willed;
- have low self-esteem; and/or
- show violent tendencies toward adults/authority.

Gangs also go after young members because they are less likely to be suspected of dealing drugs, and laws for drugs are less severe for nonadults and children. Young members will not get as harsh a jail term as teens or an adult. Children tend to trust, and have a psychological need to be liked and loved. Gang recruiters inherently realize this and take advantage of children because they are more naive and can be easily intimated. Gangs support themselves in a variety of illegal ways, including:

- trading illegal weapons;
- selling drugs;
- robberies, stealing cars;
- using extortion;
- promoting prostitution (homosexual and heterosexual); and/or
- selling stolen goods.

Gangs are organized in many different ways and manners. Traditionally, youth gangs have been organized by ethnicity or along racial lines in some turf-based community. Gang leadership can involve different generations of a family, from fathers to sons and cousins and uncles. Other gangs may be loosely structured around some common goal or ideal. People leave gangs for a variety of reasons; the prime reasons are fear of being injured or killed, or getting tired of being put in jail. Some members never really wanted to be in a gang, while others worry about hurting their families. Those who succeed in leaving seem to have found some form of God in their lives.

Effective preventative antigang strategies in schools must involve the entire educational community (Egley and Arjunan, 2002). Effective prevention requires that schools acknowledge a gang presence and establish a coordinated effort to actively investigate its extent and accurately determine who the members are, what they do, and where they congregate. Preventing gang activity is a protracted trial-and-error activity in which many different tactics may need to be employed.

Helping the Victim of Gang Violence

To help the victim of gang violence, the teacher should intervene according to the established policies of the school. If no policies exists, one should be established as soon as possible. In the meantime, students should be encouraged to avoid areas where potential conflict exists. The authorities should be notified immediately with regard to the situation and the teacher's fears. Finally, the teacher should follow up by establishing clear lines of communication with students.

SUICIDE PREVENTION

Suicide Facts

Suicide is an ever-growing problem in our society. The rates of adolescent suicide have quadrupled in the past fifty years. Suicide is presently the third leading cause of death among U.S. adolescents aged fifteen to nineteen. The statistics are startling: 61 percent of all suicides in the United States are accomplished by firearms; hanging and strangulation account for 15 percent; gas poisoning, 7 percent; and other forms, including drug overdose, 10 percent (Suicide Prevention, 2005). Each year 2 percent of girls and 1 percent of boys attempt suicide. Boys are four times more successful than girls in committing suicide. (Bostic, Rustuccia, and Schlozman, 2001; O'Carroll, Potter, and Mercy, 1994). The facts about youth and suicide provide a clear picture of the problem as it presently exists.

1. Suicide rate in young people has continually increased.
2. Suicide is uncommon in children under the age of ten, but its incidence increases after the onset of puberty and peaks at young adulthood.
3. There are many more attempted suicides than completed suicides.
4. Many youths have sought help within the previous month before the suicide.
5. There is an increased risk if the youth has a previous history of attempted suicide.
6. Many completed youth suicides are well planned and intentional.
7. Suicide has a major impact on family members and the youth's peers.
8. Copycat suicides can occur and may follow dramatic portrayals of suicides on television programs or media items (Suicide Prevention, 2005).

Warning Signs of Suicide Risk: Death or Terminal Illness of a Relative or Friend

There are five warning signs of suicide risk, according to the National Mental Health Information Center (2002):

1. divorce, separation, broken relationship, stress on family
2. loss of health, real or imaginary
3. loss of job, home, money, status, self-esteem, or personal security
4. alcohol or drug abuse
5. depression; in young people, depression may be masked by hyperactivity or acting out

Behavioral, Emotional, and Personal Indicators

It is important to understand that a child may have one or more indicators and *not* be at risk for suicide. However, the continued presence of an indicator or the presence of several indicators in combination should alert school personnel to the possibility of suicide risk. All indications of suicide, whether behavioral, emotional, or personal need to be taken seriously and addressed immediately. Behavioral indicators include:

- previous suicide attempts;
- verbal or written statements expressing suicidal tendencies;
- self-destructive behavior (for example, self-inflicted burns, cuts, and reckless or dangerous behavior);
- use of drugs and/or alcohol;
- isolation and/or withdrawal;
- school failure and/or truancy;
- deteriorating school functioning;
- neglect of personal welfare or appearance;
- running away from home;
- disciplinary crisis, such as suspension or arrest;
- unusual or prolonged crying;
- giving away personal belongings;
- inappropriately saying goodbye;
- changes in normal behavior;
- increasingly argumentative or aggressive; and/or
- eating disorders or a change in eating habits

Emotional indicators include:

- depression;
- strong and persistent bereavement concerns;
- loss of reality boundaries, or hearing voices;
- loss of emotions, increase in apathy;
- panic attacks or anxiety disorders;
- low self-esteem or extensive self-criticism;
- feelings of hopelessness; and/or
- exposure to violence or trauma.

Researchers have found that more than 90 percent of child and adolescent suicide victims had a diagnosable psychiatric disorder at the time of their death (Shaffer and Craft, 1999). Depression is the most common psychiatric disorder among youth who attempt or commit suicide. The interval between the start of depression and suicide averages seven years.

Some depressed individuals claim that self-mutilation makes them briefly feel better. By cutting or scratching themselves, they gain a sense of self-control and a way to express their bad feelings. Some therapists advise having the individual write their bad feelings on paper and then destroying the paper. Other personal indicators of suicide include:

- serious illness of oneself or a family member;
- unwanted pregnancy;
- sexual identity concerns;

- a recent humiliating event;
- family problems, including child abuse or neglect, sexual abuse, domestic violence;
- an interpersonal conflict or loss, usually with parents or a romantic relationship;
- ongoing family conflict;
- physical or sexual abuse; and/or
- impending legal or disciplinary matters.

Responding to Potentially Suicidal Students

Responding to cries for help is the responsibility of all involved. Response should be immediate, with follow-up by a trained professional. Below are six useful strategies for responding to a potentially suicidal student.

1. Treat the situation as an emergency and speak with school psychologists, guidance counselors, or social workers to decide on a course of action.
2. Follow through with a mental health clinician.
3. If a student describes suicidal thoughts, ask the student what he or she wishes would happen by this act.
4. There is no need to inquire into specific causes. It is better simply to let the student speak and to use validating comments such as, "It really hurts when someone breaks up with you," or "That sounds scary." Letting students find solutions often diminishes their fears of humiliation.
5. Never challenge the student or call his bluff; this could be disastrous.
6. If asked if you ever had similar feelings, respond, "Would that change your situation?" This focuses attention on the student and not on the educator.

Preventing Suicide

What can I do to help someone who may be suicidal? The answer is to take all signals seriously. Remember, suicidal behavior is a cry for help. We should be able to distinguish between myths and reality.

- **Myth:** "The people who talk about it don't do it." Studies have found that more than 75 percent of all completed suicides did things in the few weeks or months prior to their deaths to indicate to others that they were in deep despair. Anyone expressing suicidal feelings needs immediate attention.
- **Myth:** "Anyone who tries to kill himself has got to be crazy." Perhaps 10 percent of all suicidal people are psychotic or have delusional beliefs about reality. Most suicidal people suffer from depression, a recognized mental illness.
- **Myth:** "Those problems weren't enough to commit suicide over." It's not how bad the problem is, but how badly it's hurting the person who has it.
- **Myth:** "If someone is going to kill themselves, nothing can stop them." The fact that a person is still alive is sufficient proof that part of him wants to live. The suicidal person is ambivalent. Part of him wants not so much death as he wants the pain to end.

Suicide prevention is not a last-minute activity. Your willingness to give and get help sooner rather than later is essential to prevention. Suicidal people are afraid that trying to get help will bring them more pain or punishment. Your role is to constructively involve yourself on the side of life. Always listen but never offer or accept a deal to keep your knowledge of suicidal thoughts secret. Give the person every opportunity to unburden his troubles and ventilate his feelings. You don't need to say much since there are no magic words. Practice patience, sympathy, and acceptance while avoiding arguments or giving advice. A good practice to follow if the signals are present is to simply ask, "Are you having thoughts of suicide?" It is a myth that talking about suicide may give someone the idea to do it. People already have the idea. By asking this question you show that you care and that you take the individual seriously. It also shows you are willing to share his pain by giving him the opportunity to discharge painful feelings. Further actions you can take include the following:

- If the person is acutely suicidal, do not leave him alone.
- If the means are present, try to get rid of them. Detoxify the area.
- Urge professional help and let the person know you care and want to maintain contact.
- Agree to no secrets; when and if you are told not to tell anyone, remember that this is the part of the individual that wants to avoid more pain. It also is the part that wants to stay alive. That is the part you deal with.
- Do not try to go it alone—get professional help.

Responding to a student's suicide is very difficult because of the emotional component involved with the death of a young person. You must use tact and follow the wishes of the family, including:

- Only give out as much information as the family will allow.
- Deal with small groups to assist them to grieve appropriately.
- Place a card or book of remembrances for the family in a quiet, private spot, such as the school library, for about a month; this allows students to address their feelings of loss to the family. Do not advocate memorials, as they tend to focus on the self-destructive act and validate it. (Fraser, 1998)

CHILD ABUSE

Definitions of Child Abuse and Child Maltreatment

Until recently, child abuse has been one of the most ignored acts of our society. Most would rather believe it did not exist than deal with it. Society especially tends to deny those aspects of abuse that have traditionally been ignored, such as sexual, emotional, and educational abuse. The classical definition of **child abuse** is that an abused child is one less than eighteen years of age whose parent or other person legally responsible for his or her care does the following.

1. Inflicts or allows to be inflicted upon the child serious physical injury;
2. creates or allows to be created a substantial risk of physical injury; and/or
3. commits or allows to be committed against the child a sexual offense as defined in the penal law.

The classical definition of a **maltreated child** is one less than eighteen years of age whose physical, mental, or emotional condition has been impaired or is in danger of becoming impaired as a result of the failure of the parent or other person legally responsible for his or her care to exercise a minimum degree of care:

1. supplying the child with adequate food, clothing, shelter, education, or medical or surgical care, through financially able to do so or offered financial or other reasonable means to do so;
2. providing the child with proper supervision or guardianship;
3. unreasonably inflicting, or allowing to be inflicted, harm or a substantial risk thereof, including the infliction of excessive corporal punishment;
4. using a drug or drugs;
5. using alcoholic beverages to the extent that he loses self-control of his actions; and/or
6. committing any other act of a similarly serious nature requiring the aid of the Family Court. (Social Services Law, Sec. 412) (NYS Family Court Act Sec. 1012 (e) (f))

The following chart of physical and behavioral indicators of child abuse and neglect must not be looked at in isolation but viewed as part of an overall pattern when one is attempting to understand child abuse. The easiest way to fathom child abuse is to break it down into five general categories: physical abuse, physical neglect, sexual abuse, emotional maltreatment, and educational neglect. Table A.1 offers a ready reference for the classroom teacher to diagnose given situations that unfortunately, for many of us, will be part of our workday life.

TABLE A.1   Indicators of Child Abuse

PHYSICAL INDICATORS	BEHAVIORAL INDICATORS
Physical Abuse	

Unexplained bruises and welts:
■ on face, mouth, lips, torso, back, buttocks, thighs in various stages of healing
■ Bruises clustered forming regular patterns, reflecting shape of article used (electric cord, belt buckle)
■ Bruises regularly appear after weekend, absence or vacation
	■ Wary of adult contacts
	■ Apprehensive when others cry
	■ Behavioral extremes
	■ Aggressiveness, withdrawn
	■ Frightened of parents
	  ■ Afraid to go home
	  ■ Reports injury by parent
	■ Wears long-sleeved clothing to hide injuries

TABLE A.1   Continued

PHYSICAL INDICATORS	BEHAVIORAL INDICATORS
Unexplained swelling/dislocation/sprains: ■ On ankles, wrists, other joints ■ Unexplained burns caused by: cigar, cigarette, especially on soles, palms, back or buttocks ■ Immersion or rope burns ■ Unexplained fractures: to skull, nose, facial structure in various stages of healing ■ Multiple or spiral fractures Unexplained lacerations or abrasions: to mouth, lips, gums, eyes, external genitalia	

Physical Neglect

■ Consistent hunger, poor hygiene, inappropriate dress ■ Consistent lack of supervision, especially in dangerous activities or for long periods of time ■ Unattended dental or medical needs ■ Inadequate guardianship, abandonment ■ Delayed mental and motor development ■ Delinquency/states no caregiver	■ Begging, stealing food ■ Alcohol or drug abuse ■ Extended stay at school ■ Early arrival, late departure ■ Constant fatigue, listlessness, or falling asleep in class

Sexual Abuse

■ Difficulty walking or sitting ■ Torn, stained, or bloody underclothing ■ Pain or itching in genital area ■ Poor peer relationships ■ Venereal disease ■ Pregnancy	■ Unwilling to change for gym ■ Withdrawal, fantasy/infantile acts ■ Bizarre, sophisticated, or unusual sexual behavior ■ Delinquent or runaway ■ Reports sexual abuse by caretaker

Emotional Maltreatment

■ Speech disorder ■ Lags in physical development ■ Failure to thrive	■ Habit disorder (antisocial, destructive, etc.) ■ Behavioral extremes: compliant, shy, aggressive, demanding ■ Overly adaptive behavior: infantile or inappropriate adult, attempted suicide

Educational Neglect

■ Attendance in school infrequent	■ Child's unexplained absences is not the result of child's desire to be truant

Rules, Obligations, and Protections

Anyone with knowledge of abuse—especially teachers and officials—are required to report or cause a report to be made when they are aware of a maltreated child. Physicians, surgeons, medical personnel, school officials, social service workers, daycare workers, and law enforcement officials are all required by law to report cases of suspected child abuse or maltreatment. Teachers should recognize that they might be the last hope for an abused child.

Areas of trauma visible on a child who has been subjected to abuse can be photographed at public expense if necessary. These photographs and/or x-rays should be sent to the local child protective service in your community. All of these actions are required by law.

There are legal protections for citizens, officials, or institutions that make a report, take photographs, or take actions that result in the removal or keeping of a child in custody. Most localities have laws that offer immunity from any criminal or civil liability for reporters of abuse because these persons are presumed to have acted in good faith as long as they were acting in the discharge of their official duties. Usually confidentiality is offered to reporters by the local department of social services. The department is not permitted to release to the subject of a report data that might identify the person who made the report. The person who made the report can if he or she chooses give the central registry service permission to release his or her identity. It should be understood that there are also penalties for those who fail to report abuse (National Clearinghouse on Child Abuse and Neglect Information, 2003), including the following.

- Any person, official, or institution required by law to report a case of suspected child abuse or maltreatment that willfully fails to do so shall be guilty of a class A misdemeanor.
- Any person, official, or institution required by law to report a case of suspected child abuse or maltreatment that knowingly and willfully fails to do so shall be civilly liable for the damages caused by such failure.

Disclosure Response Procedures

There are specific procedures to follow when handling disclosures of abuse or neglect. Many students disclose abuse in school settings and with teachers they respect. Some students are unaware that their disclosures are remarkable and believe that all children have similar life experiences. They may believe that all parents use beatings or cigarette burns as a method of discipline, or use violence when they fight with each other. For many children, telling represents a giant step across a gulf of silence that has been imposed upon them all their lives. Their simple statements may be an expression of hope ("Please help me") or despair ("I can't keep this secret any more") and represent a child's sincere cry for assistance. These disclosures can occur in several different ways, as direct, indirect, disguised, or disclosures with a catch.

- *Direct disclosures.* A student announces the abuse privately or in class, perhaps during a discussion, perhaps feeling safe in doing so because of the nurturing atmosphere. If the student discloses in front of the class, acknowledge the disclosure, then tell the student that you want to talk further privately. Find a private time and place to do so.

- *Indirect disclosures.* A student alludes to abuse rather than describing it directly: "My neighbor told me to go into his bathroom." "My dad can't sleep at night." "I don't like going to my uncle's house any more." A student may not know how to speak more directly, may be embarrassed or afraid to tell, or may be trying to get around a promise to stay silent. Encourage a student to be more specific, but do not supply the words. Ask open-ended questions, such as "Can you talk about that a bit more, so I understand?" or "How do you feel about that?"

- *Disguised disclosure.* A student depicts the abuse as a friend's problem: "My friend is having problems with his stepfather." "There's this girl who told her mother of an older person who was hitting on her, but the mother thought she was making it up." "I know someone who was abused." Do not challenge the student's account. Encourage the student to talk to you further, and reassure the student that the problem is not his or her friend's fault. In time, the student may tell you that the problem is not a friend's, but his or her own.

- *Disclosure with a catch.* A student may reveal a problem, but ask you not to tell: "Something is happening to me, but this has to stay just between us." The student may want the relief of discussing it without risking that something negative will happen to the abuser. Don't make promises you can't keep. As a mandated reporter, you are legally required to report abuse. Offer your help, but inform the student immediately that you may need to consult with other appropriate persons. Students usually will proceed with a disclosure if you explain the process and offer your support.

Dos and Don'ts

Students who disclose abuse will watch your reaction carefully. They may worry that you won't believe them, or will recoil, as if their secret were an explosive devise. Remember that showing shock or disgust—or worse, disbelief—could cause the student to stop the disclosure or recant the allegation. If you appear clam and under control, the child will feel more comfortable talking to you. A teacher is often the only adult outside the family that a child can to speak to about abuse. The teacher can be a lifeline for the abused child. In order to be a safe, trusted adult for the student to come to, a teacher should follow guidelines on how to respond to a known or suspected child victim. When a student discusses an abusive situation, it is important to:

- Understand that a school staff member's role is to listen and accept, not to act as a therapist or investigator. React calmly to information given by the child. Children test adult's reactions to less significant information before risking revealing their secret. Don't act disinterested, angry, shocked, or grossed out.

- Convey a sense of caring and interest. Use active listening skills when interviewing a suspected victim. Empathy can be developed through intense listening to the child and statements such as "I care about you" and "If you feel bad, I'd like to help." Interview the child alone, as soon as possible after disclosure.

- Allow the student to relate the information in whatever way he or she finds most comfortable. Don't change the student's choice of words. When a student is disclosing information that may be considered abuse, listen carefully. Let the student tell you the information in their way. Be objective and nonjudgmental.

- State that a student has the right to tell, and that it is courageous to do so. Emphasize that abuse is not the student's fault. Word your questions so that they are nonjudgmental. Recognize your limitations in dealing with this complex, emotionally charged situation. If you are uncomfortable discussing this subject with the child, get help from the counselor to speak to the child or someone else trusted by the child.

- Give the child a sense that his or her feelings matter, and make statements such as:
  - "If you're scared, tell me."
  - "Your feelings are important and it's good to talk about them."
  - "Is there someone you are afraid of?"
  - "Is someone hurting you?"
  - "Sometimes people do things we don't like. Is anyone making you do something you don't like?"
  - "I hear you, I understand."
  - "I understand your fears."
  - "I believe you."
  - "I see how you feel."
  - "I want to help you."
  - "You seem unhappy."
  - "I want to know."
  - "You seem afraid."
  - "I'm so glad you're talking to me."

- Use open-ended questions to elicit the what, who, when, where for your report. "What is happening?" will indicate what type of abuse is occurring and to whom. "Who is doing that?" will indicate who is (are) the abuser(s). "When did it happen? Were there other times? Where were you when it happened?"

Do Not

- Do not interview the child in the presence of anyone who may influence the interview one way or the other. This includes brothers and sisters who may also have been victims.

- Do not touch the child or invade the child's space unless he or she invites you to do so.
- Do not develop rapport with the child before asking the child to disclose.
- Do not rush the interview to finish.
- Do not make promises you cannot keep.
- Do not examine or search for physical evidence; only medical staff is allowed to examine a child in case of emergency.
- Do not act as a therapist, a detective, or a child protective investigator. Your role is to listen, accept, and support the child. The only questions that you should ask are those necessary to make a report.
- Do not ask leading questions or press for answers that the student is not comfortable providing.
- Do not allow the student to feel "in trouble" or "at fault" for the abuse.
- Do not criticize or change the student's choice of words or language.
- Do not display shock, anger, disgust, or disapproval of the parents, the student, or the situation. You may feel these things, but it is unlikely to be helpful to the student to share these feelings.

Practice Exercise

Reports of suspected child abuse or maltreatment should usually be made immediately by telephone and in writing. Within forty-eight hours after the telephoned oral report has been made, most localities require a written report. In the following examples of reportable situations, explain your reasoning:

- A school principal calls his State Central Register (SCR) and reports that a ten-year old pupil told him repeatedly that he does not get enough to eat at home. The child appears pale and eats excessively at the school lunch program.
- Mary brings her ten-year-old daughter to the emergency room because of a vaginal discharge. The child is diagnosed with gonorrhea.
- A five-year-old boy is continually brought to the school nurse for an advanced case of head lice.
- A twelve-year-old student comes to school with two bruises. One is on her arm and the other on her lower back. The student claims her mother was upset and threw her against the refrigerator.
- A three-year-old is brought to the emergency room and diagnosed with second-degree immersion burns.
- A school counselor calls his State Central Registry and reports that a student has missed thirty-four out of ninety-five school days. He has only submitted an excuse for ten absences. The school has attempted to contact the parents with no success.

SEXUAL HARASSMENT

Unwelcome sexual advances, requests for sexual favors, or other verbal or physical conduct of a sexual nature constitute sexual harassment in the following.

- Submission to such conduct is made, either explicitly or implicitly, as a term or condition of an individual's employment;
- submission to or rejection of such conduct by an individual is used as the basis for employment decisions affecting the individual;
- such conduct has the purpose or effect of substantially interfering with an individual's work performance or creates an intimidating, hostile, or offensive work environment. (U.S. Equal Employment Opportunity Commission [EEOC], 2005)

The definition of sexual harassment implies a quid pro quo association that centers on a relationship in which the predator is in a position of power with regard to the victim. The marauder uses this power to interfere with the victim's performance at work and creates a harsh or distasteful work environment.

Sexual harassment has a major impact on young people. As teachers, we should understand sexual harassment and be alert to potentially unlawful and inappropriate behaviors as described in the law. It is our responsibility to be able to define and identify sexual harassment when we see it. Sexual harassment includes practices ranging from direct requests for sexual favors to hostile workplace conditions for persons of either gender, including same-sex harassment. (The hostile environment standard also applies to harassment on the basis of race, color, national origin, religion, age, and disability.) EEOC guidelines state that, with respect to conduct between employees, an employer must take immediate and appropriate corrective action if they know or suspect inappropriate conduct. This guideline can be interpreted to mean that a teacher is responsible for taking corrective action if sexual harassment is taking place within his or her class. Judgments should be made both objectively and subjectively to the reasonableness of the complaint; avoid acting rashly, as the psychological impact of a false accusation can be horrendous. The best strategies for the prevention and elimination of sexual harassment are to affirmatively raise the subject in class, express strong disapproval of any untoward actions, and develop logical consequences while employing sanctions such as referrals to a higher authority. Finally, students should be informed of their rights to raise the issue of harassment so that they understand all its implications.

RELEVANT LAWS AND DECISIONS RELATED TO SEXUAL HARASSMENT

- 1964: Title VII of the Civil Rights Act of 1964, as amended, 42 U.S.C. et seq., Prohibits Sex Discrimination
- 1972: Title IX of the Education Amendments of 1972, 20 U.S.C. et seq.
- 1998: *Onscale v. Sundowner Offshore Servs., Inc., 523 U.S. 75* (1998): Same-sex harassment can be actionable under Title VII, even when unwelcome sexual content does not express desire for sexual contact.

MINI CASE STUDY
"IS THIS REALLY SEXUAL HARASSMENT?"

Samantha Carson in your eleventh-grade social studies class is a fine student and superior athlete. She is cocaptain on the varsity swim team and has been instrumental in the team's quest for a state championship. She is quite popular with the boys and girls in your class and in school. She would appear to be a perfectly well-adjusted teenager. You have counseled her throughout the year with regard to her applying for an athletic scholarship to college. You have stressed that it is never too early to begin the application process. Samantha has always held you in high esteem, as evidenced by the beautiful porcelain vase she gave you for your birthday. You at first had declined to accept the gift but gave in to Samantha's seemingly sincere insistence.

Recently you have noticed a marked change in Samantha's attitude toward school. She appears to be angry with her classmates and distrustful of any relationships. You inquire as to her behavior and you are immediately rebuffed by Samantha yelling out "leave me alone, you're all the same." She leaves your classroom and rushes out into the hall disappearing into a crowd of students during the change of periods. You reflect on what action you should take: call her at home or wait to speak with her the following day. You decide to wait for the next day. Unfortunately, Samantha is absent for the next five days. When she returns to class she acts as if nothing has occurred and asks to see you alone after class. At your meeting she asks you if you are still her friend. You respond that you are her teacher and also a friend. She asks you to promise on your word of honor as her friend that you would not repeat what she is about to tell you. You're not sure what to do so in a rash moment you say OK. She commences to tell you that the boys on the swim team have been sexually harassing her. You ask her to be more specific about what exactly has transpired. She says the boys always say that she is "so hot" and look at her in "that way." She claims to have become self-conscious about her body and feels guilty about having led the boys on. You tell her not to worry and that you will talk to her tomorrow with some kind of solution to her dilemma.

When she leaves your class you look out the window wondering, "What did I get myself into?" You ask yourself, "How can I help Samantha? I promised not to speak to anyone else about her problem."

DISCUSSION TOPICS AND QUESTIONS TO PONDER

1. Identify the problem in this case.
2. Should the teacher have promised confidentiality with regard to Samantha's problem?
3. What can the teacher do to help?
4. Describe some actions that the teacher should not have taken.
5. Why do you think Samantha says "You're all the same"?
6. Explain your view as to whether Samantha's problem is really one of sexual harassment.

WHAT WOULD YOU DO IF . . . ?

1. Samantha accuses you of sexual harassment?
2. Samantha repents and claims she made it all up?
3. Samantha's parents want her removed from your class?

Forms and Effects of Sexual Harassment

One should realize that intentionally or inadvertently people can engage in conduct that is offensive to a reasonable person. Actions or materials that have a sexual content or derogatory element targeting specific groups or types of people can be considered objects and behaviors that may constitute harassment. Sexually harassing behavior includes the following:

- gender harassment, including sexist statements and behavior that convey insulting, degrading, or sexist attitudes;
- seductive behavior and offensive physical or verbal sexual advances;
- sexual bribery; and
- sexual assault. (Fitzgerald et al., 1988)

Forms of sexual harassment can also be seen in visual, verbal, written, and physical actions. When sexual harassment is used from a position of power, as in physical size or as in assigning grades, it is more difficult to ascertain.

FORMS OF SEXUAL HARASSMENT

Visual	posters	staring	calendars	gestures	cartoons
Verbal	jokes	whistling	compliments	gossip	innuendos
Written	love letters	email	cards	memos	promises
Physical	hugging	kissing	patting	proximity	tickling
Using Power	requests	threats	promises	references	financial aid

One potential effect of sexual harassment can be seen when a teacher is falsely accused of impropriety by a student. The teacher, as the respondent, faces reduced productivity and an interruption of any career progress. He or she also loses a sense of efficacy and autonomy, as well as altering his or her relationships with colleagues and peers. The damage to one's reputation is sometimes impossible to repair, aside from the potential for time-consuming and expensive involvement in grievances and lawsuits. In addition, student complainants and teacher respondents both face:

- anger, distrust, and guilt;
- psychological and physical symptoms related to stress; and
- disruption in their lives.

SUMMARY

Violence can be compared to an insidious virus that appears to be running rampant within the body of our nation. It has been portrayed in various forms on television, in print, on the news, and in movies and song. It is difficult to understand this germ since it can be virulent in some and hardly noticeable in others. We can question why some children act out what they see and hear and others do not. Why do bullies and gangs exist, and what effect do they have on those chronically teased students that cause them to develop a sense of self-loathing? Other teased students plot to shoot taunting peers and their presumed allies. Why are abused children in many cases hesitant to ask for help? Why has suicide become an option for so many children? It's almost impossible to answer these questions with any significant degree of accuracy. We really are unable to specify and pinpoint what causes children in general to behave violently. What we can do is discuss the causes and types of misbehavior that can lead to violence. We still are unable to profile or identify violence-prone individuals with any great degree of authority. We can, however, explore the core procedures and actions to take in dealing with the various forms and shapes of violence. Proper preventative actions can deter violence and enhance safety in our classrooms and society.

This Appendix has focused on some of the primary causes for the violence created by children in society—specifically bullying, gangs, suicide, sexual harassment, and child abuse—because they exemplify the violence so prevalent in our minds. We explored these five core forms of violence to gain understanding, raise sensitivity, and prepare the reader to deal with them. We want to spotlight the importance of understanding the potential for violence that exists in every child. Children come to school carrying all the good and bad that they have been exposed to in their lives. To co-opt these negative deficits, teachers must reflect on the management style they employ. In so doing, the reader and practitioner will be able to create a safe, secure learning environment for all children.

KEY TERMS TO FOCUS ON

risk factors for violence

strategies for preventing bullying

gangs and recruitment of members

suicide indicators and response

child abuse physical and behavioral indicators: Dos and Don'ts

sexual harassment

DISCUSSION QUESTIONS

1. Describe the five types of misbehavior commonly associated with children and schools.

2. Why is the public's perception of a crisis in conflict with the studies that report a declining rate of school violence?

3. How would you assess the strategies for preventing bullying?

4. Why are so many children drawn to gang membership?

5. How would you react if a potentially suicidal student came to you and asked you to promise not to tell anyone about his or her feelings?

SEXUAL HARASSMENT TRUE OR FALSE

Determine and discuss whether the following statements are true or false.

1. A person must state that a behavior was unwelcome in order to advance a legitimate claim of sexual harassment.

2. If a teacher hears a rumor that members of her class are engaging in harassment, she must investigate immediately.

3. If a child comes to you and claims to have been harassed, the intentions of the perpetrator are irrelevant.

4. A legal finding of a hostile work (class) environment occurs only if a behavior occurs repeatedly.

5. You should always honor promises of confidentiality when a student asks for it.

MINI CASES FROM THE FIELD

Analyze the following brief case studies using the IOSIE method. Reflect upon how you as the teacher would react in each situation presented. Each of the cases can be presented in class in a role-play format until a solution is found.

1. Mary wears long-sleeved shirts all the time, even on the warmest days. She does not have a weight problem and seems to function fairly well in your tenth-grade mathematics class. Mary has no apparent academic problems. She appears to be shy and withdrawn, very rarely volunteering to answer any class discussion questions. You notice that her nose seems to be constantly running. When you inquire about her condition she claims it's just a nagging cold. You have spoken with her other teachers who all seem to feel there may be something wrong with Mary. After analyzing this case using the IOSIE method, determine if this a case of drug abuse. Justify your response.

2. Billy is a loud, abusive second grader. He teases the other children in class, especially those who are smaller. You have

spoken to Billy and scolded him on many occasions with regard to his aggressiveness. He claims he is only playing and would never hurt anyone. You note that despite his denials he seems to enjoy frightening and intimidating weaker children. You have spoken to his parents, who see no problem with Billy. They claim he is a normal male child and suggest that you look more closely at the behavior of the other children and leave their child alone. After analyzing this case using the IOSIE method, determine the appropriate way to react to the bullying exhibited in this case.

3. Jane, a quiet eighth grader, is crying hysterically in the back of your classroom. When you ask her what is the problem, she replies, "No one likes me" and "Sometimes I wish I were dead." You ask her if anyone has done anything to her and she claims everyone hates her. Jane has always been a good student, but has difficulty making friends. She is ignored by the boys and shunned by the girls in her class. By looking at her you assume it is a

weight problem, since Jane is grossly over-weight. After analyzing this case using the IOSIE method, determine if it is a potential suicide case. And if it is, what is your role as the classroom teacher?

4. Carl, a special education student, shows up to your eleventh grade class wearing gang colors and a gang jacket. He has always been quiet in class, preferring to fade into the background rather than stand out, due to his learning disability. You have noted that a gradual change is taking place in the way Carl relates to his main-stream classmates. You have seen him making fun of the physically smaller class-mates and calling them derogatory names that incite them. When you tell him to stop, he claims he is only teasing. Some of the boys in your class have come to you privately and told you that Carl had threatened them if they complained about him. After analyzing this case using the IOSIE method, determine if this case is a gang problem, a bullying problem, or both. Explain your answer.

REFERENCES

ACT Against Violence. 2002. *Early violence prevention.* American Psychological Association. Retrieved at www.actagainstviolence.com

Board of Education of the City of New Board of Education Suicide Reference Guide for Chancellor's Regulation A–755.

Borduin, C. 1999. Multisystemic treatment of criminality and violence in adolescents. *Journal of the American Academy of Child and Adolescent Psychiatry* 39(3), 242–49.

Bostic, J., Rustuccia, C., and Schlozman, S. 2001. October. The shrink in the classroom: The suicidal student. *Educational Leadership* 59(2), 81–82.

Briggs, D. 1996, Sept. Turning conflicts into learning experiences. *Educational Leadership* 54(1), 60–63.

Curwin, R. 1997, December. Discipline with dignity: Beyond obedience. *The Education Digest,* 11–14.

Curwin, R. 1992. *Rediscovering hope: Our greatest teaching strategy.* Bloomington IN: National Educational Service.

Curwin, R., and Mendler, A. N. 1999. Zero tolerance for zero tolerance. *Kappan* 81(2), 119–20.

Curwin, R., and Mendler, A. 1997. *As tough as necessary: Countering violence, aggression, and hostility in our schools.* Alexandria, VA: Association for Supervision and Curriculum Development.

Curwin, R., and Mendler, A. 1988. Packaged discipline programs: Let the buyer beware. *Educational Leadership* 46(2), 68–71.

Dohrn, B. 1997. Youth violence: False fears and hard truths. *Educational Leadership* 55(2), 45–47.

Dwyer, K., Osher, D., and Warger, C. 1998. *Early warning, timely response: A guide to safe schools.* Bethesda, MD: National Association of School Psychologists.

Egley, A., and Arjunan, M. 2002. Highlights of the 2000 national youth gang survey. Washington, DC: U.S. Department of Justice, Office of Juvenile Justice and Delinquency Prevention.

Ewing, C. P. 2000, January/February. Sensible zero tolerance protects students. *The Harvard Education Letter, Research Online.* Retrieved September 3, 2005 at http://gseweb.harvard.edu/

First, J. 2000, January/February. *Protection for whom? At what price? The Harvard Education Letter. Research Online.* Retrieved August 31, 2005 at http://gseweb.harvard.edu/

Fitzgerald, L. S. et al. 1988. The incidence and dimensions of sexual harassment in academia and the workplace. *Journal of Vocational Behavior* 32: 152–75.

Frankel, F. 1996. *Good friends are hard to find.* Glendale, CA: Perspective Publishing.

Fraser, J. 1998, Winter. *Responding to suicide* (Children, Youth, and Family Background Report No. 6). Pittsburgh, PA: University of Pittsburgh.

Froschi, M., Sprung, B., and Mullin-Rindler, N. 2001. *Quit it! A teacher's guide on teasing and bullying for use with students in grades K–3.* New York: Educational Equity Concepts, Inc., Wellesley College Center for Research on Women, and the NEA Professional Library.

Garbarino, J. 1999. Young murderers. *American Educator* 23(2), 4–9, 46–47.

Hurst, M. D. 2005. Safety check. *Education Week* 24(33): 31–33.

Indicators of School Crime and Safety. 2004. National Center for Educational Statistics. Retrieved June, 10, 2004 from http://nces.ed.gov/pubsearch/pubsinfo.asp?pubid=2005002

Johnson, S., and Muhlhausen, D. 2005, March 21. *North American transnational youth gangs: Breaking the chain of violence. The Heritage Foundation.* Retrieved September 9, 2005 at www.heritage.org

Lal, S. R., Lal, D., and Achilles, C. R. 1993. *Handbook on gangs in schools: Strategies to reduce gang related activities.* Newbury Park, CA: Corwin Press.

Lowry, R., et al. 1999. School violence, substance use, and availability of illegal drugs on school property among U.S. high school students. *Journal of School Health* 69(9), 347–55.

Mager, F. R., and Pipe, P. 1997. *Analyzing performance problems: Or you really oughta wanna.* (3d ed.). Atlanta, GA: The Center for Effective Performance, Inc.

National Center for Educational Statistics, Institute of Education Sciences. 2004. *Indicators of school crime and safety 2000.* Washington DC: U.S. Departments of Education.

National Clearinghouse on Child Abuse and Neglect Information. 2003. Child abuse and neglect state statues series: Reporting penalties. Retrieved at www.mhric.org

National Institute of Child Health and Human Development (NICHD). 2001, April 24. *Bullying widespread in US schools.* Retrieved at www.nichd.nih.gov/bullying

National Mental Health Information Center. 2002, December 12. *Teen mental health problems: What are the warning signs?* Retrieved May 2, 2005 at www.Mentalhealth.samhsa.gov

O'Carroll, P. W., Potter, L. B., and Mercy, J. A. 1994. Programs for the prevention of suicide among adolescents and young adults. *Morbidity and Mortality Weekly Report,* 43(RR-6), 1–7.

Office of Juvenile Justice and Delinquency Prevention. (2003–2004). *Annual Report.* U.S. Justice Department. Retrieved May 23, 2005 at www.ojjdp.ncjrs.org

Olweus, D. 2003, March. A profile of bullying at school. *Educational Leadership* 60(6), 12–17.

Phillips, P. 1997, May. The conflict wall. *Educational Leadership* 54(8), 43–44.

Posey, K. C. 1995. *How to handle bullies, teasers, and other meanies.* Highland City, FL: Rainbow Books.

Reaves, J. 2001, March 9. Why he's in the headlines. Retrieved May 26, 2005 at www.warroom.com?school/%20shooting/charleswilliams.htms

Remboldt, C. 1998. Making violence unacceptable. *Educational Leadership* 56(1), 32–38.

Ritter, J. 2002, June 20. AMA puts doctors on look out for bullying. *Chicago Sun Times,* p. 1.

Rossman, S. B., and Morley, E. 1996. Introduction to safe schools: Policies and practices. *Education and Urban Society* 28(4), 395–411.

Schlozman, S. C. 2002, October. The shrink in the classroom: Fighting school violence. *Educational Leadership,* 60(2), 89–90.

Suicide Prevention. 2005. Retrieved at www.members.tripod.com/kittn/index.html. Contact Suicide Prevention Resources, Box 7693, FDR Station, New York, NY 10150-1914 for more information.

Shaffer, D., and Craft, L. 1999. Methods of adolescent suicide prevention. *Journal of Clinical Psychiatry* 60(2), 70–74.

Smith, F. L. 1994. Fighting back. *Executive Educator* 16(10), 35–37.

Spitzer, R. J. 1999. The gun dispute. *American Educator* 23(2), 10–15.

Stein, N., and Sjostrom, L. 2001. *Bullyproof: A teacher's guide on teasing and bullying for use with fourth and fifth grade students.* NEA and the Wellesley College Center for Research on Women. *The 1998 Annual Report on School Safety.* 1998, October. U.S. Department of Education. Retrieved June 10, 2004 from www.ed.gov/pub/AnnSchoolRept98

Twemlow, S. W., Fonagy, P., and Sacco, F. C. 2001. An innovative and psychodynamically influenced approach to reduce school violence. *Journal of the American Academy of Child and Adolescent Psychiatry* 40(3), 377–79.

Twemlow, S. W., Fonagy, P., Sacco, F. C., O'Toole, M. E., and Vernberg, E. 2002. Premeditated mass shootings in schools: Threat assessment. *Journal of the American Academy of Child and Adolescent Psychiatry* 41(4), 475–77.

U.S. Equal Employment Opportunity Commission [EEOC] Clearinghouse. 2005, March 2. *Sexual harassment.* Retrieved at www.eeoc.gov/types/sexual_harassment.html

Viadero, D. 2003, January 15. Tormentors. *Education Week* 24–27.

Vossekuil, B. Reddy, M., Fern, R., Borum, R., and Modzeleski, W. 2000. *U.S.S.S. Safe School Initiative: An interim report of the prevention of targeted violence in schools.* Washington, DC: U.S. Secret Service, National Threat Assessment Center.

U.S. Department of Education. 2001, February/March. *Community Update* 85, 1–8.

Reports noted above are available online. They can be downloaded from the Safe and Drug-Free Schools' Web site at www.ed.gov/offices/OESE/SDFS/news.html

Sample pledges for nonviolence can be found and downloaded from www.ncsu.edu/cpsv/SAVE/save pledges.html

CLASSROOM MANAGEMENT QUIZ

Now that you have read about the variety of classroom management models in Chapters 4 through 6, take this quiz. This quiz can be used to assist you in understanding and developing your personal classroom-management strategy. Those statements that you are drawn to can be understood as the basis for your own management plan.

In the space provided, place the letters that correctly identify the classroom management strategies the statement represents: AU = authoritarian; BM = behavior modification; I = intimidation; GG = group guidance; IE = instructional/eclectic; TP = tolerant/permissive; and SE = socio-emotional.

1. ___ The central role of teachers is to maintain order and discipline by controlling student behavior.

2. ___ Classroom climate greatly influences learning and teachers greatly influence the nature of that climate.

3. ___ Teachers should reward acceptable student behavior and avoid rewarding unacceptable student behavior.

4. ___ Personalized or individualized curriculums can eliminate most classroom management problems.

5. ___ Teachers should address the situation, not character or personality, when dealing with a problem.

6. ___ Teachers should not impose limits on students, as this will keep them from reaching full potential.

7. ___ Logical consequences minimizes the potential for the negative side effects that can accompany other forms of punishment.

8. ___ Effective management begins with the ability to control each student through the use of force if necessary.

9. ___ Teachers should always be fair and firm in dealing with students, as consistency is very important.

10. ___ Teachers should help students understand, accept, and follow established rules and regulations.

11. ___ A well-managed token system is an effective means of promoting appropriate student behavior.

12. ___ The teacher should be tolerant of all forms of student behavior.

13. ___ Students should be allowed to suffer the consequences of their behavior unless those consequences involve physical danger.

14. ___ Teachers should behave in ways that let students know that they know what is going on.

15. ___ A central role of teachers is the establishment and maintenance of positive teacher-student relations.

16. ___ The use and threat of punishment can be very effective management tools when used appropriately.

17. ___ The teacher should recognize that rewards are unique to the individual student.

18. ___ Appropriate classroom activities usually ensure appropriate student behavior, as they decrease the potential for frustration and boredom.

19. ___ The appropriate use of mild desist behaviors can be both effective and efficient in controlling student behavior.

20. ___ Teachers should treat students with respect and be committed to helping them develop self-responsibility and feelings of self worth.

21. ___ Teachers should never punish a student unless there is adequate evidence to establish guilt beyond a reasonable doubt.

22. ___ The teacher should help students develop a high level of cohesiveness and productive norms.

23. ___ Teachers should operate on the assumption that both appropriate and inappropriate student behaviors are learned.

24. ___ The teacher should understand that disruptive students often misbehave because they have been given inappropriate learning tasks.

25. ___ The manner in which the teacher communicates with students is decisively important.

26. ___ Teachers should use sarcasm very carefully and only after good interpersonal relationships have been established.

27. ___ Teachers should always act in a businesslike and dignified manner when interacting with students.

28. ___ The teacher should observe and/or question students to obtain clues concerning potential rewards.

29. ___ Classroom meetings and group problem-solving sessions can be very effective means of solving certain managerial problems.

30. ___ Teachers should "separate the sin from the sinner" when dealing with a student who has behaved inappropriately.

Assertive discipline The basic premise is to insist on proper behavior from students, following through with well-organized procedures when children do not behave. Assertive discipline is a system in which punishment is consistently meted out for rule infractions.

Attributes of the successful teacher These are usually related to the *caring sharing approach* to classroom management, which consists of specific qualities such as being approachable, having patience, being truthful and supportive, and having warmth and an obvious love of children.

Authentic assessments of classroom management and learning These include portfolios, projects, and performances. By definition, behavioral problems occur within the realm of real-life activities and therefore are authentic.

Authoritarian practice This practice is teacher-centered and focused on the teacher's complete control of the classroom. It requires the teacher to establish and enforce rules by issuing commands and orders as a prime objective for gaining classroom control and student obedience.

Behavior modification B. F. Skinner (1904–1990), the father of behavioral psychology, claimed our choices are determined by the environmental conditions under which we live. He found that students' behavior could be controlled through a program of reinforcement acted upon through outside stimuli.

Behavior window Thomas Gordon developed this concept, a visual device to help clarify the concept of problem ownership for students and teachers.

Behavioral model B. F. Skinner (1968) formulated the principles for shaping behavior, and his followers use his principles for discipline and shaping classroom behavior.

Causes of misbehavior These include five categories: frustration, ignorance, conflict, displacement, and rules.

Character education Character education programs promote core ethical values as a basis for good character, and focus on teaching a recognized set of values while using interactive teaching strategies and promoting critical thinking skills.

Characteristics of the best and worst teachers The best teachers have a sense of humor, make classes interesting, have knowledge of their subjects, explain things clearly, and spend time helping students; the worst teachers are dull, rarely explain things clearly, show favoritism, and have poor attitudes.

Characteristics of the professional educator Professional educators have pedagogical knowledge, a clearly defined theoretical content knowledge base, and are certified and able to meet licensing requirements. They also must be lifetime learners, intellectually curious, responsible, and empathetic.

Child abuse When a parent or other person legally responsible for the care of a child less than eighteen years of age allows, inflicts, or allows to be inflicted upon the child serious physical injury; creates or allows to be created against the child a substantial risk of physical injury; or commits or allows to be committed against the child a sexual offense as defined in the penal law.

Choice (control) theories Satisfying four basic psychological needs, which developer William Glasser views as genetic: belonging and love; power and achievement; fun and enjoying work; and freedom and the ability to make choices.

Classroom management A four-stage analytic pluralistic process where the teacher specifies desirable conditions, analyzes existing conditions, uses management strategies, and assesses effectiveness.

Classrooms of effective teachers Ecological environmental factors evident in a classroom's physical organization, which can be used as indicators of a teacher's effectiveness.

Congruent communication A process of conveying acceptance instead of rejection and avoiding blaming or shaming.

Consequences management approaches Management models that utilize behavior reward systems combined with consequences, both negative and positive, to change student behavior. Consequences agreed upon by students may support procedures established to deal with improper actions.

Constructivist model The assumption that individuals construct their own knowledge based on their schemata of existing beliefs.

Content knowledge The quality or capacity brought to class by all teachers related to their knowledge or lack of content expertise.

Cooperative discipline Cooperative discipline is a management program that combines a group guidance approach with character building. Cooperative discipline was developed by Linda Albert (1996) and based on the work of Rudolf Dreikurs, who spoke of group discussions, shared responsibility, and recognition of consequences as appropriate management techniques.

Criterion reference tests These tests, also known as teacher-prepared tests, measure an individual's ability in regard to specific criteria.

Curwin and Mendler model This model, developed by Richard Curwin and Allen Mendler (1988, 1999), focuses on chronically misbehaving students. Its major contribution to school discipline has been in the development of strategies for improving classroom behavior through maximizing student dignity and hope.

Deficient performance Deficient performance, or inadequate performance, implies fault with a student whose performance does not match the teacher's predisposed levels of achievement.

Definition of teacher attributes A teacher attribute is a quality that can be inherent within one's being, accidentally acquired by nature, or gained through life experience.

Determining beliefs Classroom management beliefs can be developed by teachers understanding their individual likes and dislikes as well as their unrealized bias through a process of self-reflection and analysis.

Determining practices Classroom management practices can be developed by understanding and addressing the psychological needs of students.

Determining skills Classroom management skills can be developed through reflection, observation, or response to the teacher skills checklist survey.

Discipline Building responsibility, self-control, and self-discipline; not a form of punishment.

Effective momentum model Psychologist Jacob Kounin found that effective lesson management led to good behavior in the classroom.

Effective teaching behaviors When a teacher brings about intended learning objectives; emphasis is placed on what students learn, not on what the instructor teaches.

Efficacy in action The belief that learners can control their own success through effective effort. The Efficacy Belief System states that one becomes smart by working hard and that being smart is not a trait one is born with, but something achieved through effort.

Environmental model The environmental model primarily concentrates on a child's social environment, working with or helping to develop the positive aspects of a child's immediate environments: home, school, and neighborhood.

Five positions of control The five positions of control are the punisher, guilter, buddy, monitor, and manager. *Manager* is considered the highest level of control for students because effective management means that individual responsibility has been achieved.

Gangs and gang recruitment Early discussions about the negative consequences of gang membership and providing children with positive ways to get their personal needs met can discourage gang membership. School must be viewed as a neutral zone for gangs, where gang leaders should be dealt with in a respectful but firm manner.

Ginott model This discipline model is based primarily on interpersonal communication methods that encourage humanitarian and productive classroom environments. The model was developed by psychologist Haim Ginott (1976), who maintained that discipline was made up of little victories in interaction between student and teacher.

Goals of misbehavior The four immediate goals include attention, power, revenge, and avoidance of failure.

Group management approaches These preventative, not interventionist, management strategies tend to focus on group pressure to move toward proper behavior.

Group process practice This practice is a sociopsychological approach based on group social psychology and group dynamics. It attempts to maneuver or cajole students into behaving. Discipline and control are achieved as the result of working with the group or class within the confines of the classroom. Group process practice is also known as *group guidance approach.*

I-messages These are nonconfrontational statements that one uses to communicate with students; one tells what one personally thinks or feels about another's behavior and its consequences. Students will alter their misbehavior when teachers deliver appropriately constructed I-messages.

Individual guidance management The focus in this therapeutic approach to classroom management is on developing good interpersonal relationships with students to guide them to take responsibility for their actions.

Instructional practice Good practice is based on the basic concept that good lessons prevent management problems. Effective momentum theory provides the theoretical rationale for this practice.

Interstate New Teacher Assessment and Support Consortium (INTASC) A form of teacher assessment used by thirty-five states as an avenue for creating national standards for teaching practices.

Intimidation practice A teacher-centered intimidating behavior approach, which is seen by many as ineffective in most classroom situations. An exception might be yelling or harsh loud desists used to stop a fight or prevent physical violence.

IOSIE This classroom management method can be used when analyzing any act of misbehavior within the classroom. IOSIE stands for *identify, objectives, solution, implement,* and *evaluate.*

Instructional paradigm The traditional approach to classroom instruction in which the teacher provides instruction.

Jones model This concept draws theoretically and conceptually from the knowledge base of behavior modification, proximity research from anthropology, and neurobiology on how the brain functions. The basic assumptions are that children need to be controlled to behave properly and that teachers can achieve control through nonverbal cues and movements calculated to bring them physically closer and closer to students.

Judicious discipline A comprehensive approach to democratic classroom management based on the constitutional principles of personal rights balanced against societal needs, in which students are taught to govern their own behaviors by assessing their actions in terms of time, place, and manner.

Keys to effective teaching Management, methods, mastery, expectations, and personality play a major part in the growth of all teachers.

Learning paradigm A teaching approach where the primary concern is the production of learning by the learner.

Learning zone concept In this strategy for motivating all to learn, there are three dimensions, or zones, in which learning occurs: *too easy, challenging,* or *too hard for the time being.* Children are placed in the position of seeing where they are and where they are expected to go.

Logical consequences In this management theory developed in Vienna, Austria, by psychiatrist Rudolf Dreikurs (1897–1972), democratic principles are central to discipline. The basic premise is that children should be given a choice rather than forced to behave as directed. People are believed to act according to their own subjective appraisal of the reality that surrounds them; when they assess the consequences associated with their behaviors, their actions become more knowledgeable.

Mager and Pipe model This model synthesizes the process of analyzing performance problems in the classroom by stressing the meaning of performance discrepancy as opposed to deficient, or inadequate, performance.

Maltreated child This is a child under eighteen years of age whose physical, mental, or emotional condition has been impaired or is in danger of becoming impaired as a result of the failure of the parent or other person legally responsible for his or her care to exercise a minimum degree of care with regard to basic necessities of life and providing proper supervision.

Management style Management style is the personality, beliefs, skills, and practices a teacher uses in managing a class. One's management style can be altered intentionally through study and life experiences.

National Board for Professional Teaching Standards (NBPTS) This organization sets standards that describe the highest level of teaching in different disciplines and with students at different developmental levels.

Norm-referenced tests Standardized tests allow us to compare one individual with other individuals. Scores are usually reported in the form of percentiles.

Objective tests for classroom management These measures are used to appraise and evaluate the validity and reliability of the results of the actions a teacher has taken to rectify a specific management problem.

Objective tests for learning Objective tests are at the lower thinking levels of knowledge and comprehension: who, what, where and when. Matching, completion, and true–false items are the usual objective means used for assessing student memory and recall, and are useful in covering large bodies of material.

Paradigms for teaching See *instructional paradigm* and *learning paradigm.*

Peer mediation Developed by Crawford and Schrumpf (1988), peer mediation is based on the idea that behavioral change should not come through a process of coercion, but should occur in an educational setting where students can reflect on their actions and negotiate alternative solutions using the skills of negotiation, reasoning, and compromise.

Performance discrepancy The difference between actual performance and desired performance, which can be remedied in many instances by the actions of the teacher.

Permissive practice A student-centered approach focused on maximizing student freedom in a natural way. The role of the teacher is not to interfere but to allow free student expression.

Positive action model Carol Gerber Allred (1996) developed this model—based on the philosophy that we feel good about ourselves when we do positive actions—to measure the success of a school and classroom instruction and behavior.

Preparing for the first day of school A teacher should review the keys to effective teaching—management, mastery, expectations, methods, and personality—and follow four practical suggestions: assign student seats randomly; teach procedures; start classes by having assignments labeled as "do now on the board"; and let students experience success.

Principles of professional development for teachers and students A platform from which to begin pedagogical and professional growth; the content of professional development should focus on what students are to learn and how to address the problems students may have in learning that material.

Procedures A means to teach students how to accomplish classroom activities without the use of punishment.

Professionalism and teaching experience Both are acquired over time. Professionalism should be the end product of all teaching experiences.

Psychodynamic model A guidance model that looks primarily inside the child, viewing behavior as reflective of internal feelings and conflicts, while emotions generate human behavior.

Punishment A concept considered arbitrary and capricious, rarely leading to self-discipline in classroom situations.

Reality therapy A method of educational counseling and human interaction that doesn't infringe on the rights of others and allows teachers to implement choice (control) theory.

Reasons for assessment Reasons for assessment are both diagnostic and evaluative tools that assist teachers in measuring student learning and, in addition, provide teachers with similar tools to help them evaluate the solutions they wish to achieve when attempting to resolve classroom management problems.

Reflection When a teacher assesses the success of students and their own effectiveness in helping to facilitate their own success.

Reliability When a test yields similar results when it is repeated over a short period of time or when an equivalent form of the text is used; a reliable test can be viewed as consistent, dependable, and stable.

Restitution model Diane Chelsom Gossen (1993) developed an internally motivational model in which students were expected to discipline themselves. This model was an outgrowth of Gossen's work with William Glasser and his Control Theory and Reality Therapy model.

Risk factors for violence characteristics A low verbal IQ, immature moral reasoning, poor parental modeling, poor social skills, and lack of social supports have all been associated with the development of violent and aggressive acts among youth. However, these risk factors by themselves will not identify every violent student.

Sexual harassment Unwelcome sexual advances, consisting of requests for sexual favors and other verbal or physical conduct of a sexual nature, which result in a threat to one's employment, grades, job, and social status, and interferes with one's performance.

Skillstreaming Developed by Arnold P. Goldstein and Ellen McGinnis (1988, 1992) this model is a psychological–educational design based on behavioral analysis processes and philosophy. Goldstein and McGinnis's view proposes that the teaching of social skills is now the role of the school.

Social systems theories This theory proposes that to understand behavior, one should take into account the ecology or context beyond the immediate situation in which an individual is functioning; that an individual is intertwined by human relationships in big and small social networks.

Socioemotional practice Also known as *individual guidance,* socioemotional practice has its roots in counseling and clinical psychology. It advances the belief that positive teacher–student relationships are necessary if effective classroom management and instruction is to occur.

Spectrum of teacher control Classroom management strategies fall on a spectrum from *most teacher control* to *moderate teacher control* to *least teacher control*, which then can be crossreferenced with strategies that offer consequences or empathy through individual or group guidance techniques.

Strategies for preventing bullying The four basic principles for the prevention of bullying are: providing warm positive interest and involvement from adults; providing a consistent application of nonpunitive, nonphysical sanctions for unacceptable behavior or violations of rules; establishing firm limits on unacceptable behavior; and having an adult as the authority and role model. It is the role of the teacher to teach bullies alternate ways to relate to others, and to teach victims the skills necessary to avoid the actions of bullies. This can be done through the process of skillstreaming, peer mediation, or conflict resolution.

Subjective assessments for learning Essay questions focus on higher-order thinking skills by requiring children to analyze, describe, synthesize, and compare.

Subjective tests for classroom management Higher-order thinking skills are used to judge real-life situations in a classroom.

Suicide indicators and response *Indicators* are usually grouped into three categories: behavioral indicators, such as previous attempts at suicide; emotional indicators, such as ongoing depression; and personal circumstances, such as unwanted pregnancy. *Response* is the responsibility of all involved; reaction should be immediate, and follow-up by a trained professional is imperative.

Teacher effectiveness training Psychologist Thomas Gordon developed two programs: one that trained parents and one that focused on training teachers in behavior management. Gordon's primary goal was to improve the quality of interactions between teachers and students. A major premise of teacher effectiveness training is that the only true effective discipline is the self-control that occurs internally in each child.

Testing practices The basic types of tests most commonly administered by teachers are the shortanswer question, the essay question, and the oral question.

Three ego-states Eric Berne defines the three egostates as "consistent patterns of feelings and experiences directly related to corresponding consistent patterns of behavior" (1966). He considered each of these states an entire system of thought, feeling, and behavior from which we interact with each other.

Traditional model This strategy is based on an approach that uses a "bag of tricks" or a "cookbook practice" that usually consists of lists of dos and don'ts that teachers have acquired over the years.

Transactional analysis This method, created by California psychiatrist Eric Berne (1964, 1966), deals with behavioral disorders by understanding what the subconscious mind has learned by interacting with others and by understanding that experiences are part of each individual's total being and become part of the way he or she behaves. For example, the behavior exhibited by students is subconsciously designed to get reactions and to see how others feel about them.

Types of misbehavior Misbehavior can be classified into five general categories: moral, personal, legal, safety, and educational.

Usability The criterion for selecting a test, such as: Is the test easy for the student to understand? Is the test easy to administer and score? and Is the test appropriate in its degree of difficulty?

Validity How well a test measures what it is represented as measuring.

INDEX